646.19 Ba
Bays, Carter.
The encyclopedia of early
American sewing machines :

DEMCO

THE ENCYCLOPEDIA OF EARLY AMERICAN & ANTIQUE

Sewing Machines

Third Edition

IDENTIFICATION & VALUES

Carter Bays

COLLECTOR BOOKS
A Division of Schroeder Publishing Co., Inc.

On the front cover (clockwise from top): Thomson, 1860 (p. 227); Singer, 1910 (p. 225); Wheeler & Wilson prototype, 1852 (p. 12); Unknown "paw foot" variety, 1865 (p. 186).

On the back cover: The Free, 1920 (p. 385); Shaw and Clark, 1865 (p. 190); Singer "Turtleback," 1859 (p. 215).

Cover design by Beth Summers
Book design by Marty Turner
Photography by Carter Bays

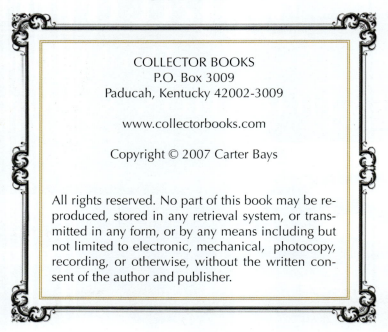

COLLECTOR BOOKS
P.O. Box 3009
Paducah, Kentucky 42002-3009

www.collectorbooks.com

Copyright © 2007 Carter Bays

All rights reserved. No part of this book may be reproduced, stored in any retrieval system, or transmitted in any form, or by any means including but not limited to electronic, mechanical, photocopy, recording, or otherwise, without the written consent of the author and publisher.

The current values in this book should be used only as a guide. They are not intended to set prices, which vary from one section of the country to another. Auction prices as well as dealer prices vary greatly and are affected by condition as well as demand. Neither the author nor the publisher assumes responsibility for any losses that might be incurred as a result of consulting this guide.

Searching for a Publisher?

We are always looking for people knowledgeable within their fields. If you feel that there is a real need for a book on your collectible subject and have a large comprehensive collection, contact Collector Books.

Contents

Acknowledgments 4

Introduction 4

The History of the Sewing Machine 5
   Its Earliest Invention 5
   Elias Howe, Jr. 7
   Isaac Merrit Singer 8
   Allen Benjamin Wilson 10
   William O. Grover 14
   The Sewing Machine Combination 15
   1856 – 1877: The Growth Years and Beyond 16
   Endnotes 18

Figure 2-99. See page 94 for more information.

Sewing Machine Manufacturers
from 1850 to 1880 19
   Types of Stitches 19
   How to Evaluate a Machine 20
   Value Scale 20
   Rarity and Value of Unknown Machines 20
   Rarity and Value of Later Machines 20
   Serial Numbers 20
   Patent Dates 21
   An Alphabetical List of Machines 21

Early Toy Sewing Machines 279

The Restoration of Early Sewing Machines 307
   Metal Restoration 307
   Wood Restoration 308
   Veneer Replacement 309
   Replacing and Repairing Parts 309

Figure 3-19. See page 287 for more information.

Bibliography 310

Appendix A:
Some Data from *One Hundred Years
of American Commerce* 312

Figure 3-43. See page 296 for more information.

Appendix B:
Dating Machines by Serial Numbers 315

Appendix C:
Patent Models and Unidentified Machines 316

Appendix D:
Evolution of the "Modern" (Vintage)
Sewing Machine 337

Appendix E:
Singer Manufacturing Machines
(1900 – 1910) 374

Appendix F:
"The Great Factory" 379

Appendix G:
A Comprehensive List of Vintage Sewing
Machines (circa 1900 – 1925) 384

Appendix H:
Some Photographs of Vintage
Sewing Machines 408

Appendix I:
Early Photographs 420

Index 430

Rarity/Value Codes: A Price Guide 431

I wish to thank my daughter, Virginia Bays, who wrote most of the history chapter and transcribed my original ramblings from audio to computer disk. These ramblings eventually (and very gradually) became the bulk of this book.

I also wish to thank the many collectors and others who have contributed their time and/or photographs of their machines and other material in order to make this project better. These include Gary Wacks, Gene Bishop, Graham Forsdyke, Elizabeth and Ned Brown, Claire Toschi, Ginny Meinig, Margie Abel, Louisa Llull, George Collord, Larry Meeker, Ellie Holbein, Judd Caplovich, Dennis Clark, Jane Les, Peter Frei, Theresa Powers, Connie Williams, and Harold Miller of the State Historical Society of Wisconsin. Barbara Janssen of the Smithsonian deserves special thanks for her help over the years. And Judd Caplovich deserves mention for his able assistance editing the (semi) final version of the first edition.

Almost all the illustrations in this book are from the collection of the author. The exceptions are indicated below.

Margie Abel: 3-62.
Harry Berzak: 2-144
Gene Bishop: 2-110, 3-22.
Elizabeth and Ned Brown: 2-276.
Judd Caplovich: 2-291.
George Collord: 2-158.
Peter Frei: 2-289.
Ellie Holbein: 2-11.
Jane Les: 3-25.
Louisa Llull: 3-61.
Larry Meeker: 2-147, 2-233.
The National Museum of American History (Smithsonian photo number is given next to figure number):
1-2 (45525B), 1-4 (45572D), 1-7 (45505B), 1-10 (32003G), 2-16 (48440B), 2-52 (70013), 2-131 (764870), 2-149 (48440G), 2-263 (48216L), 2-347 (83-1241).
Theresa Powers: 2-208, 3-55.
Cathy Racine: 2-83.
Gary Wacks: 2-8, 2-9, 2-14, 2-40, 2-46, 2-58, 2-74, 2-82, 2-84, 2-89, 2-122, 2-129, 2-134, 2-136, 2-157, 2-224, 2-247, 2-248, 2-268, 2-274, 2-280, 2-282, 2-323, 2-324, 2-334, 2-335, 2-336, 3-20, 3-23, 3-48, 3-49, 3-50, 3-51, 3-52, 3-53.
Connie Williams: 2-250, 3-45.
The following individuals kindly supplied photos for their vintage machines: Gilchrist – Naomi Cloer; Macy's – Cynthia Wilson; Run Easy – Carol Sonnier; Winner – Lisa A. DeHart.

The continued demand for this book has led inevitably to a third edition, which is greatly improved over the second. Most machines have been rephotographed; new machines have been added and the rarity/value indicators have been updated. There are more than 100 new figures, bringing the total to almost 600.

Carter Bays
February 2006

The History of the Sewing Machine

Its Earliest Invention

The America of the present is an industrial nation with a high standard of living provided by a multitude of labor-saving devices that make our day-to-day lives easier. The nineteenth century was one of those periods, rare in the history of mankind, that radically changed the substance of everyday life. Although the Industrial Revolution began in the previous century, it reached its fullest potential during the 1800s. The sewing machine played an important part in these vast changes.

Cloth production had been revolutionized by new looms, but there was no means of quickly making the cloth into clothes. Ready-made apparel was simply non-existent. The sewing machine was the key to taking the new, inexpensive cloth and quickly making it into cheap clothing. But even before cloth was being commercially produced on a large scale, inventive men were watching their wives and trying to imitate human-made stitches with mechanized speed.

When the idea of attaching two pieces of cloth (or leather, leaves, bark, etc.) with a strand of thread (or twine, yarn, vine, etc.) and a needle (or thorn) formed in some Neolithic brain, there was probably little thought of the myriad uses it foretold. Countless items found around the home are created by sewing: clothes, shoes, curtains, and quilts, to name just a few. It therefore seems natural, given both the inventiveness of eighteenth and nineteenth century man and that so many once-unheard-of machines were coming into use (such as the steam engine), that attention would be turned towards a sewing machine.

The first recorded attempt to create a mechanical means of sewing was made by an Englishman, Thomas Saint, who was interested in shoe production. He received British patent No. 1,764 on July 17, 1790. A drawing among the patent papers shows a machine that would have used an awl to first punch a hole in the leather it was designed to sew and then pass thread through the hole with a forked needle. A hook would retain the thread, which would then be looped together to form a chain stitch. In general shape, Saint's machine is similar to the industrial machines made 60 years later: it has an overhanging arm, a cloth plate, and spool holder.[1]

The sewing machine that Saint conceived was overlooked until 1873, when a manufacturer named Newton Wilson uncovered it on a trip to the patent office.[2] The reason for its obscurity is evident in the patent title — "An Entire New Method of Making... Shoes... and Other Articles..." Why Saint never chose to develop his idea is unknown, but it is almost certain that he never made a model. When Wilson Built one to the specifications of the plan, it would not produce stitches without modification.[3] Saint either may not have had the mechanical genius to perfect a machine or he may simply not have seen the greater implications of his specialized invention, a shortsightedness that was rampant during the early stages of the Industrial Revolution. Regardless of the reasons, Saint's machine, though the first recorded sewing machine, has little connection to the machine that was introduced to American society in the 1850s.

The sewing machine is one of those devices that seems to have been created simultaneously by tinkerers and inventors all over the world. There were a number of patents granted throughout Europe during the early years of the nineteenth century, each offering a different solution to the problem of finding a mechanized means of making a stitch in a piece of cloth, leather, or rope. It is difficult to say how much, if any, information was shared among these inventors. More than likely, each was working independently.

Most inventors tackled a specific problem, frequently embroidery or leather-stitching; in some cases, an even slimmer target was made: binding together cord, finishing the edges of knit hats, etc. It is perhaps because of a limited range of vision that these early inventors lacked the motivation to perfect their machines. The huge advantages of something like a loom are obvious from the outset, since large segments of society were required to engage in the task of making cloth, and all people used it. When a machine was geared for a highly specific task such as embroidery, it generally lacked the ability to serve a broad range of other sewing functions, and thus was not worth the effort to develop.

It is therefore interesting to note that only one of the early machines was designed to replace plain sewing. This exception is found in a French patent issued to Stone and Henderson in 1804, for a seam-sewing machine.[4] These inventors, however, while appreciating the implications of their work, suffered from what proved to be a major stumbling block for all early sewing machine inventors — they attempted to replicate the sewing action of a human hand. That is to say, the early inventors were using hand sewing as their model, and were not attempting to create a stitch which was peculiarly adaptable to mechanization.

One early inventor who deserves a place of honor in the realm of sewing machine history is Barthelemy Thimonnier, if only for his perseverance. While no single person can be credited as the sole inventor of the sewing machine, there is little doubt that this French tailor was the first to see his machine in commercial operation. Thimonnier patented a machine in 1830 that formed a chain stitch with a hooked needle and a looper, the same stitch an embroiderer might use. Although his machine was not terribly speedy initially, he ultimately perfected it, and by 1841 it sewed 200 stitches per minute.[5] He made 80 of these machines, all of which were put to use in his shop making clothing for the French army.

Thimonnier was a tailor, not a machinist or inventor, and this machine of his was truly a labor of love, which is not to say that he didn't believe he could make money with it. It is probably only because of his broader vision that he succeeded in perfecting his machine at all, because his early version saved little labor and was expensive to construct. He did not have the sort of background that would incline him to create an entirely new stitch; he was a tailor and must naturally have envisioned a machine that formed stitches in a manner with which he was familiar. One can only guess that the thing that made him persist where others quit was his ability to see the widespread potential that a machine might produce. As a tailor, he must also have been accustomed to hand sewing, and thus would have spent many weary hours plying a needle. This experience would support a desire to create a machine that would do away with such drudgery.

Regardless of Thimonnier's intentions — whether they were to make a fortune for himself or to free the women who spent many weary hours enslaved to needle and thread — other tailors of Paris saw the sewing machine not as a godsend, but as an enemy to be feared; in 1841, an angry mob destroyed all of Thimonnier's machines. Why, one might ask, would a group of tailors attempt to wipe out a machine that promised to be so useful for their businesses? The answer, of course, lies in fear and prejudice. The fear of lost jobs was one of the largest obstacles all sewing machine inventors faced. In France, England, and the United States, there was an overwhelming prejudice that depicted the sewing machine manufacturer as an evil interloper unfairly pricing machines beyond the means of the common citizen. These fears were something that Thimonnier was never able to overcome.

Thimonnier devoted the remainder of his life to perfecting his machine, and he did receive two more patents, one French and one English. In a final attempt to show the world his marvelous creation, he sent his machine to the 1851 exhibition at the Crystal Palace in London. Once again, fate was against him, for the judges never saw his machine; it was lost in transit. Moreover, it is unlikely anything would have come of the machine's appearance at the exhibition, since the newspapers took almost no notice of other machines that were there. The only mention of any machine was published in an Italian paper,[6] and even that was in a very derogatory tone.

On the American scene, the first attempt at a general purpose sewing machine was reportedly made by Walter Hunt, a professional inventor. Around 1834, Hunt built a machine that used an eye-pointed needle and a shuttle to form a lockstitch. Hunt was a man of mechanical genius, and it is therefore fitting that he was the first to take a new approach, casting aside handsewing as a model and creating a stitch that was uniquely suited for mechanized formation. His machine must have been superior to all others that came before it and quite equal to the best early efforts of Elias Howe, who worked nearly a decade later. In 1836, it was described as "working like a charm."[7]

But Hunt is not a name that many know today, and he certainly has not been recognized as the father of the sewing machine, as have both Howe and Singer. Hunt's name was lost for a time until Singer uncovered it in a search to find pre-Howe machines while fighting a patent battle against Howe. Hunt was an inventor; his livelihood was inventing devices, not marketing them. He studied a problem, produced a solution, sold the rights to the idea, and tackled the next item of interest. Hunt's attitude toward his work is clearly illustrated by the example of the safety pin, which he also invented. In need of $15.00 to pay back a debt, Hunt conceived of and made a prototype for the safety pin in about three hours' time. His return for this feat was a $400.00 payment received for exclusive rights to the idea.[8]

Another revealing anecdote illustrates the contemporary attitude that influenced Hunt's rejection of his machine, as well as the struggle of Thimonnier, Howe, and Singer. Caroline Hunt, the inventor's 15-year-old daughter, was given the opportunity to go into business manufacturing corsets with the aid of her father's machine. She declined for moral reasons, feeling that the sewing device would be detrimental to the condition of the poor seamstress, whose subsistence-level jobs would be taken away by mechanization. Thus, the fear of unknown — and erroneously predicted — consequences once again squelched what would prove to be one of the most successful mechanical devices of the century.

ELIAS HOWE, JR.

Figure 1-1. Elias Howe, Jr., circa 1865.

The biggest step towards a practical sewing machine came in 1846, when Elias Howe received his first patent. Although Howe is frequently credited as being the inventor of the sewing machine, this was obviously not the case. He did not even take out the first American patent for a sewing machine, as there were four others issued before his.

To appreciate fully the background of Howe's invention, we must go back some seven years and find Howe, a young man of 20, working in a machine shop in Boston. Ari Davis, the shop owner, was solicited to aid two gentlemen in the perfection of a knitting machine. Davis, uninterested in the machine, asked the men why they were bothering with it and suggested they make a sewing machine instead. In response to their insistence that it couldn't be done, Davis asserted that he could make one himself. "Well, you do it, Davis, and I'll insure you an independent fortune," was the intriguing reply.[9] This statement, never acted upon by Davis, was the seed of an idea planted in Elias Howe's brain. Such a snippet of conversation must have had more impact on him because of his youth and financial condition; if Howe had been older, more cynical, and wealthier, he might never have had the inclination to create a machine for sewing. His goal was always money; it was definitely never to free the weary fingers of womankind.

By 1843, Howe certainly was in need of an independent fortune. Married, with three children, his future as a journeyman machinist did not look promising, especially considering his unfortunate lameness and sickliness, a problem from childhood. The seed had been planted four years earlier and it must have germinated well, for Howe was convinced that a fortune would be his if only he could make a sewing machine. With twentieth century hindsight, one would guess that this point was obvious to more individuals than just Howe, but to Saint, Hunt, and a host of others, it was not so clear.

Howe diligently and painstakingly devoted all his efforts to produce a workable machine. He began by mimicking his wife's hand motions, but aborted the idea and ultimately devised a lockstitch using two threads and a shuttle. During this period, Howe was financially supported by an old school friend, George Fisher, who was to have equal rights to the patent. By 1845, Howe had produced a machine that was workable enough to sew the primary seams on two suits of clothes — one each for him and his partner.

Howe then required a means of getting word out to the public. He set up his machine in the Quincy Hall Clothing Manufactory in Boston and offered free demonstrations. At this point he proposed a contest, matching his sewing machine to the efforts of five seamstresses. Howe was successful in this battle; he completed five seams before any of the seamstresses had completed one.

Howe never stopped attempting to improve his machine, and by 1846 the patent model incorporated several innovations (figure 1-2). A baster plate suspended the cloth vertically and fed it through the machine, a moving arm carried the thread through the cloth with a curved needle (only incidentally was it eye pointed) and a lifting rod retained a loop through which the shuttle passed a second thread, locking the loop in place.

Howe's machine sewed about 250 stitches per minute, a reasonably fast speed, but a great deal of effort was required on the part of the operator. The cloth had to be removed from the baster plate and rehung at very short intervals. No curved work could be accomplished, and therefore hand-finishing was required to complete any article of clothing (it was no accident that Howe challenged the seamstresses to sew straight seams).

Then there was the problem of cost. Each machine would cost the customer about $300.00,[10] and a number of machines would be needed for any moderately sizeable tailor shop. Moreover, there would be the additional expenditure of a machinist, for any repairs — and there would be many — would have to be done from scratch, as no interchangeable replacement parts could be made, each machine being a unique, hand-tooled effort.

Howe was thus disappointed with his lack of success. It was certainly admired as an "extraordinary invention,"[11] but this did not ensure a flood of orders, and such puffery was commonplace for newly exposed inventions in scientific journals. It must have been thoroughly discouraging to Howe, who was doubtless bolstered only by youthful dreams of fortune. The disappointment proved too much for his partner George Fisher, who finally grew disgusted with both Howe and his machine.

Howe must have decided that England was a more advanced nation and more likely to embrace such a marvelous invention, for he sent his brother, Amasa B. Howe (who would later play a large role in sewing machine manufacture), to London, machine in hand. Amasa made what must have seemed like a wonderful deal to Howe. A corset maker, William Thomas, paid 250 pounds for the patent rights for England, promising to pay a three-pound royalty for every machine sold. This would later prove to be Howe's favorite way of making money: letting others manufacture, while he reaped royalties. In 1847, Howe himself set sail for London, Thomas having hired him for three pounds a week to adapt his machine to the manufacture of corsets. Howe brought with him his patent model and papers.[12]

At this point, life must have been looking up for Howe; he was assured of money to feed his family for the moment, and saw promises of plenty of royalties in the future. Unfortunately, the inventor was not to have an easy time of it — in fact quite the opposite. Thomas never fulfilled his promise of payments; he further proceeded in firing Howe after the inventor had served his purpose in adapting the machine. Howe was forced to return to America penniless, without patent papers and model (which he had pawned in England for passage home), and just in time to see his wife die. He also arrived on the American scene in time to see others beginning to profit from his idea. Key among those was Isaac Merrit Singer, who would become his chief rival.

Figure 1-2. Howe's patent model, 1846.

Isaac Merrit Singer

The story of Singer begins when the entrepreneur was a Shakespearean actor on the stage. To be an actor was Singer's first love; he never thought of himself as anything else, and his dramatic persona was certainly a key part of his ability to market sewing machines successfully. Singer was, in fact, the most interesting of the early rulers of the sewing machine industry. He was the son of an immigrant, the personification of the American Dream that every foreigner coming to Ellis Island was striving to capture. He left a machinist's apprenticeship at an early age to form a band of travelling players. The stage must have been appealing to him, not only as a means of satisfying his histrionic nature, but also as a method of touring the country, which, among other things, kept him from being pinned down by one wife.

Singer was certainly a handsome figure, and he managed to attract two wives and father five children by the time he was 35 (these numbers eventually escalated to approximately five and twenty-two). For all of his faults, he never denied support to his children or wives, and his enthusiasm for inventing may be attributed to the needs of a large family in two households.

Singer had some experience as a machinist and inventor. In 1839 he sold, for $2,000.00, the patent rights to a horse-powered drilling machine, which he conceived of while working as a laborer in Chicago between acting jobs. This money was immediately invested in his acting career, using it to form the Merrit Players. In 1844, when the troupe, never successful, was no longer able to support him, he took a job in a print shop.

Always looking for a way to better himself financially, Singer was again struck with a patentable idea — this time for a type-carving machine. His powers of persuasion were apparently as effective on men as women, for he succeeded in finding himself a source of money in the form of George B. Zieber, who provided the funds for promoting the machine in Boston. This undertaking was never to prove successful, but it led to Singer's introduction to the idea of a sewing machine.

In 1850, Singer and Zieber were working in the machine shop of Orson C. Phelps, who manufactured, among other things, a Blodgett and Lerow sewing machine. Phelps was having difficulty with these machines; they were constantly being brought back for repairs, and only one of every dozen worked well enough to be saleable.[13] It was obvious that the design needed improvement; hence Phelps called upon Singer's inventiveness and Zieber's capital to do just that. However, it took some persuasion to convince Singer to abandon his type-carving machine in favor of something that belonged in the realm of the feminine. Zieber quoted him as having said, "You want to do away with the only thing that keeps women quiet — their sewing!" Singer was finally persuaded to work on the new invention, but his interest was obvious from the outset: "I don't give a damn for the invention, the dimes are what I'm after."[14]

Once he applied himself to the task, Singer was apparently quick to point out and correct the flaws of the Blodgett and Lerow machine. He thought of moving the shuttle in a line rather than a circle, and also decided to replace the curved needle with a straight one, which moved vertically rather than in an arc. On the strength of Singer's assurances that his plan would work, the three men entered a partnership, and Singer was given $40.00, the last of Zieber's ready assets, with which to build a prototype (figure 1-4).[15]

Figure 1-3. Isaac Merrit Singer (from Lewton).

The story of this first Singer sewing machine is a dramatic one, if we are to believe Singer:

> I worked day and night, sleeping but three or four hours out of ... the day ... The machine was completed the night of the eleventh day ... that evening ... we commenced trying it. The first attempt to sew was unsuccessful ... Sick at heart, about midnight I started with Zieber to the hotel where I boarded ... Zieber asked me if I had noticed that the loops of thread on the upper side of the cloth came from the needle. It then flashed upon me that I had forgotten to adjust the tension ... I went back to the shop. I adjusted the tension, tried the machine, and sewed five stitches perfectly, when the thread broke. The perfection of those stitches satisfied me that the machine was a success, and I stopped work ... and had a sound sleep. By three o'clock the next day I had the machine finished, and started with it to New York ... to get out a patent for it.[16]

After this wonderful turn of events, Singer, Zieber, and Phelps were faced with marketing their machine. Jenny Lind, the name of a famous singer of the day, was decided upon as the name for the product, but this idea was cast aside, and the name of the inventor was taken instead. At $125.00, the Singer Sewing Machine was guaranteed to run well for a year, and advertisements promoted it as "an ornament to any lady's sewing apartment."[17]

Singer and his partners did have a great advantage over other manufacturers of the time. Their machine was much more practical than what was in use, and Singer himself was a brilliant salesman, a trait no doubt aided by his acting background. Singer, as Howe had done, offered demonstrations of his invention. He toured the country, attracting onlookers with notices of dramatic

Figure 1-4. Singer's patent model, 1851.

recitations and displays of mechanical wonder. In those early years, the sewing machine was a hard item to sell. While Singer's machine was a more satisfactory device than others that came before it, the public had to be convinced of this. Previous sewing machines had been clumsy and subject to frequent repair; they created a prejudice against, rather than a demand for, the item. It was certainly not clear that any real money would come of the invention. Blodgett himself, one of the early pioneers with the Blodgett and Lerow machine, told Singer that he was "an idiot to try and make sewing machines to sell," that "sewing machines would never come into use," and that no money would ever be made from their manufacture.[18]

Singer had other concerns. He was determined to reap the maximum benefit from his invention and did not intend to share the profits with the likes of Zieber and Phelps. Their usefulness to him was over; he therefore used every means in his power to trick them out of their rights. Zieber, in the midst of a serious illness, was duped into signing away his shares, and Phelps was simply bullied out. Singer did, however, need a partner. A lawyer's services were rendered necessary by the heavy patent litigation that was infesting the sewing machine market in the early 1850s. Edward Clark proved the perfect ally and was accepted as an equal partner without contributing any financial support. The combination of the two men was a formidable one; they managed to create what would become the preeminent sewing machine company of the century and the leader of American industry's invasion of foreign markets.

ALLEN BENJAMIN WILSON

The man who is most universally recognized as having contributed more to the mechanical development of the sewing machine than any other is Allen Benjamin Wilson. In comparison to Singer and Howe, his story is not as dramatic, but it is certainly as important. It is unclear what prompted Wilson to direct his mind towards the development of a sewing machine, but we can be certain that he did not have the benefit of seeing one in use, since, as a cabinetmaker's apprentice in Michigan, he had no knowledge of the developments in New England.

The subject was mentioned in a letter of 1847, but it was not until 1849 that he built a working model, which used a double-pointed shuttle to form a lock stitch at both ends of its curved path (figure 1-6). Wilson was not lucky in this endeavor, nor was he ever as financially successful as any of the other sewing machine inventors, despite the marked advancements he brought to the field. He had perfected his machine by 1850 and was successful in his patent application, but he was forced to hand over half of the rights to a company that erroneously claimed control of the double-pointed shuttle.

Not to be discouraged by this setback, Wilson simply turned his attentions toward an entirely new way of forming a stitch. Thus his rotary hook patent was born. The rotary hook device (figure 1-7) was far simpler, yet more effective,

Figure 1-5. Allan Benjamin Wilson (from Urquhart).

than anything that came before it. A rotating hook retained the thread that the needle brought below the cloth plate, and made a large loop through which a shuttle could easily pass. Wilson added to this improvement a design for a stationary bobbin, which effectively eliminated any possible claim by another patentee.

Wilson formed a partnership with Nathaniel Wheeler, who financed the production of Wheeler & Wilson sewing machines, the compact size and smooth works of which were a tribute to the inventive genius of the latter. As can be seen in figure 1-9, Wheeler & Wilson machines were smaller and more decorative than other brands, and suited to home rather than manufacturing use. In this respect, they differ greatly from the clunky early creations of Singer.

Another of Wilson's universally used contributions came in 1854 with the patent of his four-motion feed, which greatly improved the job of feeding the cloth through the machine. Rather than the large, toothed wheels that were previously commonly used, Wilson conceived of a small, toothed plate that would drop down, move back, press up against the cloth, and move it forward, thus feeding it across the cloth plate with great accuracy and uniformity of stitch. This feature was not only widely adopted in the 1850s, but is also used on almost every home sewing machine today.

The Wheeler & Wilson company was an early leader in

the industry, and the mechanical genius of A. B. Wilson was the main reason behind its success. But Wilson was never given the credit that was his due. Many refer to Singer as the maker of the first practical sewing machine, but Wilson succeeded before Singer did and greatly surpassed Singer's efforts in the process. Wilson, never healthy, retired from the company in 1853. He, like Walter Hunt, had a mind for inventions, not business. History seems to have been written by the claims of businessmen rather than by the facts themselves. If Wheeler and Wilson had been the consummate promoters that Singer and Clark were, the name Allen B. Wilson would be known today by more people than just a few enthusiasts.

Figure 1-6. Wilson made this prototype double-pointed shuttle machine in 1849. He received a patent for the device in 1850.

Figure 1-7. Wilson's 1851 patent for a rotary hook.

Figure 1-8. An 1852 A. B. Wilson prototype. This machine apparently never went into production. It utilizes the patented rotary hook and stationary bobbin and has no serial number. The typical model that was sold resembled the machine in figure 1-9.

Figure 1-9. Comparison between an 1853 A. B. Wilson (left) and an 1853 Singer machine.

WILLIAM O. GROVER

The final inventor deserving credit as one of the pioneers in the early days of sewing machine history is William O. Grover. Grover, a Boston tailor, had the foresight as early as 1849 to realize that the sewing machine would be a highly valuable invention. He took a different approach in his attempts to build one. Realizing that hand motions were not ideally suited for machine replication, Grover focused his efforts on creating a new stitch. In 1851, he patented a machine that produced the two-thread chain stitch (figure 1-10), which had the advantage of using two complete spools of thread, eliminating the necessity of winding thread onto a bobbin. The stitch was complicated and involved a series of interlocking knots. As Frederick Lewton points out:

> It is remarkable that during his experiments he did not discover the single thread chain stitch ... it is probable that, working on the assumption that it was absolutely necessary to use two threads, the idea of using one thread could not find room to develop in his brain.

It is certainly surprising that he was able to overcome the many difficulties that his new stitch created. The two-thread chain stitch uses more than twice as much thread as the ordinary lockstitch, and a bulky seam is created, which is advantageous for embroidery work but generally not desired in plain sewing.

Grover was quite astute in his choice of a partner. Orlando B. Potter, a lawyer, would prove quite useful during the rampant patent litigation of the early 1850s. The Grover and Baker Company, which had been formed under Grover's association with another tailor by the name of William E. Baker, was very successful through the 1870s.

Figure 1-10. Grover and Baker's patent model, 1851.

The Sewing Machine Combination

The mechanical difficulties of producing a machine that was practical for home and manufacturing use were thus overcome by the early 1850s, but the key ingredients to a workable machine were not covered by any one patent. The essential features had been devised by a variety of men: the lockstitch, eye-pointed needle, shuttle, horizontal cloth plate with overhanging arm, continuous feed, tension controls, presser foot, and the propensity for curved as well as straight seams.[19]

Elias Howe, Jr., was unwilling to let any of the innovations that fell under his patent be used by manufacturers without compensation to himself. He was the initiator of what would become one of the fiercest periods of legal arbitration any industry has ever seen. Upon his return to America, the impoverished inventor, witnessing the relative success of sewing machines that incorporated some of his features, was determined to make his own fortune by forcing others to pay royalties on each machine produced.

According to an obviously slanted pamphlet published by the Howe Machine Company in 1876, Howe's claims were justly felt and his terms would have been readily agreed to, had not one company incited a revolt among the others: "that one (I. M. Singer) induced the others to resist, and the only remedy was a resort to the courts."[20] The promoters of the Howe machine were naturally anxious to place the blame of an infamous legal melee on anyone other than the "honored" name of Elias Howe, but it is incorrect as well as unfair to blame Isaac Singer. It would also be unfair to charge Howe as the only aggressor in these conflicts. While he no doubt spurred them, it seems likely that such battles would have been waged without him if only on a smaller scale, as no other patentee laid claim to so many basic principles necessary for the machine.

Regardless of the instigator, the legal proceedings that followed were a source of frustration to all of the many companies who were producing machines during this period. The case that overshadowed all of the others was one between Howe and Singer. It was during these proceedings that, in an effort to break Howe's claims to having made the first operating sewing machine in the United States, Singer discovered the prior work of Walter Hunt. Unfortunately for Singer, Hunt was never able to find the original working model that he had created some 20 years earlier. Howe's claims were upheld; Singer lost the battle and was forced to remit $15,000.00. Howe's power over other manufacturers was strengthened in the process.

It should be noted that one of the key innovations that Howe was given indisputable patent rights to was that of the eye-pointed needle. Not only did Howe not invent the eye-pointed needle, but in his original patent papers he never even claimed it as his own idea. The courts evidently felt a desire to fix upon someone the promise of a fortune.

Howe at this point had a great deal of control over the market. Any manufacturer who used his patents was required to pay him a royalty of $25.00 per machine. But Howe was not the only obstacle these companies had to overcome. There was a great deal of litigation over other sewing machine patent rights independent of Howe's claims, and every company was touched by it. It was clear that everyone was suffering, and that the situation had to be resolved in the interests of mutual prosperity. The solution to this problem was the formation of the United States' first patent pool. At the instigation of Orlando Potter, president of the Grover and Baker Company, the Sewing Machine Combination was formed in 1856. Potter's idea was brilliant; it not only succeeded in eliminating the legal exercises that faced the major manufacturers of the period, it also gave them virtual control over the market. Wheeler, Wilson and Company, I. M. Singer and Company, Grover and Baker, and Elias Howe created a pool of patents, each contributing the most important ones they held. These patents included the eye-pointed needle used in combination with a shuttle (Howe patent), the four-motion feed (A. B. Wilson patent), the vertically moving needle above a horizontal work surface (Bachelder patent), and others.[21]

This combination of patents covered all of the functions necessary for a practical sewing machine. The three companies were required to pay Elias Howe $5.00 for each machine sold in the United States and $1.00 for each machine sold overseas. In addition, licenses were granted to other manufacturers — Howe stipulated that there must be at least 24 — at the price of $15.00 per machine. Part of the license fee was put into a fund that covered any legal expenses incurred in the process of protecting the Combination's patent rights.

The Combination lasted, with minor changes, for over 20 years. Howe dropped out of it in 1867 when his patent expired, and final dissolution came in 1877 when the last patent (a Bachelder feed patent bought by Singer during the 1850s) expired. While it lasted, the Sewing Machine Combination was a model business organization. It was criticized for the power it held, and many an editorial was written against it, claiming it priced sewing machines beyond what the common family could afford and thus added to "the manual work and unending drudgery of the wives and daughters of farmers and mechanical laborers."[22] The critics had a valid argument, since by the 1870s the average cost to the manufacturer was $12.00, while the average retail price was $65.00. But such profits were far from those of the 1850s, when every sewing machine company faced an uphill battle simply to establish itself.

1856 – 1877: The Growth Years and Beyond

As can be surmised by the virulent attacks against Thimonnier, and the resounding failure of Howe's sewing machine, it was not an easy process to convince the public that the invention that would eventually find a place in every home was desirable at all. There were several reasons behind this lack of popularity; the cost was exorbitant, the machines were not easily fixed, the labor they would save was that of a woman's, whose time was not considered to be of consequence by the man who made the purchasing decisions, and women could not possibly understand and operate anything so mechanically difficult anyway, or so the prevailing opinion claimed. The real story of the American sewing machine and its popularization is not one of inventors, but one of businessmen, for without a doubt, the promotion of the sewing machine shaped public view more than any inherent qualities of the machine itself, as is clearly shown by the popularity of Singer's machine over the mechanically better Wheeler and Wilson.

The first obstacle that stood between the sewing machine and the populace was that of cost. Each machine was more or less hand made at great expense. This and the license and legal costs, which as we have seen were quite high, all contributed to a price of about $125.00 per machine, and the average yearly income was around $500.00. Most households could obviously not afford such an outlay, and thus manufacturers were the primary supporters in the early days of the industry.

Solutions to this problem came in various forms. Sewing circles were formed in which a group of families would pool their resources to buy a machine that was shared by all. Churches and other organizations might purchase a machine for the use of their members. But to the greedy capitalist, these solutions were unsatisfactory, for they made a single sale to numerous potential customers. A far more preferable scheme was laid out by Edward Clark of the I. M. Singer Company. If a family could only amass a few dollars at a time towards the purchase of a sewing machine, then why not enable the manufacturer to take payments in small bits rather than in one large sum.

The basic premise of the hire/purchase plan, as it came to be known, was that a sewing machine could be rented, after a down payment of about $5.00 had been made, for the sum of $3.00 – 5.00 a month. Payments would be credited toward the final purchase of the machine. Not only did this system open up the market to a greater number of customers and increase sales, it also meant that the price charged for a machine could be raised by quite a bit, which the manufacturers justified by citing the credit risks they took (which were very real). It seems that it was just as true in the nineteenth century as it is today that consumers would "rather pay one hundred dollars for a machine in monthly installments of five dollars, than fifty dollars outright, although able to do so."[23] The plan was definitely a popular one — the other manufacturers quickly followed Singer's lead, and thus one of the foundations of our modern economy was born: buying on credit.

While it is certain that the hire/purchase plan did do a great deal of good by enabling a larger segment of the public to benefit from a labor-saving device (and that segment doubtless needed it the most), some drawbacks became evident when less scrupulous businessmen began to take advantage of the unwary with schemes theretofore unheard of. There were reports of foreclosures on machines that were nearly paid for, during which violence sometimes ensued. In one scheme, a bogus manufacturer would assure a woman of steady income: she could make the required payments for purchase of the machine with the work the company provided her. After a few weeks of sewing goods for the company (during which time the only compensation for the woman's labor was a credit towards the purchase of the machine), the woman would cease to receive assignments, and the machine would be repossessed upon her failure to pay off the balance. Thus, these wily agents received free labor at a minimum of trouble to themselves.[24] Such abuses of the hire/purchase system, while they may have cast some undue suspicion upon the more reputable names in the industry, apparently did not affect the rise of sales. In 1855, Singer reported 883 machines sold; this figure rose dramatically to 2,564 in 1856, when the plan went into effect.

The name Singer did not become synonymous with the sewing machine in many parts of the world without just cause. Promotion was the key to popularity, and Singer's personal flair, as well as Clark's business acumen, were the keys to the company's success. Without Clark's innovations, the industry as a whole would not have fared as well as it did. In addition to the hire/purchase plan, which was pivotal in opening up the market, Clark formulated another promotion, one that would have still more lasting influence. In 1857, the I. M. Singer Company announced a "Liberal plan of exchanging Singer's new and latest improved sewing machines for old or unimproved sewing machines of every kind." The price allowed for the trade-in was the considerable sum of 50 dollars, which must have seemed an irresistible deal. The benefits of the idea were quickly felt by the company, whose sales rose another 40% that year.

The benefits of the trade-in scheme were twofold. First was the added incentive to purchase a new model, if the consumer happened to be lucky enough to have an old model already, although in 1857 there were not that many improvements on the latest machines to make such an additional investment worthwhile. Second was the successful elimination of thousands of cheap used machines that might hamper the sales of new machines, for all of the trade-ins were destined to be melted down and used for scrap metal. Clark was candid about his intentions in a manner unheard of today: "These worthless machines now stand directly in the way of the sale of good ones. Their existence causes great pecuniary loss to us."[25]

The early process of manufacture, namely that of individually handcrafting all parts, led to more evils than just high cost. Any repairs that needed to be made could not be achieved by the simple substitution of a replacement part for the offending piece. There was not sufficient standardization from machine to machine; every part had to be specially fitted. If we are fortunate enough to have at our disposal two identical early models — Singer or otherwise — we can observe the effect of this method of construction. Placed side by side, two examples of the same early Singer model appear identical to the casual observer. However, upon closer inspection, one finds tiny differences in the internal workings. Thus, a certain lever on the first machine might be $1/32''$ longer than the same lever on the second machine. On some early models, these differences occur in each and every part, down to the tiniest screw.

It is more than just coincidence that the introduction of mass production, which would solve the above problems, occurred shortly after the formation of the Combination. The early sewing machine capitalists were reluctant to pour money into new factories during the litigious climate of the early 1850s, for one could never be sure that one's business might not be sued out of existence. Encouraged by the formation of the Combination and the legal stability it engendered, as well as the growing popularity of the sewing machine, companies were more willing to spend large sums on factories that employed the most modern manufacturing techniques.

Mass production had begun during the early 1850s with the development of specialized equipment to stamp out identical parts for Colt pistols. It was logical for the sewing machine manufacturers to realize the potential of machinery that could produce an endless supply of absolutely identical and interchangeable parts. Thus, by 1857, the I. M. Singer Company had completed a factory of the most modern design, which, as much as the sewing machine itself, was the beginning of a new chapter in the Industrial Revolution. This factory and others to follow were to revolutionize the way all durable consumer goods were manufactured. A comparison between the old and new methods is succinctly given in this description of a similar sewing machine factory built in Bridgeport, Connecticut, by the Wheeler & Wilson Company:

This was a tiresome job when all was done by hand; when each part of each machine was fitted to its fellows by cutting and filing, and when the parts of two machines must be kept separate. Now all are so exactly alike that a thousand pieces are finished and thrown into a box together, and each one forming a part of a machine, and never requiring the stroke of a file to adjust it, though the parts may be a thousand miles away from each other.[26]

The final step in this process involved parts being placed in bins in front of workers, each of whom would assemble complete machines (the day of Henry Ford and the assembly line had not yet arrived). The products of these workers, the complete machines, were inspected, and the workers were then paid by the piece.

An immediate implication of mass production was that small sewing machine companies could contract with larger ones to be supplied with all the working parts for a machine, which the smaller company could then assemble and stamp its own name on. Or a large company could ship parts to remote areas and assemble its machines there, thus minimizing loss due to damage that might occur in transport. It was cheaper for a shipper to lose a few small mass-produced parts than to lose entire machines.

By 1870, if a company, large or small, wished to stay in business, it had to utilize mass-produced parts. Scores of companies came and went during these early days. In some cases, their demise was due to newly patented but otherwise poorly functioning mechanisms for forming a stitch, but in many cases these companies failed because of their lack of capital to construct the expensive factories required for part production. Yet the large companies flourished, and by 1877, when the Sewing Machine Combination disbanded, the industry was in the midst of exponential growth as far as the overall sale of sewing machines was concerned. But while almost every family in the USA was acquiring a sewing machine (and many for the second or third time), the total number of companies in the business of actual manufacture of these machines was decreasing.

By 1900, through mergers and bankruptcies, there were only a dozen or so prospering sewing machine companies actually manufacturing machines for home use. These companies all made excellent machines, and most offered their services to any business, small or large, that wished to have its own named sewing machine. Thus the "Sears, Roebuck" sewing machine and the "Spee Dee" sewing machine were both manufactured by the National Sewing Machine Company and probably differed only in the stenciled gold lettering. Several thousand such names sprang up during the early twentieth century — most only existed for a short time and almost all are long since forgotten today, along with many of the giants of the prior generation, such as Grover and Baker. Not forgotten are the technology and business acumen that were spawned by the early sewing machine companies. These features have become an integral part of the national fabric today.

Endnotes

[1] Cooper, p. 4.

[2] Brandon, p. 55.

[3] Cooper, p. 4.

[4] Ibid., p. 6.

[5] Ibid., p. 11.

[6] Brandon, p. 57.

[7] Lewton, p. 563.

[8] Ibid., p. 562.

[9] Parton, p. 527.

[10] Brandon, p. 63.

[11] Scientific American, Sept. 26, 1846, p. 4.

[12] In 1844, in England, John Fisher was granted a patent for an eye pointed needle and shuttle. Although two threads were used in the stitch, Fisher's machine was designed for embroiderywork and did not produce a lockstitch. Nevertheless, Thomas, having bought Howe's patent rights, was not allowed to claim the eye pointed needle and shuttle due to Fisher's prior patent.

[13] Brandon, p. 43.

[14] Ibid., p. 44.

[15] The original prototype has been lost. This machine probably reflects the appearance of the prototype. See Cooper, p. 31.

[16] Parton, p. 536; also Lewton, p. 571. There are at least three slightly different versions of this dramatic recollection.

[17] Brandon, p. 50.

[18] Ibid., p. 52.

[19] Ibid., p. 73.

[20] The 1876 Howe Sewing Machine Exhibition Catalogue, p. 6.

[21] Details were addressed in the so-called "Albany Agreement" of 1856. Nine patents (including Howe's 1846 patent) were involved in the agreement. The patents do not include A. B. Wilson's stationary bobbin, but this patent was utilized by Sloat's Elliptic sewing machine as early as 1858. It is possible that a private arrangement was made between Sloat and the Wheeler & Wilson Company; however, it is also possible that patents were added to those of the original Albany agreement as new licensees joined the combination.

[22] Scientific American, 28; January 25, 1873, p. 49.

[23] Scientific American, as quoted in Brandon, p. 117.

[24] Coons, p. 77.

[25] Brandon, p. 119.

[26] New York Daily Tribune, May 22, 1863, p. 8.

Sewing Machine Manufacturers from 1850 to 1880

This section reflects most U.S. manufacturers from the 1850 – 1880 period, and a few after 1880, that one might encounter. It deals specifically with machines designed for home use. The reader should note that only a representative selection of the different manufacturers of clones of SINGER NEW FAMILY and WILLCOX & GIBBS machines have been given. The same applies to the "modern" machine styles that appeared in great quantities starting shortly before 1880 and continuing through 1925 (see appendices D, G, and H). Note that cross-referenced machines are given in capital letters.

Types of Stitches

An attempt has been made to indicate what type of stitch each machine sews. With minor variations, the stitching mechanisms on almost all sewing machines designed for home use fall into the following six categories (see figure 2-1):

1) **Shuttle Lockstitch**
   (example: Singer New Family)

2) **Stationary Bobbin Lockstitch**
   (example: Wheeler & Wilson)

3) **Two-thread Chain Stitch**
   (example: Grover & Baker). A large number of variant mechanisms formed this stitch.

4) **Single-thread Chain Stitch with Revolving Hook**
   (example: Willcox & Gibbs)

5) **Single-thread Chain Stitch with Reciprocating Hook**
   (examples: New England and Shaw & Clark)

6) **Running Stitch**
   (example: Madame Demorest)

Figure 2-1. The six most common stitches used on sewing machines designed for home use. All but the running stitch are from drawings in Gilbert.

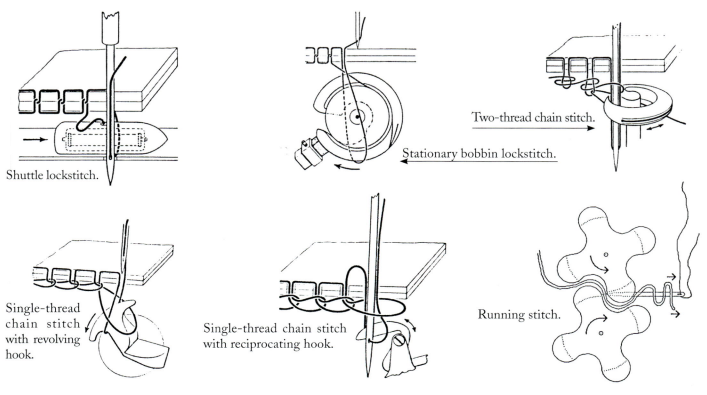

Shuttle lockstitch.

Stationary bobbin lockstitch.

Two-thread chain stitch.

Single-thread chain stitch with revolving hook.

Single-thread chain stitch with reciprocating hook.

Running stitch.

One should note that the two lockstitches are identical, but the two single thread chain stitches differ slightly. The revolving Willcox & Gibbs hook imparts a half twist to the loop of the chain, whereas other methods do not. The two-thread chain stitch was formed by several different mechanisms; hence there are minor variants of the stitch. The running stitch is similar to a stitch that a human might form with a needle and thread.

How to Evaluate a Machine

Usually hand-operated machines are more common, because it was easier to save a small hand-operated machine (for example, in the attic) than a complete treadle machine. Hence, for two machines of similar vintage where the same number of treadle and hand models were made, you will find many more hand machines than treadle examples. Naturally, a head alone, without its treadle stand, is less valuable than a complete treadle machine. Completely enclosed wood cabinets are rarer and more valuable than the typical treadle models with iron legs. Heads inlaid with mother-of-pearl are more rare than those that are not and are always worth more than the usual value for a head.

One should not base an evaluation of a machine on its sewing ability. Many of the sewing machine manufacturing companies that sprang up in the early days of the industry made machines that did not sew well; hence few were sold, and the result is that many of the rarest machines hardly sew at all!

Each illustration (and occasional text) is accompanied with a rarity/value (r/v) code, with r reflecting the quantities surviving and v indicating a relative dollar value for the machine. Unless otherwise indicated, the rarity/value codes apply to the example illustrated. If variants are discussed, they will be given individual r/v codes. Of course, trying to estimate the number of surviving examples of any mass-produced nineteenth century object is risky at best — hence these rarity codes, which are given below, should be utilized with caution.

- **X** (Extremely rare)
- **R** (Rare)
- **O** (Occasionally found)
- **F** (Frequently found)
- **A** (Abundant)
- **U** (Cannot establish rarity due to insufficient data)

Value Scale

It is extremely difficult to pin down accurately the value for a particular sewing machine. This task is made even harder when one considers that price can (and does) vary widely over time. For example, during the past five to ten years, many early toy sewing machines have doubled in value, whereas many scarce full-sized machines have seen their values drop in half. Furthermore, a great deal depends upon the condition of the machine.

With the above caveat in mind, a 1 through 10 numbering system has been implemented in which 10 implies the highest value. Each number will reflect a rather wide range, which is not unreasonable since individual machines can vary so much. Codes and values are located on page 431.

Rarity and Value of Unknown Machines

It is difficult to place an accurate dollar amount on a machine for which no market value has been established. Much depends upon the age, condition, and distinction of the example. Thus, the machine of a newly discovered manufacturer that is identical to the Singer New Family might be historically important, but would probably command marginal interest to the collector and hence not be of great monetary value. However, a heretofore unknown model from a known manufacturer that is highly unusual in appearance and was made before 1860 would command a high price.

Rarity and Value of Later Machines

By 1890, the overall features and shape of sewing machines designed for home use had pretty much stabilized. With few exceptions, all machines looked just about alike except for their cabinets. Yet thousands of different brand names appeared stenciled on the sides of these machines (see Appendices G and H). Undoubtedly, some of these names are quite rare and whimsical — for instance, the Husband and Patrandry sewing machine — while others are more mundane (there were at least three Acme sewing machines). Regardless of the rarity, the value of such machines must be guided by the individual appeal. If a name or a treadle stand is ordinary, the value will be quite low — regardless of how rare the machine might be. Typical value codes would thus be 1 – 2 for a standard iron-leg treadle machine and 2 – 3 for an enclosed wooden cabinet model or an exotically named or highly carved version. (See appendix D for some typical examples.)

Serial Numbers

Frequently you will find numbers stamped in various places on one machine, for example, under the cloth plate or on machine parts themselves. These numbers are usually not serial numbers. The serial number, when it is present at all, will usually appear stamped on the top surface of the cloth plate, but there are many exceptions. One should exercise caution when using serial numbers to ascertain rarity or to date a machine (see appendix B). Serial numbers are not necessarily an honest depiction of how many machines had been produced at that point. Furthermore, some manufacturers restarted serial numbers when changing models. But since there is little else to go by — except of course the patent dates that appear on many machines — one cannot be faulted for using every bit of information presented by a machine, as long as one's approach is scientific.

Patent Dates

As with serial numbers, the same caution is recommended when attempting to date a machine by using the patent dates that frequently appear stamped on the cloth plate or other parts. One would like to believe that a machine stamped with "Sept. 10, 1846" was made in 1846; however, the appearance of this date merely means that Howe's patent was employed — the machine itself was actually made many years later, possibly as late as the 1870s. Of course, one can usually infer that a machine was made no earlier than the latest patent date, or that a machine with several early patents was probably made earlier than one with a long list of later ones.

An Alphabetical List of Machines

A. B. HOWE: See Howe.

AETNA: Popular for ten years starting around 1868, about 30,000 were made by Planer, Braunsdorf & Co. of Boston. There are several versions of this machine, including a small family model and larger heavy-duty models, each with specific functions. The Aetna "A" (figure 2-2) was sometimes called the New Family Sewing Machine; its design was obviously based on the SINGER NEW FAMILY. Similarly, the Aetna #2 (figure 2-4) appears to be copied from the SINGER #2. When examining the serial numbers on these machines, one should realize that one sequence was probably used for all models; hence it is difficult to tell how many of each model were made. Moreover, the serial number sequence was probably continued from the predecessor company, PLANER AND KAYSER.

AKINS & FELTHOUSEN: This machine may have been the predecessor to the LESTER sewing machine, because an example that looks like a Lester has turned up with no identification other than the inscription, "Akins & Felthousen's Patent, August 5th 1851." According to Cooper, the company was in business in 1855 in Ithaca, New York.

AMERICAN (figure 2-5): Little is known about this machine except that the company was based in New York. According to Cooper, a company by that name was in business in 1854. The figure depicts a machine made in 1866. This company bears no relation to the later AMERICAN (see next).

AMERICAN (Buttonhole, Overseaming, and Sewing Machine): Made in Philadelphia for about twenty years beginning in 1867, the most typical mechanism (figure 2-6) was manufactured in considerable quantities. A less common and earlier model is actually the true "buttonhole machine." It is distinctive because of its decorative open iron work (figure 2-7) and the extra mechanism above and below, which could be engaged to sew a buttonhole (actually, a seam along the edge of the buttonhole). Both models seem to have been made concurrently in the first few years of the company's existence. The buttonhole feature was phased out as a family machine option, possibly because adequate and economical attachments were made that performed the same function. Hence this feature does not appear on the later family machines, which are nevertheless frequently marked "American BHO" (for *B*utton*h*ole and *O*verseaming). The company also produced hand-operated machines (figures 2-8 and 2-9), some of which apparently were embossed with the names of local distributors (figure 2-10).

Figure 2-2. Aetna "A" (O/5), circa 1870.

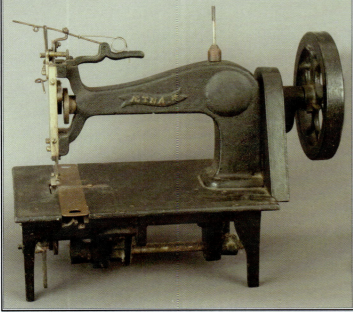

Figure 2-3. Aetna (R/6), circa 1870. This machine was designed for home and manufacturing use. It is intermediate in size between the machines in figures 2-2 and 2-4.

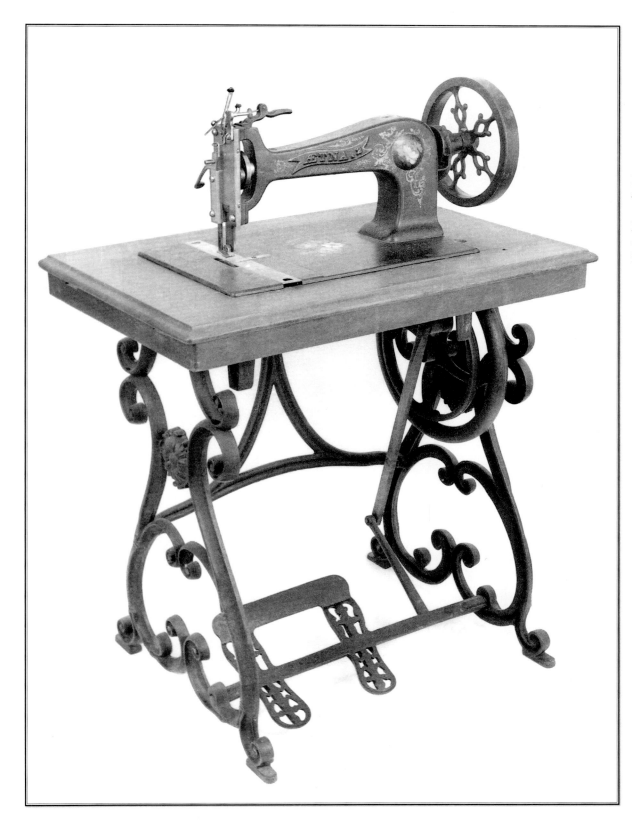

Figure 2-4. Aetna #2 (R/6), circa 1870. This rather large machine was designed for sewing heavy material.

Figure 2-5. American (U/7 or 8), circa 1866. Not much is known about this machine, except that it is unrelated to the machines in figures 2-6 through 2-10.

Figure 2-6. American (A/3), circa 1875.

Figure 2-7. American (O/5), circa 1870. This machine has the buttonhold feature. The electric motor was made around 1915 and could be added to any treadle machine of the period.

AMERICAN EAGLE SEWING MACHINE: See Woodruff.

AMERICAN HAND (figure 2-11): As the illustration shows, this machine superficially resembles a pair of scissors; hence, these models were sometimes called SEWING SHEARS, a term that applies to this as well as a number of other machines made in somewhat similar styles. This machine sews a lockstitch, utilizing a tiny shuttle containing an even tinier bobbin. The American Hand is attractively made out of nickel-plated steel, and several thousand were sold during the 1880s and 1890s.

AMERICAN MAGNETIC (figure 2-12): About 600 of these shuttle lockstitch machines were supposed to have been manufactured in 1853 and 1854 by a factory in Ithaca, New York. However, this figure is rather doubtful, as only three manufacturers had produced that many machines by 1854. More than likely, fewer than two or three hundred were actually made, and only one example is known to have survived. A huge grooved flywheel across the back of the machine drives the L-shaped arm, which was fitted with a ceramic bearing. Despite its clumsy appearance, this is the earliest known machine that has a mechanism that can reverse the direction of the stitch while the operator is in midseam. Notwithstanding this one technological advantage, the reason for its quick demise is plain to anyone who attempts to use it: it does not sew well! Many of the earliest sewing machine manufacturing companies had this same problem; hence, one frequently finds that the rarest machines today usually did not work well during their own time.

ASHLAND (figure 2-13): Except for a difference in the arm mechanism, this machine is almost a clone of the WILLCOX & GIBBS, utilizing its popular revolving hook and outward appearance. The Ashland Machine Co. was based in Ashland, Ohio, and may have produced a large number of these later (circa 1900) machines, as the machine illustrated has a serial number of more than 100,000.

ATWATER (figures 2-14, 2-228): This was usually sold as a hand-operated machine, although treadle versions have turned up. Widely advertised in the 1860s, it was known as "Atwater's $15.00 Sewing Machine." The PAW FOOT base was very common for the era, and several machines share the same design. The Atwater is one of the more desirable of this type and is unique in the simplicity of its mechanism, which accounts for its advertised cheapness. Mr. Atwater, of Berlin, Connecticut, received an 1857 patent for a machine in which the needle is the only moving part involved in stitchmaking, and the underside of the machine is nearly bare of mechanism. During its descent, the needle is forced between a small piece of glass and a piece of leather. The stitch is formed during the next descent of the needle, when the loop remaining from the previous descent is penetrated. Though simply constructed, the Atwater was apparently satisfactory as a sewing device, because quite a few were sold.

BANNER (figure 2-15): This Canadian treadle machine was made during the 1870s and employs a shuttle mechanism that moves in an arc, a common motion for later machines. The upper part of the head closely resembles the earlier CHICOPEE, implying that there may be a connection between the two companies. About 10,000 were made.

BARTHOLF: This New York company, founded by Abraham Bartholf, was one of the very earliest to manufacture sewing machines. It produced a machine with the primitive BLODGETT & LEROW mechanism (figure 2-16) and appears to have made the prototype itself (figure 2-35). At the same time, it began to manufacture its own version of a sewing machine, replacing the faulty Blodgett revolving shuttle mechanism with a reciprocating version (figures 2-17, 2-18). Quite likely, fewer than 100 of these machines were made, and the company soon switched to a more typical-looking (for that early period) machine, which was its model from about 1854 to 1860 (figure 2-19). Its next model, shown in figure 2-20, was made until 1865, when the company went out of business. About 6,000 machines were produced under the Bartholf name, the vast majority being the two later types.

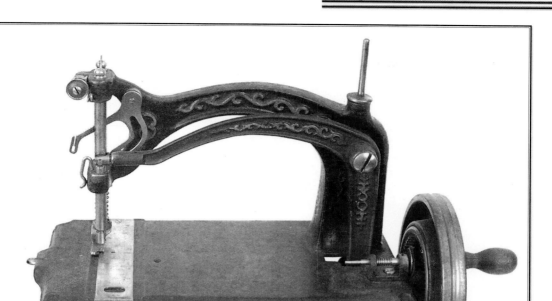

Figure 2-8. American (O/4), circa 1875.

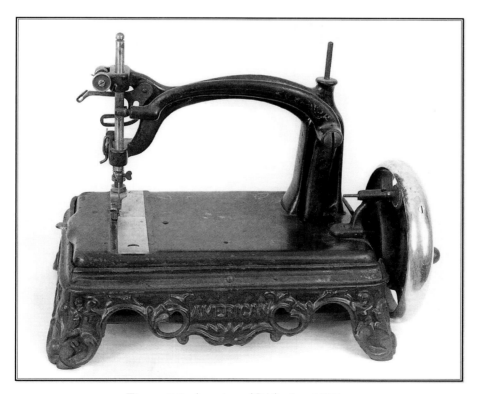

Figure 2-9. American (O/4), circa 1875.

Sewing Machine Manufacturers from 1850 to 1880

Figure 2-10. American (R/6), mounted on a base that has been embossed with the name of a local company.

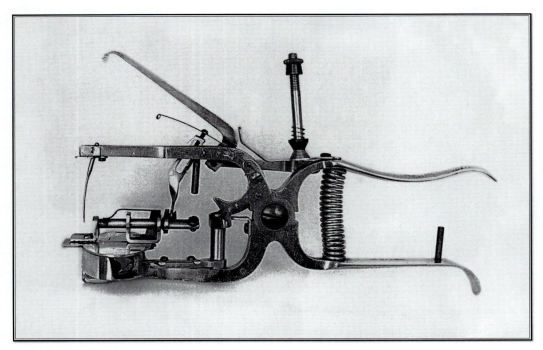

Figure 2-11. American Hand (O/6), circa 1880.

Figure 2-12. American Magnetic (X/10), 1853. The stand for this machine appears to be its shipping crate.

Figure 2-13. Ashland (U/4), circa 1885.

BARTLETT: The example shown in figure 2-21 is typical of most Bartlett machines. Manufactured from about 1866 to after 1870, the Bartlett was primarily sold as a hand-operated model, although an optional treadle table could be purchased. These machines were made by the Goodspeed & Wyman Company, Winchendon, Massachusetts, and later by the Bartlett Sewing Machine Company, New York City. Another type of machine produced by the same company was called the Bartlett NOVELTY (figure 2-22). It appears to have been made concurrently with the more common variety, but in fewer numbers. Bartlett's seldom-encountered last model is shown in figure 2-23 and has a mechanism similar to that of the machine in figure 2-21. A total of 5,000 – 6,000 of all kinds were made. Precise dating is difficult, since not all Bartlett machines were stamped with serial numbers. The serial number for the Bartlett Novelty is painted on the body of the machine just above the wheel. The serial number of the more usual variety, if present at all, is stamped on the cloth plate.

BARTRAM & FANTON (figures 2-24, 2-25, 2-26): According to the chart in appendix B, the Bartram & Fanton Company of Danbury, Connecticut, supposedly produced machines from 1867 to 1875, but the total output of the company is unknown. To add to the confusion, serial numbers are not necessarily stamped on the machines, and when they are, do not appear to reflect precise quantities made. At least one treadle example has been embossed on the cloth plate with, "Cast or pat'd Jan 30th 1866. R.D.O. Smith patent agent, Washington, D.C." Although the Bartram & Fanton superficially resembles the WILLCOX & GIBBS, the chain stitching mechanism is entirely different, and, unlike the Willcox & Gibbs, the machine appears to have been manufactured only as a treadle variety. The treadle example illustrated sports a milk glass spool holder, which appears to be original to the machine.

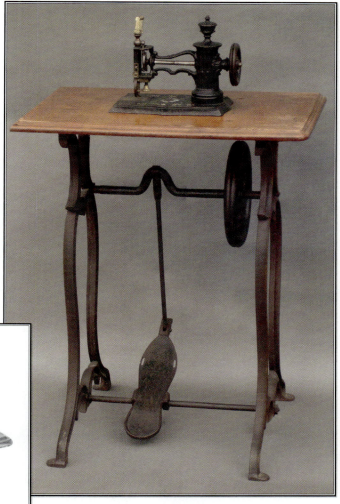

Figure 2-14. Atwater (R/7), circa 1865. The treadle version is encountered much less frequently than the more typical "paw foot" version (see figure 2-228). Although many treadle machines powered by foot-shaped pedals are rather common, this only applies when the pedals are shaped like two feet. Single foot pedal powered machines are all rare to extremely rare.

Fig. 2-15. Banner, circa 1875. Although this machine was made in Canada, it is illustrated here since it could be mistaken for a machine made in the USA.

Figure 2-16. Blodgett & Lerow version of the Bartholf (X/10), 1853. Very few of these were produced starting in 1850. At the same time, Bartholf was manufacturing machines employing its own mechanism (see figure 2-17). Note that the elaborate gold decoration so often found on later machines is usually absent from the very earliest models, which were mainly concerned with just functioning properly.

Sewing Machine Manufacturers from 1850 to 1880

Figure 2-17. Bartholf (X/10), 1850. This machine, serial number 10, was the first model produced by Bartholf using its own design (a reciprocating shuttle) rather than the Blodgett & Lerow design (a revolving shuttle) of figure 2-16. Note the similarity between the stands and the hand cranks of figures 2-16, 2-17, and 2-35. (The wood handle has been slid off to further illustrate this similarity.)

Figure 2-18. Detail of the shuttle race for the Bartholf machine of figure 2-17. Note the circular race for the machine in figure 2-16. But here the entire circle was not used; only a small arc was employed for the to-and-fro motion of the shuttle. Apparently the Bartholf company had several unused carcasses of its version of the Blodgett & Lerow machine, which it adapted for its own mechanism. The Blodgett mechanism, which involved a circular shuttle path, was rather unreliable (see Blodgett and Lerow, figure 2-35). The very earliest machines were still works in progress, so to speak; reliability (and hence stability of design) did not begin until about 1852 – 1853.

Sewing Machine Manufacturers from 1850 to 1880

Figure 2-19. Bartholf (R/8), the second model, circa 1859.

Figure 2-20. Bartholf (R/8), the last model, circa 1863.

Figure 2-21. Bartlett (O/5), the most typical type, circa 1868.

BATTELLE (figure 2-27): The company that distributed this machine was based in Worcester, Massachusetts, and apparently produced sewing machines from the mid-1850s through the mid-1860s. This machine is a very early example of a "waxed thread" machine, meaning that the heavy-duty thread was passed through a wax tray for lubrication. It is quite heavy and boxy — in fact the cams underneath are almost six inches across. The machine may have been manufactured by the LEAVITT company.

BECKWITH: About 30,000 of these chain stitch machines were made during the 1870s by a New York–based company, which also apparently shipped machines overseas in large numbers. There are three distinct types, all of which are hand operated. The first (figure 2-28) is painted black with gold designs. The second is similar to the first, except nickel plated (figure 2-29). The third and apparently the most popular type can be differentiated by its curved arm (figure 2-30). All three were designed to be clamped onto a table. The Beckwith is a very light machine and can be easily tucked away in the corner of an attic or sewing room; hence many have survived.

BELLE (figure 2-31): This is a later treadle machine that derives much of its charm from its diminutive size. It features a WILLCOX & GIBBS mechanism — hence the name Belle Automatic, since the tension on all later Willcox & Gibbs type machines never needs to be adjusted.

BIRD SEWING MACHINE: See WOODRUFF.

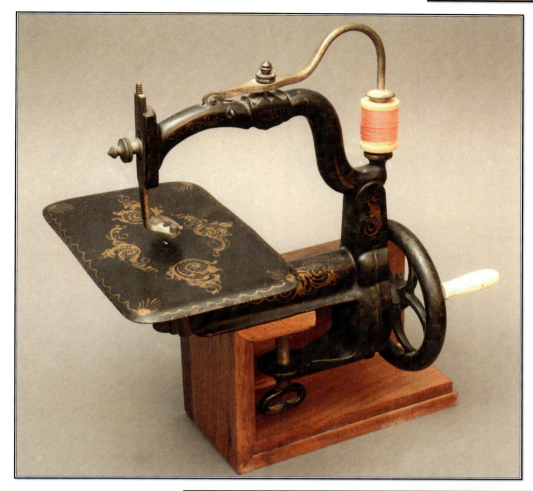

Figure 2-22. Bartlett Novelty (R/6), circa 1868.

Figure 2-23. Bartlett (R/5), the last model, circa 1870.

Figure 2-24. Bartram & Fanton (X/8), 1867. Although this machine superficially resembles the Willcox and Gibbs (figure 2-334), the mechanism is entirely different. Probably only a few hundred of these were produced before the company switched to its typical design with the flattened top.

Figure 2-25. Bartram & Fanton (R/7), circa 1868.

Figure 2-26. Detail of the typical Bartram and Fanton head.

BISHOP (figures 2-32, 2-33): The example shown has no manufacturer's name on it, but is marked: "William H. Johnson's patent March 7, 1854, Feb. 26 1858, H. H. Bishop's patent, Dec. 7, 1858." Hence, calling the machine a Bishop may be incorrect. Designed for treadle use, the machine sews a two-thread chain stitch.

BLEES (figure 2-34): Made mainly as a treadle variety, about 15,000 Blees machines were manufactured starting in 1870. It is a cumbersome-looking machine whose design appears to have been based upon the SINGER LETTER "A" of a decade earlier. The place of manufacture was Bordentown, New Jersey, but the company had its headquarters in New York City, for the machines display hand-painted gold lettering that says, "Blees S. M. Co. New York." Interestingly, the company appeared to be quite successful during its short span, but abruptly ceased manufacture after 1877.

BLODGETT & LEROW (figure 2-35): Blodgett & Lerow actually refers to a type of mechanism rather than to a specific manufacturer; however, any examples are quite rare, so from the standpoint of a collector, the maker is not important. The principle behind this machine was the revolving shuttle, patented in 1849 by S. C. Blodgett. It is a unique and unsatisfactory solution to the problem of making a machine that sews. With every turn of the crank, the shuttle revolves in a circular race and a stitch is formed, but the thread also gets an extra twist due to the circular motion of the shuttle. Because of this drawback, the mechanism did not enjoy much commercial success and was made for only a brief period, from 1849 to 1853. A Smithsonian example was manufactured by Goddard, Rice & Co. of Worcester, Massachusetts, and another example (figure 2-16) was made by BARTHOLF.

Figure 2-27. Battelle (X/9), circa 1858.

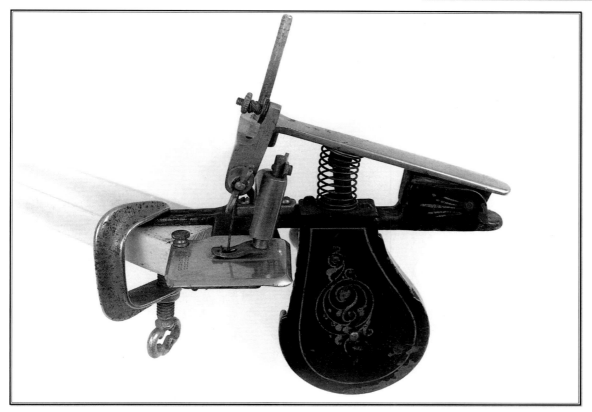

Figure 2-28. Beckwith (O/6), circa 1873.

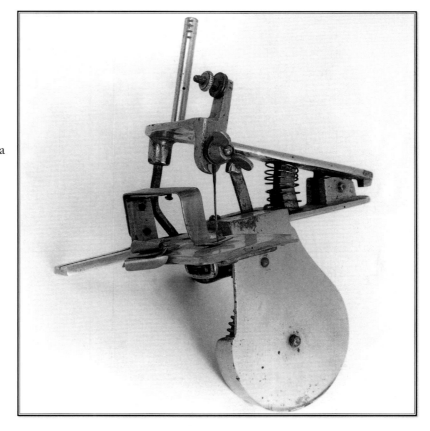

Figure 2-29. Beckwith (O/6), circa 1873. This machine is nickel plated.

Figure 2-30. Beckwith (O/6), circa 1875. This is the largest and probably the most frequently found type.

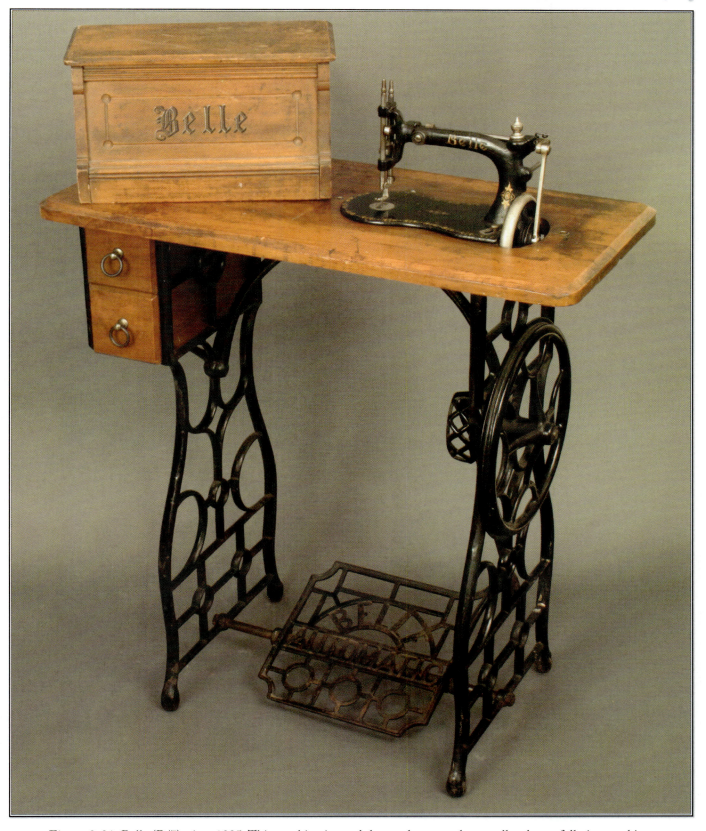

Figure 2-31. Belle (R/7), circa 1885. This machine is much larger than a toy but smaller than a full-size machine.

Figure 2-32. Bishop (X/9), circa 1859.

Figure 2-33. Mechanism detail of the Bishop machine (figure 2-32), which sews a two-thread chain stitch.

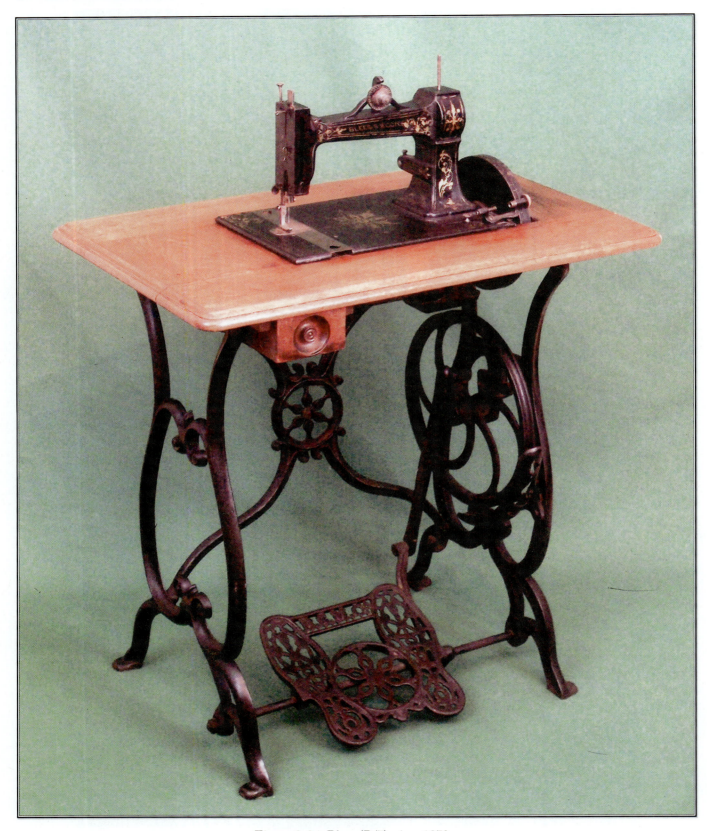

Figure 2-34. Blees (R/7), circa 1872.

Figure 2-35. Blodgett & Lerow (X/10), 1849. This appears to be the prototype, and was probably custom made by the Bartholf company (note the similarity of the hand cranks in figures 2-16, 2-17, and 2-35). The shuttle revolves in a circle, and hence imparts a twist in the thread for every stitch. This faulty mechanism design was only manufactured for a short while. (See also figure I-1.)

Sewing Machine Manufacturers from 1850 to 1880

BOSWORTH: Made for a short period of time by Charles Bosworth of Petersham, Massachusetts, this chain stitch treadle machine excelled as a decorative parlor piece. The table is nicely scalloped, and the dainty treadle legs are painted bright gold. Unfortunately, none of this helps the Bosworth sew. Its main cause for failure was due to a tiny pawl that was used to advance the cloth. The machine had the unfortunate characteristic that, if operated backwards (which was easy to do accidentally), the pawl attempted to advance the cloth while the needle was still penetrating; hence, this small device is frequently broken off. Probably about 1,500 Bosworth family machines (figures 2-36, 2-37, 2-38) were made and sold for $25.00 each during the early 1860s. Even this limited popularity can probably be attributed to their decorativeness and low price rather than usefulness. Subsequently, Mr. Bosworth sold heavier, and presumably more useful, commercial models, such as an 1870 machine designed for sewing hats (figure 2-39). Interestingly, this later machine revived the long discarded revolving shuttle principle (see BLODGETT & LEROW), but solved the problem of thread twisting by maintaining a cam-driven finger-like projection that kept in contact with a specially shaped bobbin. The purpose of this device was to keep the bobbin from turning as the shuttle revolved, hence preventing the thread from twisting.

BOUDOIR (figures 2-41 and 2-42): Although this is now a rare machine, it was rather popular during the 1860s and was widely advertised. The mechanism sews a two-thread chain stitch and appears to have been designed mainly for treadle use. Minor variations have been found for both the mechanism and the head design, as well as various treadle models. According to Cooper, the machine was manufactured in Chicago, although it may also have been made in the eastern U.S.

BOYNTON (figure 2-43): This machine employs 1858 and 1859 patents by Boynton and may actually have been manufactured under another name. Although the machine is hand operated, another version (figure 2-44) is embossed "patent treadle sewing machine, Nov. 2. 58" and yet is only about 4" high. An arm containing a large flywheel can be attached to the machine, allowing the operator to sew two stitches with each turn of the handle (one revolution of the larger wheel). At least three different models of machines with this same overall appearance were made.

BRADFORD & BARBER (figure 2-45): This Boston company made heavy-duty sewing machines from 1859 until about 1866. The machines are large, heavy, and noisy, and utilize a complicated mechanism and waxed thread to sew a single- thread chain stitch. Perhaps it was thought that if the material was three times as heavy, the machine should be made with three times as many cams and levers. The extremely large flywheel has both a handle for manual operation and a groove ready for use with a belt drive. This particular boxy design was popular during the 1860s for machines of its type, namely those that sewed leather or other heavy materials.

BUCKEYE (figures 2-46, 2-47): The Buckeye was a popular shuttle machine manufactured by the W. G. WILSON Sewing Machine Company of Cleveland, Ohio, during the early 1870s. Ready to be used as a hand-operated machine, the Buckeye could also be mounted on a separately purchased stand; hence, complete treadle machines sometimes have handles on the machine flywheel. The Buckeye (and many other hand-operated machines) has threaded holes under the head base so that the customer could attach the head to a treadle table by means of a large bolt or two.

BUELL (figures 2-48, 2-49): This unusual machine was made around 1859 by A. B. Buell of Westmoreland, New York. Underneath, it has been clearly stamped "Lathbury's Patent," which refers to a patent of July 7, 1857. Very few Buells were produced — probably between 1,000 and 2,000.

BUSY BEE (figure 2-50): This heretofore unknown machine appears to be more or less typical of the small cheap hand-operated models that were sold during the 1860s. Its maker is unknown.

CENTENNIAL: See McLEAN AND HOOPER.

Figure 2-36. Bosworth (R/8), circa 1861. The iron stand sports its original gold paint.

Sewing Machine Manufacturers from 1850 to 1880

Figure 2-37. Detail of the Bosworth, figure 2-36. During this period, hand-painted flowers and other motifs were common.

Figure 2-38. Mechanism detail for the Bosworth machine of figure 2-37. This single-thread chain stitch device was simple but flawed (see text).

Sewing Machine Manufacturers from 1850 to 1880

Figure 2-39. Bosworth (X/8), circa 1870.

Figure 2-40. Boudoir (R/7), circa 1865. This particular treadle stand design was one of the most typical of the period. (See figures 2-46, 2-250, etc.)

Figure 2-41. Boudoir (R/7), circa 1862.

Figure 2-42. Mechanism for the Boudoir machine of figure 2-41. Over the years, this mechanism, which sews a two-thread chain stitch, varied slightly.

Figure 2-43. Boynton (R/7), circa 1860.

Figure 2-44. Boynton (R/7), circa 1860. The cloth plate is embossed, "patent treadle sewing machine."

Figure 2-45. Bradford & Barber (X/7), circa 1865. This waxed thread machine is extremely heavy.

Figure 2-46. Buckeye (O/5), circa 1870.

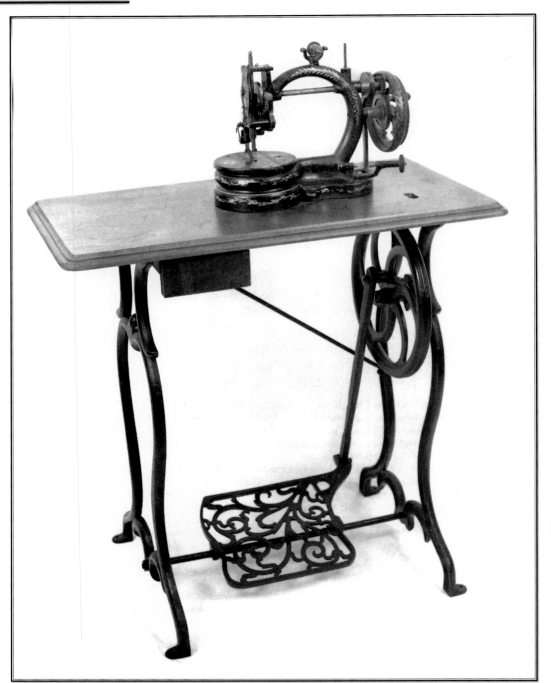

CHERUB (figure 2-51): The Cherub, which was probably made by D. W. Clark of Bridgeport, Connecticut, sews a single-thread chain stitch. It is one of the most desired small figural machines and appears to have been made for a very brief period during the late 1850s. The machine shown differs somewhat from a Smithsonian example but is the same small size (about 5" across).

CHICOPEE (figure 2-52): This machine was made from 1868 to 1869 by the Chicopee Sewing Machine Co., Chicopee Falls, Massachusetts. The head greatly resembles the BANNER sewing machine, but the two may be unrelated.

CLARK'S REVOLVING LOOPER (figures 2-53, 2-54): About 3,000 of these machines were produced from the late 1850s to 1861 by the Lamson, Goodnow & Yale Co. of Windsor, Vermont. Designed to be powered either by hand or by treadle, they are most frequently found in hand-operated form; the complete treadle variety is considerably scarcer. This machine produces a two-thread chain stitch similar to a GROVER & BAKER stitch.

COMMON SENSE: See FAMILY for an explanation; also see NEW ENGLAND, GOLD MEDAL.

CUTE (figure 2-55): This hand-operated chain stitch model was designed to be clamped to a table. The machine was made during the 1880s and is unusual in that the mechanism for translating the motion from the flywheel to the needle shaft contains no gears, yet one revolution of the flywheel causes two revolutions of the needle shaft. Frequently the name *Cute* has worn off the side of the arm, where it was stenciled in gold. Probably around 2,000 – 4,000 of these little machines were manufactured.

Figure 2-47. Buckeye (R/6), circa 1877, hand-operated version.

Figure 2-48. Buell (R/8), 1859.

Sewing Machine Manufacturers from 1850 to 1880

Figure 2-49. Mechanism for the Buell machine (figure 2-48), which produces a single-thread chain stitch. Written on the long arm is "Lathbury's Pat.," which probably refers to his 1857 patent.

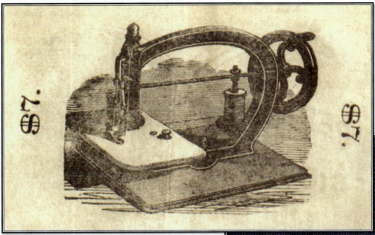

Figure 2-50. Busy Bee (U/5 or 6), circa 1865. Little is known about this machine except that it apparently cost $7.00.

Figure 2-51. Cherub (X/9), circa 1853.

DAISY: The Daisy was a full-fledged treadle machine made in Cleveland, Ohio, during the 1880s (figure 2-56). It should not be confused with the child's LITTLE DAISY treadle sewing machine. Particulars on the numbers made are not known.

DAVIS: This treadle-powered shuttle lockstitch machine was later known as the Vertical Feed Sewing Machine due to its needle feed mechanism. Of the early examples, 3,000 – 5,000 were made during the 1860s (figure 2-57). The early version is somewhat more crude in appearance than the modern Davis of the 1880s, which was manufactured by the hundreds of thousands from about 1875 well through the turn of the century (figure 2-58). The early models were produced by the Davis Sewing Machine Co. in Watertown, New York. Later the company moved to Dayton, Ohio.

DEMOREST: See MADAME DEMOREST.

DIAMOND IMPROVED: See FRANKLIN.

DOMESTIC: One of the most successful lockstitch machines of the late 1800s, the Domestic was manufactured well into the twentieth century. According to Cooper, the machine was made first in Newark, New Jersey, and later in Cleveland, Ohio. The very earliest models (around 1865) may have been made by William A. Mack of Norwalk, Ohio (see MACK). Trade cards from about 1880 to 1885 indicate that New York City was the company headquarters. The head has a high arm, a popular modern design of that period. Many thousands of these treadle machines were sold, including one that was mounted on a fancy stand similar to the elaborate fancy FLORENCE stand (figure 2-59). The company advertised widely and produced a large variety of trade cards, many of which are quite whimsical and are collectors items in their own right (see figures D-17 and D-21).

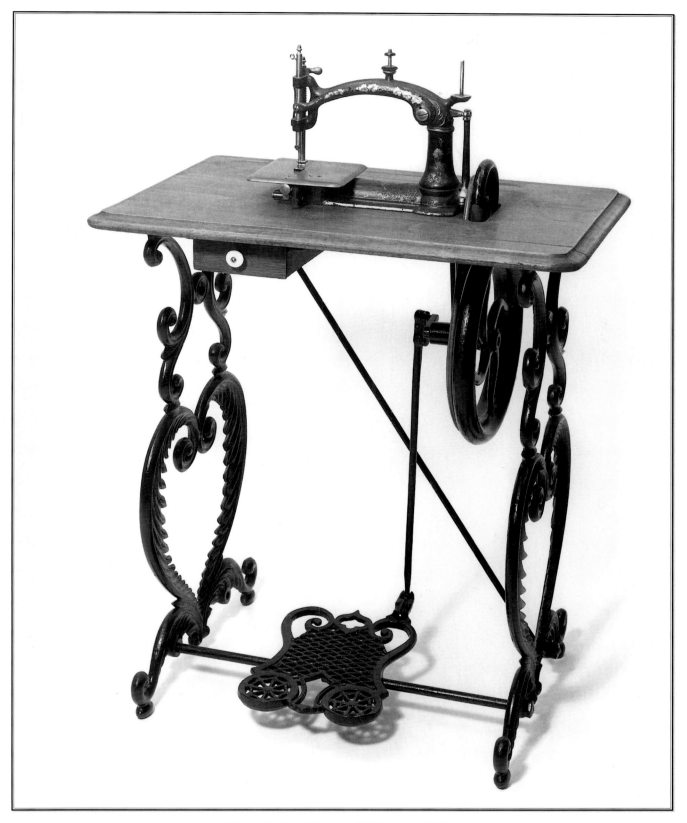

Figure 2-52. Chicopee (X/8), circa 1870.

Figure 2-53. Clark's Revolving Looper (R/7), circa 1860. It could be mounted on a treadle stand or operated by hand.

Figure 2-54. Detail of the machine in figure 2-53.

DORCAS (figure 2-61): One of the very earliest machines made, its production lasted for about five years, starting in 1853. It sews a shuttle lockstitch and is somewhat similar in appearance to the Singer No. 1. The example shown is from a small advertisement that appeared in the Salem Observer (Massachusetts), May 13, 1854. The American Sewing Machine Company mentioned in the advertisement probably has no connection with the later AMERICAN company.

ELASTIC MOTION (figures 2-62, 2-63, 2-64): Made during the mid-1880s in Brooklyn, New York, this machine employs a WILLCOX & GIBBS type of revolving-hook chain stitch mechanism. Sold only as a treadle model, the stand is intricately cast, with little vines decorating the legs. It is likely that about 2,000 were made.

ELDREDGE (A/2): Made during the latter two decades of the nineteenth century and on into the twentieth by the Eldredge Sewing Machine Co. of Belvidere, Illinois, the Eldredge Automatic is essentially a WILLCOX & GIBBS clone and is identical to that machine in appearance. It was, however, very successful in its own right, although not nearly as many of it were sold as of the true Willcox & Gibbs. Probably more than 100,000 were manufactured.

Figure 2-55. Cute (R/6), circa 1880.

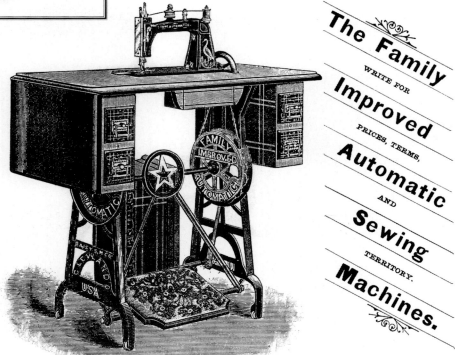

Figure 2-56. Daisy (U/6), circa 1885.

Sewing Machine Manufacturers from 1850 to 1880

Figure 2-57. Davis (R/5), circa 1869. This is the first model produced.

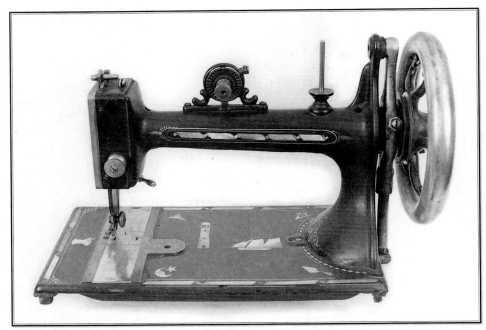

Figure 2-58. Davis (O/3), circa 1878. This particular example is heavily embossed with mother-of-pearl, and hence is somewhat more valuable than the typical model (A/1). An example of a 1910 Davis is depicted on the front cover of this book.

Figure 2-59. Domestic (R/5), circa 1870. This fancy example is not encountered nearly as frequently as the more mundane versions (A/1).

ELLIPTIC: Known also as Sloat's Elliptic, this stationary bobbin lockstitch machine was made by at least five different companies, although the number of actual manufacturing facilities may be fewer. The George B. Sloat Company of Philadelphia produced the very first machines (figure 2-65) for a short time starting in 1858, but the head style was soon modified to that shown in figure 2-66 and was never altered again. The most common treadle model (figure 2-67), if there is such thing for the Elliptic, is similar in appearance to a WHEELER & WILSON and was in fact made by the Wheeler & Wilson company from 1861 to about 1867. Several companies sold the Elliptic on a fancy stand (figure 2-68); note minor differences between this stand and that of the FLORENCE. All Elliptic machines incorporate a stationary-bobbin lockstitch mechanism and apparently were made as treadle models in America, although hand-operated versions have appeared in Europe.

Figure 2-60. Domestic (O/3), circa 1880. It is unusual to find a "high arm" type of machine with mother-of-pearl inlay.

Another manufacturer of the Elliptic was the Lester Manufacturing Co. of Richmond, Virginia (see LESTER), which made, among others, a model that was housed in a finely carved full cabinet (figure 2-69). Lester versions of the Elliptic were only manufactured for a few months starting in 1860; hence this cabinet variety is rather rare. Later in 1860, the Lester company was renamed the Union Sewing Machine Co., and other Elliptic styles were produced under that name for a short period, until sometime after the outbreak of the Civil War.

Several different stands for the Elliptic incorporate a mirror and a pair of pincushions; these amenities appear on plain, fancy, and full-cabinet varieties. Including all manufacturers, about 30,000 Elliptic sewing machines were made, but serial numbers do not necessarily indicate such quantities, as more low-numbered machines have surfaced than is statistically likely. Possibly the numbers were restarted when the Wheeler & Wilson company began manufacturing these machines during the early 1860s, and then again when the Elliptic Sewing Machine Co. of New York commenced their manufacture in 1867. Occasionally, neither a name nor a serial number appears on the machine. Except for the 1858 model, the machine heads are all identical — regardless of their company of origin.

Figure 2-61. Dorcas (X/9), circa 1854.

EMPIRE: With manufacturing facilities based in New York, this was a moderately successful lockstitch treadle machine made for a few years starting around 1863. The Empire Number One (figures 2-70, 2-71) was sold in a variety of treadle stand styles, the most typical form featuring a simple metal table (as opposed to the usual wood surface). About 15,000 Number One models were made. The Improved Empire followed, with a head that began to resemble the REMINGTON, which descended from the Empire line. Improved Empires, unlike their predecessors, have only been found with wooden tabletops. It is not known exactly when production of the Empire ceased, but advertisements show that the improved model was being sold in 1866 and in 1871. Approximately 10,000 – 15,000 Improved Empire machines were produced (figure 2-72).

EMPIRE: This PAW FOOT model sews a chain stitch and is similar to other paw foot varieties. These machines probably were not made by the Empire company that produced lockstitch machines.

Figure 2-62. Elastic Motion (R/7), circa 1885.

Sewing Machine Manufacturers from 1850 to 1880

Figure 2-63. Detail of the Elastic Motion head, figure 2-62. This machine could be pivoted about its center to view (and perhaps adjust) the mechanism. See also figure 2-163 (the Manhattan) for a machine with this same ability.

Figure 2-64. Detail of the Elastic Motion in figure 2-62, showing the tiny vines embossed into the legs.

Figure 2-65. Elliptic (R/6, head only), circa 1858. The earliest model.

Figure 2-66. Elliptic (O/4, head only), circa 1865. The typical version.

Figure 2-67. Elliptic (O/5), circa 1865. Several types of stands were sold. This is a typical one.

Figure 2-68. Elliptic (R/7), circa 1865. The fancy version.

Sewing Machine Manufacturers from 1850 to 1880

Figure 2-69. Elliptic (X/8), as manufactured by the Lester sewing machine company, circa 1860.

Figure 2-70. Empire model number one (R/7), circa 1865. This example is inlaid with mother-of-pearl. Most versions are not as elaborately decorated and are mounted on a metal table (R/6).

Figure 2-71. Detail of the Empire in figure 2-70.

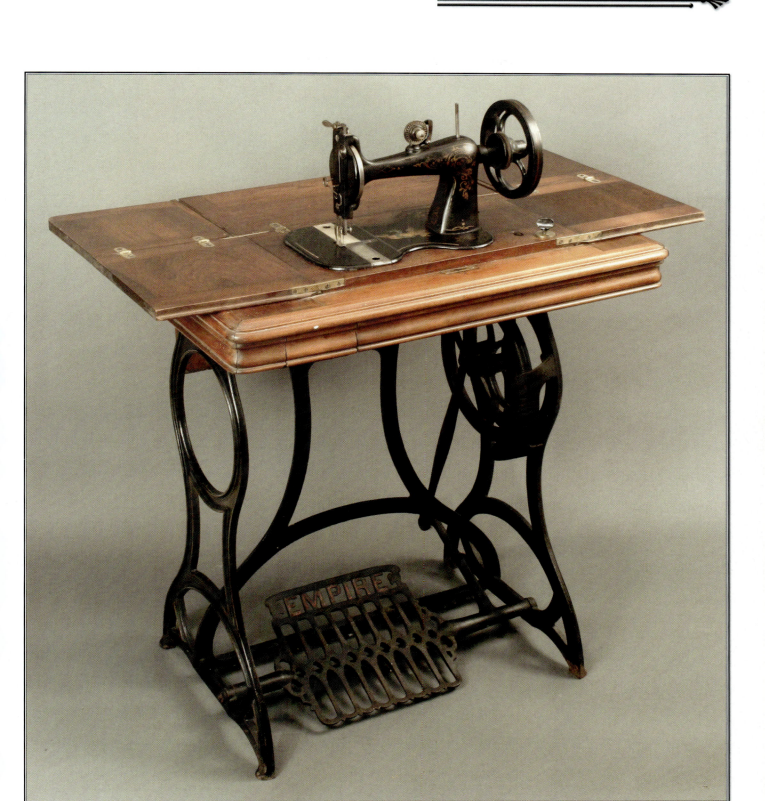

Figure 2-72. Empire (R/5), circa 1868, the improved version. The box cover unfolds to increase the table surface. This type of cover, which many makers featured, was called a "folding case."

Figure 2-73. The machine of figure 2-72 sports a somewhat whimsical hand-painted cherub tooting a couple of horns.

ERIE: See GRANT BROTHERS.

F & W AUTOMATIC (figure 2-74): This machine was made for about 20 years by the Foley and Williams company of Chicago, starting around 1895. It is one of a large number of machines that employs components of the WILLCOX & GIBBS mechanism without actually looking like a clone, although the resemblance is certainly there. The machine was designed mainly for hand use and, though quite small (about 6" long), is not a toy.

FAIRY (figure 2-75): Made during the 1880s by the Secor Sewing Machine Company of Bridgeport, Connecticut, the Fairy is a small hand-operated machine painted dark green and packaged in a wooden box. The stitch forming mechanism utilizes the WILLCOX & GIBBS revolving hook. The machine, like many other smaller hand varieties, was equipped with a clamp to affix it to a table. Figure 2-76 illustrates the machine in its original box.

FAIRY: see MADAME DEMOREST. Fairy is the other name by which the Madame Demorest has been known.

FAMILY: Many small hand-operated machines were sold as Family machines or COMMON SENSE sewing machines, meaning they were practical and cheap, yet suitable for home use. Some machines, such as the GOLD MEDAL and NEW ENGLAND varieties, were frequently sold with no identification and no place of manufacture given. Presumably this was done in some cases in order to avoid paying royalties to the Sewing Machine Combination (page 15).

FAMILY GEM (figure 2-77): This running stitch machine appears to be modeled after the MADAME DEMOREST. Differences can be discerned by comparing figures 2-159 and 2-77; particularly noteworthy is the oval emblem on the Family Gem, which is positioned precisely where the Madame Demorest face would be. The raised scrollwork and one of the patent dates are identical on the two machines. If you are lucky enough to find this machine complete with box and instructions, you will note that the printed enclosure has neither manufacturer name nor location. Many companies made machines but did not pay royalties to the Sewing Machine Combination. Presumably, it was easier to avoid litigation if a precise place of manufacture was hard to trace.

FETTER AND JONES (figures 2-78, 2-79): The rather crude mechanism of the Fetter and Jones sews a two-thread chain stitch and resembles somewhat the hand operated version of the NETTLETON AND RAYMOND. This machine was manufactured during the late 1850s; it is not known how many were made, but apparently the machine was sold only as a hand operated model.

FIGURAL MACHINES: This is a present-day characterization of a class of machines rather than any one machine. Figural refers to the fact that some early machines incorporated a theme into their appearance. Typical figural machines are the CHERUB, SQUIRREL, FOLIAGE, HENDRICKS, WOODRUFF, SEAMSTRESS FRIEND, and (arguably) the MADAME DEMOREST and the horse version of the W. G. WILSON.

FINKLE & LYON: The earliest of these machines were made starting in 1856 (figure 2-80) and are stamped "M. Finkle, New York," although Cooper gives the manufacturer as M. Finkle of Boston. Possibly the factory for these early models was in Boston and the company offices were in New York. Sold mainly as a treadle model, the M. Finkle machine sews a shuttle lockstitch. In 1859, the company changed its name to Finkle & Lyon (figure 2-81), and in 1872, to the VICTOR sewing machine company, which remained in business until 1888.

Sewing Machine Manufacturers from 1850 to 1880

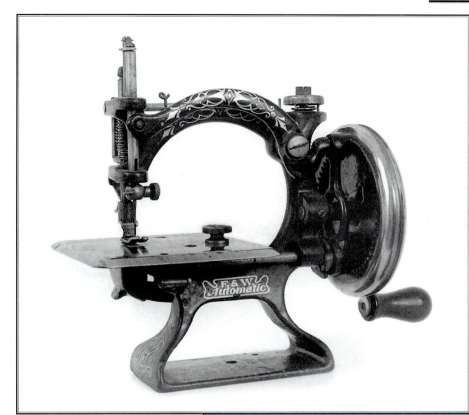

Figure 2-74. F & W Automatic (F/3), circa 1900.

Figure 2-75. Fairy (R/6), circa 1885.

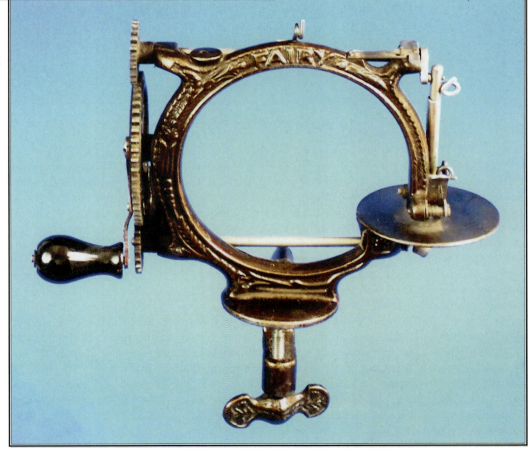

Figure 2-76. Fairy, showing placement in the original box.

FLORENCE (figure 2-82): One of the most unusual-looking sewing machines, the Florence was also one of the most popular. Manufactured in Florence, Massachusetts, the first machines were made around 1860, and production continued for almost 20 years. During this period, about 150,000 shuttle lockstitch machines were made. Although all Florence heads were designed for treadle use, there was a specially made portable platform that could be hooked up to the head for operation under hand power (figure 2-83). The most desirable treadle Florence has an elaborate iron stand (figure 2-84). Though common, it has a relatively high value due to its spectacular appearance.

Although the usual placement of the head allowed sewing in a left to right direction, the company also produced a model with the flywheel across the back (figure 2-85), which facilitated sewing from back to front (and from front to back — the Florence had a stitch-reversal mechanism). Throughout its production era, two standard forms of the machine were constructed. One model featured the movable arm on the left (see figures 82 and 84), while on the other model the movable arm was on the right (see figures 83 and 85). Empirical evidence indicates that the "left" form was the earlier of the two, but both forms are quite common.

As for the machine in figure 86, it is likely a Florence, but unfortunately the round cloth plate was missing when the machine was found. However, the mechanism underneath is the same as the more usual Florence models.

FOLIAGE (figure 2-87): Of all the FIGURAL machines, the Foliage is one of the most frequently found today, although it is by no means common. Only five inches across, the Foliage sews a single-thread chain stitch and is constructed of solid brass. It was made from 1858 to about 1860 by D. W. Clark of Bridgeport, Connecticut. Based upon the serial numbers, it appears that about 1,000 – 1,500 Foliage machines were made.

Figure 2-77. Family Gem (R/6), circa 1865.

Figure 2-78. Fetter and Jones (X/8), circa 1859.

Figure 2-79. Mechanism detail for the Fetter and Jones machine of figure 2-78.

Figure 2-80. Finkle (R/7), circa 1856. The first model.

Figure 2-81. Finkle & Lyon (O/4), circa 1865. The second model.

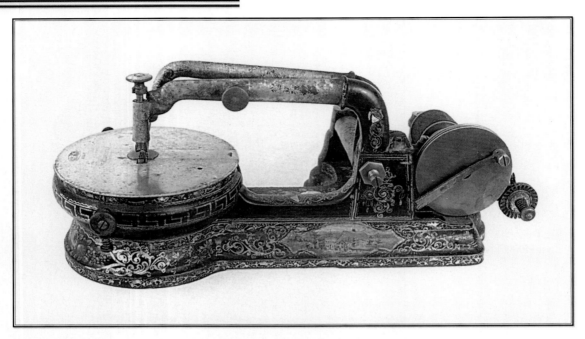

Figure 2-82. Florence (A/3, head only), circa 1863. Florence heads were frequently highly decorated, although not usually to the extreme of this example.

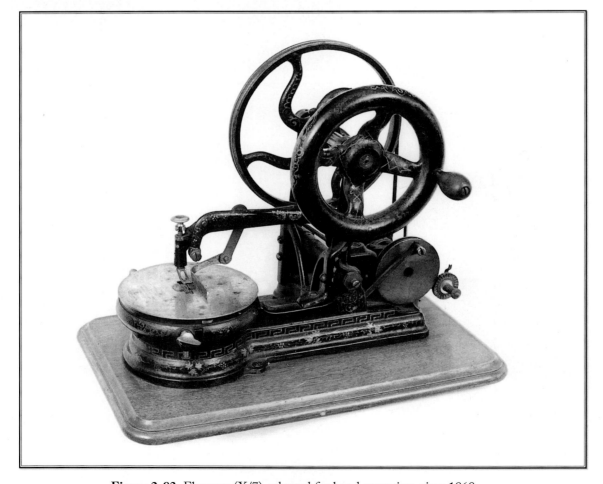

Figure 2-83. Florence (X/7), adapted for hand operation, circa 1868.

Figure 2-84. Florence (F/5), circa 1865. This is the popular Fancy Florence stand.

Figure 2-85. Florence (O/5), circa 1865. This version is called the "back feed" model. Another model allowed sewing from left to right.

Figure 2-86. Probably a Florence (U/6). The cloth plate is missing; hence, one cannot identify the machine for certain.

Figure 2-87. Foliage (R/7), circa 1859. This is the most common of the small brass machines.

Figure 2-88. Folsom (O/6), circa 1865.

Sewing Machine Manufacturers from 1850 to 1880

FOLSOM (figures 2-88, 2-189, 2-218): The Folsom company, which was based in Winchendon, Massachusetts, made many different styles of hand-operated machines. The model that is normally identified as a Folsom is shown in figure 2-88, but the manufacturer also produced a NEW ENGLAND style machine (figure 2-189) and a PAW FOOT type machine (figure 2-218). At least two different mechanisms are found on the various models, which produce both two-thread and single-thread chain stitches. Several thousand Folsoms were manufactured between 1865 and 1872.

FRANKLIN: Judging by the quantity that has survived, a few thousand Franklins were made, mainly in two different styles. Both styles are treadle powered and sew a two-thread chain stitch. The earlier version appears in figure 2-89; the later version (figure 2-90) is a slightly less angular rendition of the first and has the name DIAMOND IMPROVED printed in gilt next to the needle descent plate. It is unfortunate that this printed name is the only means by which the machine can be identified, since after some use, the gilding gets worn away. The Franklin is interesting in that it is one of few treadle machines that are powered directly by friction rather than belt. The flywheel makes direct contact with a two inch rubber ring that is on the surface of a vertical drive wheel under the machine. A rare third style of this machine, produced for a very short time, utilizes a horizontal rubber ring (figure 2-91). This style occasionally goes by the name MEDALLION.

The company was based in Mason Village, New Hampshire, and produced machines from about 1867 to 1870. Several advertisements for it were run in Harper's Weekly during this period. These ads started with the quotation, "Economy is Wealth (Franklin)." In 1870, an ad appeared in Harper's Bazaar stating that, "for circulars and reduced prices, address J. C. Ottis & Co., or Franklin and Diamond S. M. Co., Box 397, Boston, Massachusetts."

Figure 2-89. Franklin (R/7), circa 1869. The earlier version.

Figure 2-90. Franklin (R/6), circa 1870. This was made somewhat later than the other models. It is also called the Diamond Improved.

Figure 2-91. Franklin (X/7), circa 1868. This unusual hand-operated model features a horizontal friction drive mechanism. There is also a treadle version.

Figure 2-92. Mechanism detail for the hand-operated Franklin machine depicted in figure 2-91.

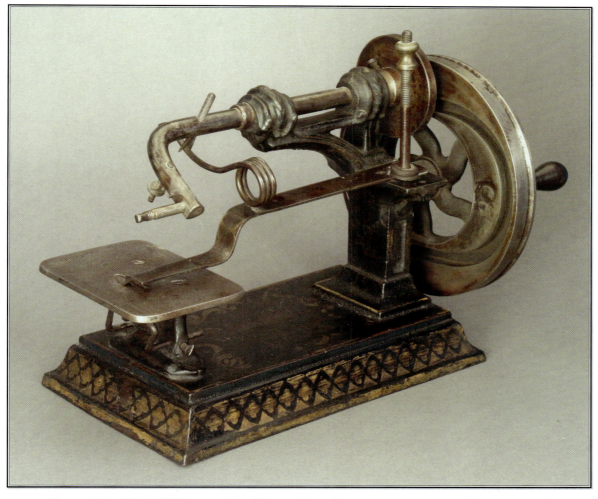

Figure 2-93. Gibbs (X/7), circa 1858. The model in figure 2-94 is more typically encountered.

GIBBS (figures 2-93, 2-94): This machine was based upon a patent by J. E. A. Gibbs, but bears little resemblance to his highly successful revolving-hook sewing machine, the WILLCOX & GIBBS. Designed to be operated by hand, the mechanism sews a simple chain stitch and goes about it in a very strange way. Examples that have turned up have serial numbers greater than 10,000; however, it is difficult to believe that this many were made.

GLOBE: The FOLSOM was also sold under the name Globe.

GOLD MEDAL: The name Gold Medal was placed on several different types of sewing machines — there are running stitch (figure 2-98), chain stitch, and lockstitch machines called Gold Medal. The type that is currently most often associated with the name Gold Medal is the hand-operated variety shown in figure 2-95. It was made by Johnson, Clark & Co., which became the Gold Medal Sewing Machine Co., both of Orange, Massachusetts. The least common of this type is shown in figure 2-96. Its round shape causes confusion with the BARTLETT, but similarities end with the outward appearance, as the mechanisms are distinct. More than 50,000 Gold Medal machines were made, with both round and rectangular cloth plates, from the late 1860s through the mid-1870s. Although this machine is one of the most commonly found types, it was relatively forgotten until about 1975.

The company also produced a totally different Gold Medal machine (figure 2-97), a shuttle lockstitch model. These machines were also known by HOME SHUTTLE and other names. The machine was designed to be hand or treadle operated, as is evidenced by the fact that even the treadle models have handles on the flywheel. Probably around 75,000 were made throughout the 1870s. Several other companies produced machines of a similar style.

Sewing Machine Manufacturers from 1850 to 1880

Figure 2-94. Gibbs (R/7), circa 1858.

Figure 2-95. Gold Medal (F/3), circa 1870. This popular machine has both round and rectangular cloth plates.

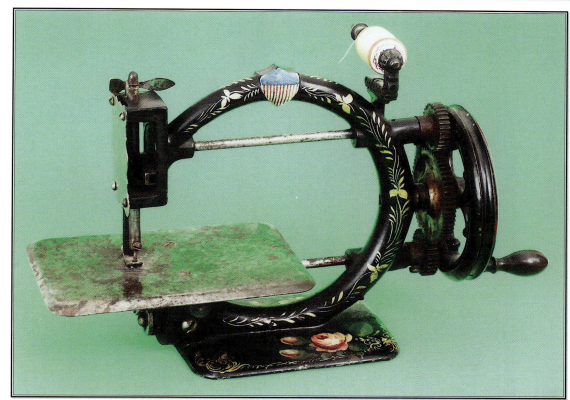

Figure 2-96. Gold Medal (O/4). The mechanism is identical to the machine in figure 2-95.

Figure 2-97. Gold Medal (F/4), circa 1875. This machine is also a variant of the Home Shuttle, and the version here goes by the name Champion.

Figure 2-98. Gold Medal (R/6). This running stitch machine had no relationship to the machines of figures 2-95 through 2-97.

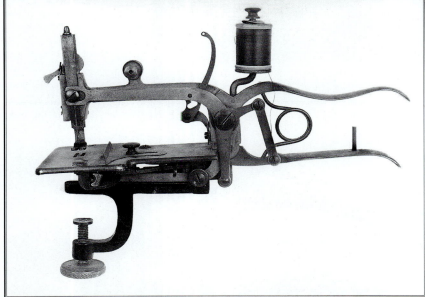

Figure 2-99. Goodbody (R/6), circa 1888.

in terms of numbers made by a single manufacturer, there were so many similar ones produced that the value is not high.

GRANITE STATE (figures 2-227 and 2-233): This PAW FOOT variety may come in two forms. Figure 2-233 illustrates a machine that is imprinted with "The Granite State" on the base. And the machine in figure 2-227 is strikingly similar to one depicted in a brochure that illustrates a treadle version. Also on that brochure: "The Granite State/Family Sewing Machine/manufactured and for sale by/G. W. Spencer & Company/East Chester, N. H." Both varieties probably date from the mid-1860s.

GOODBODY (figure 2-99): One of several machines collectively known as SEWING SHEARS, the Goodbody was made in Bridgeport, Connecticut, during the 1880s. It has a tiny shuttle and bobbin and will sew a lockstitch, but not for very long without a thread change. Since these machines, like so many others, did not display serial numbers, it is difficult to say exactly how many were made, but a few thousand would be a likely estimate.

GOODRICH (O/2): Of Chicago manufacture, the Goodrich is typical of a large number of machines made by several different manufacturers from the late 1870s through the 1890s that identically copied the extremely popular SINGER NEW FAMILY machine of the preceding decade. Even after Singer had dropped the New Family and changed to a more modern high-arm model, the old design persisted in popularity, especially in Europe. Although machines of this general type may be scarce

GRANT BROTHERS (figure 2-191): The machine that is now known as the Grant Brothers machine is somewhat different in appearance from some similar machines, which have been grouped under the name NEW ENGLAND. But it, like the others, forms a single-thread chain stitch using Raymond's patented chain stitch looper. During the late 1860s and early 1870s, Grant Brothers machines were made by a Philadelphia-based company of the same name. There is some confusion about the true name for this machine, as it was one of many types that were sold under the name FAMILY Machine or COMMON SENSE Sewing Machine. During the late 1870s, an identical model was sold as the UNIVERSAL Underfeed Hand Machine, and the same type of machine was also sold by the Buffalo- and Chicago-based ERIE sewing machine company.

Figure 2-100. Greenman & True (X/9), circa 1860. This machine is actually an early Leavitt model.

Sewing Machine Manufacturers from 1850 to 1880

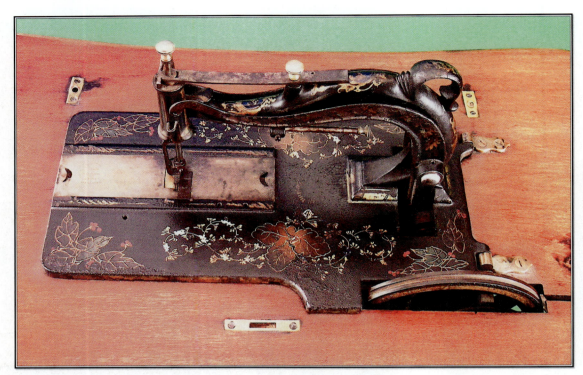

Figure 2-101. Detail of the machine in figure 2-100.

Figure 2-102. Mechanism for the Greenman & True of figure 2-101.

Figure 2-103. Griswold (X/9), circa 1875.

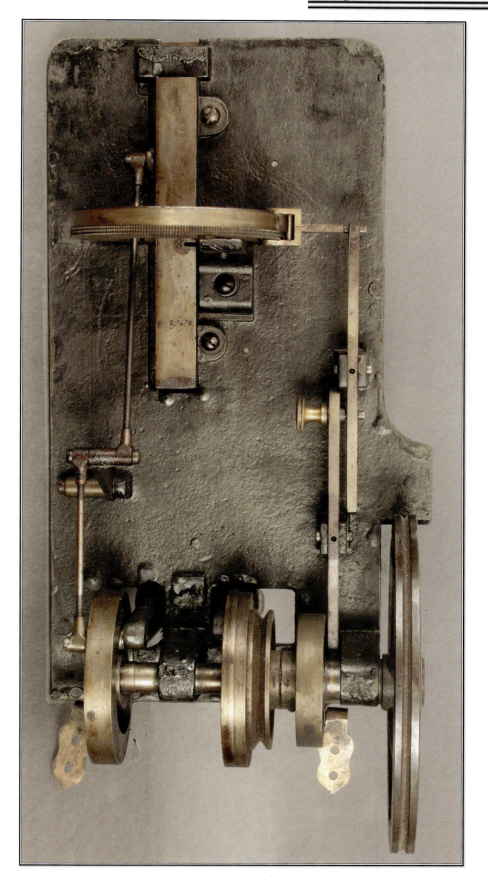

Figure 2-104. Grover & Baker (R/8). The earliest model, this version was made from about 1852 to 1860.

Interestingly, the advertising illustrations for the Erie, Universal, and Grant Brothers versions are from the identical woodcut. Since the Grant Brothers version was sold about ten years before the other varieties, one can justify the present day preference of that name over the others. Occasionally, a top feed version is found (figure 2-192); this model is considerably scarcer than the underfeed variety and presumably was not sold as the Underfeed machine.

GREENMAN AND TRUE (figures 2-100, 2-101, 2-102): The machine illustrated is at present popularly called the Greenman and True. It was, however, made for a very short time around 1860 by the LEAVITT Sewing Machine Company of Boston; perhaps the Leavitt name would be more appropriate. Nevertheless, there is a machine called the Greenman and True made by the Greenman & True Manufacturing Company of Norwich, Connecticut. This was probably manufactured in the Leavitt factory, for it is identical to the machine illustrated. The mechanism produces a shuttle lockstitch, and the machine was made only as a treadle model. The example illustrated is stamped "Leavitt" and has a serial number of 1729. Probably no more than a couple of thousand were made, and it is therefore very rare and desirable. There is a number on the underside of the cloth plate, but it is not the serial number, which is stamped clearly on top.

GRISWOLD: Little is known about this machine, and the number produced can only be guessed. It was probably made for a brief period during the late 1870s by a company founded by the patentee, Leo Griswold. The example shown in figure 2-103 sews a lockstitch and is the only example known of a sewing machine with the flywheel placed in such an odd position.

Sewing Machine Manufacturers from 1850 to 1880

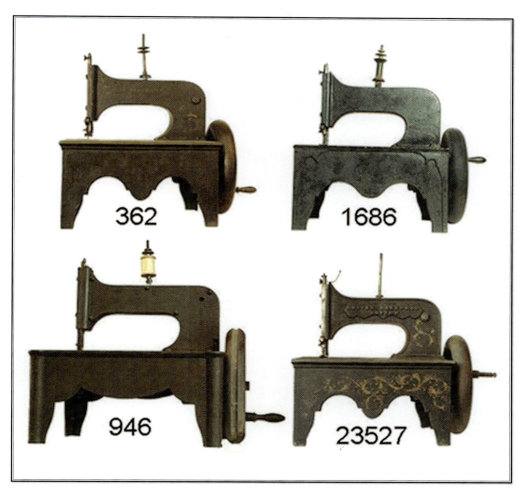

Figure 2-105. Note the minor variations in these early Grover & Baker models. The numbers under each machine are the serial numbers. All of these machines employ the double-thread chain stitch mechanism shown in figure 2-107 (see also figure 2-1). The machine with the serial number 946 is illustrated at the same scale as the others; it is extremely heavy — the flywheel alone is 10" in diameter and the sewing surface is 15½" across. These very early "heavy duty" machines were all quite large.

GROVER & BAKER: Grover, Baker & Co. of Boston, one of the original members of the Sewing Machine Combination, made more than 500,000 machines from the early 1850s through the late 1870s, eventually merging with the DOMESTIC Sewing Machine Co. There were many different models produced: chain stitch or lockstitch, portable, family, and manufacturing or industrial. A large disparity of rarity and value exists over the whole spectrum of Grover & Baker machines; hence, several examples have been illustrated. Although some Grover & Baker forms are rather common, all are more or less desirable. Perhaps the higher value associated with even fairly common Grover & Baker machines is due to their historical importance and unusual appearance.

The earliest machines, shown in figures 2-104 and 2-105, are very heavy models that sew the typical Grover & Baker two-thread chain stitch. Produced throughout the 1850s, probably no more than a few thousand of this type were made. One should note that all these machines, even those made in 1852, employ the four-motion feed patented by A. B. Wilson in 1854. W. O. Grover and W. E. Baker obtained a patent for essentially the same device in 1852, but it was later determined that Wilson had mentioned a similar mechanism in his 1851 patent for a rotary hook; hence, Wilson was credited with the patent.

Figure 2-106 shows a portable case for a Grover & Baker that was designed for home use and was the first such American portable sewing machine; for this case, the company had an exclusive patent. These machines were sold starting in 1855 and the patent was granted in 1856. The design was quite popular, and portable models similar to the ones illustrated continued to be made throughout the life of the company. Of course, during such a long production span, some changes occurred in the design. The earliest model was made up to about 1860. The machines pictured in figures 2-109 and 2-110 are later versions, made during the 1860s and 1870s. Although the later portables were made for a longer period of time, they do not seem to turn up as frequently today as do the earlier models. All sew the two-thread stitch, but the earlier examples are much more finely crafted, with great precision evident in all moving parts. Occasionally, the later model is found perched upon small spool-turned legs; this version was apparently made for the market in Europe.

Sewing Machine Manufacturers from 1850 to 1880

Figure 2-106. Grover & Baker (O/6). The first portable sewing machine, circa 1855.

Figure 2-107. Mechanism for early two-thread chain stitch Grover & Baker models. The workmanship on these machines was quite good, and in fact deteriorated somewhat when the mechanism changed around 1860 (see figure 2-117).

Sewing Machine Manufacturers from 1850 to 1880

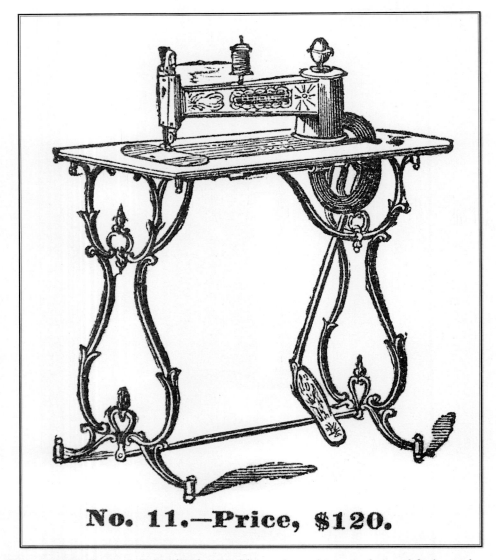

Figure 2-108. Grover & Baker (X/8), 1856. This early machine was designed for heavy duty.

The treadle version of this machine is found with several different iron stands and cabinets, the kind in figure 2-111 being one of the most common. The stand in figure 2-112 is one of the most desirable forms for present day collectors of Grover & Baker treadle machines, and the one pictured in figure 2-113 turns up occasionally. Figure 2-114 shows an early cabinet model typical of the mid-1850s. Figure 2-115 shows an 1860 machine with a table made of slate painted to look like marble. Note also the mother-of-pearl inlay on the head. Grover & Baker, as well as other manufacturers, embellished many of its deluxe models with mother-of-pearl inlay and silver plating.

Figure 2-109. Grover & Baker (O/6). Later version of the portable model, circa 1864.

Figure 2-110. Grover & Baker (O/6). The latest version of the portable model, circa 1875.

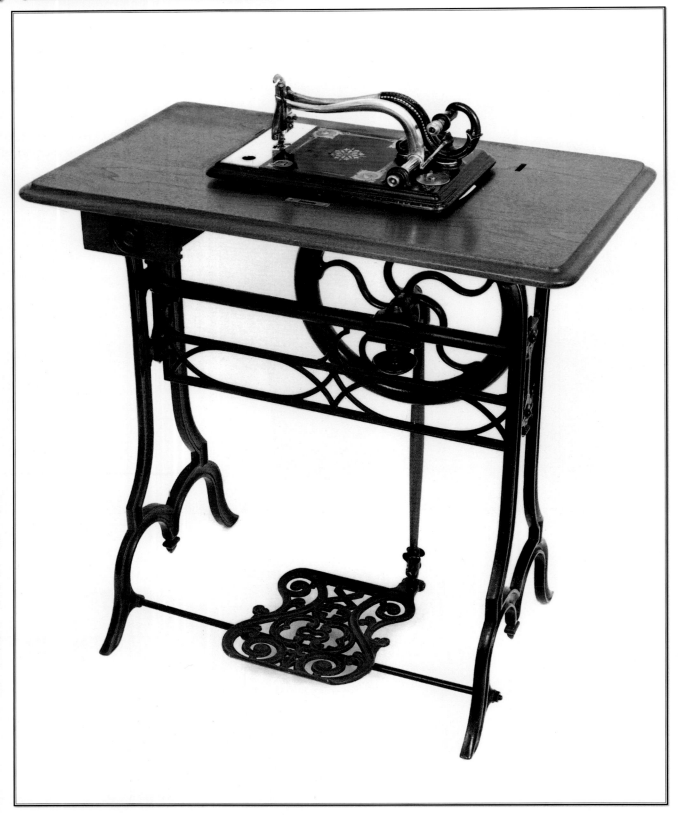

Figure 2-111. Grover & Baker (F/4). A typical treadle model, circa 1865.

Sewing Machine Manufacturers from 1850 to 1880

Figure 2-112. Grover & Baker (R/7). The fancy version, circa 1859.

Figure 2-113. Grover & Baker (O/5), circa 1861.

Sewing Machine Manufacturers from 1850 to 1880

Figure 2-114. Grover & Baker (R/8). The earliest cabinet model, circa 1857.

Sewing Machine Manufacturers from 1850 to 1880

Figure 2-115. Grover & Baker (X/7, this version; O/6, other cabinet versions). A later cabinet model, circa 1861. This particular version features a tabletop made of slate that has been painted to look like marble and a head that has been silver plated.

Sewing Machine Manufacturers from 1850 to 1880

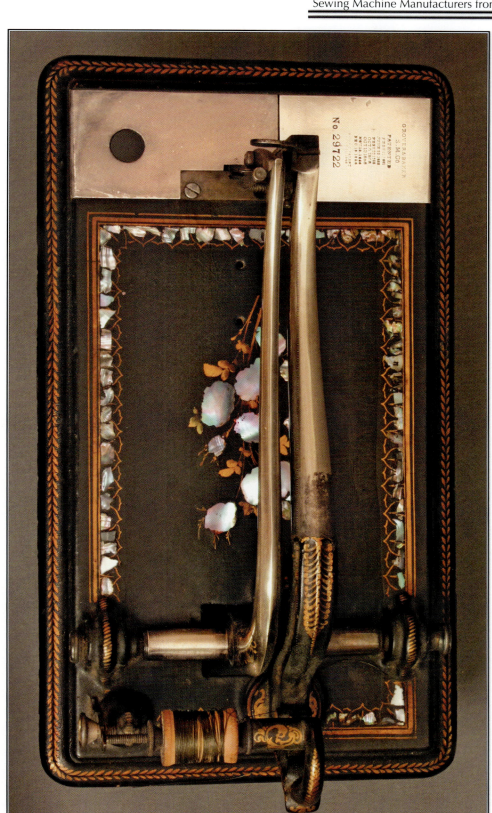

Figure 2-116. Detail of the head, figure 2-115.

Figure 2-117. Mechanism for the machine of figure 2-116. The stitch-forming horizontal looper was the same as that on earlier machines, but the driving mechanics were simpler and not as finely made. This form was on all two-thread chain stitch Grover & Baker machines from around 1861 until the company ceased making them in the mid-1870s.

Figure 2-118. Grover & Baker (O/4). The lockstitch machine, circa 1870.

Figure 2-119. Grover & Baker (U/4), circa 1878. The last model, made when the company merged with the Domestic Sewing Machine Company.

Although the Grover & Baker company was famous for the two-thread chain stitch, which William O. Grover invented, the company also produced lockstitch machines (figure 2-118). The mechanism forms its stitch using a shuttle that moves in a horizontal arc motion, similar to most early twentieth century shuttle machines. The last model Grover & Baker lockstitch machine was made during the late 1870s (figure 2-119) and is almost identical to the DOMESTIC, which is not surprising, since the Domestic company bought out the Grover & Baker company at that time.

HANCOCK (figures 2-120, 2-121): The small Hancock machine was made for about ten years, starting around 1867. Two different varieties have typically turned up; both were used exclusively as hand-operated models that clamped to tables. The single-thread chain stitch is formed using a needle that has a hook at the end for pulling a loop of thread back up through the cloth. Several thousand Hancocks were made, but serial numbers are not present. A much later turn-of-the-century version of the machine's mechanism was revived under the names SOEZY and others (see figure 3-35).

HARDIE (figure 2-122): This machine is similar in design to the HOOK machine, but twice as large (about 5" high). It was made during the early 1860s.

HEBERLING (figure 2-123): The Heberling is a hand-operated running-stitch machine akin to the MADAME DEMOREST and the FAMILY GEM. About 5,000 were made during the 1880s by the Heberling Running Stitch Sewing Machine Co. in Mt. Pleasant, Ohio. Although Mt. Pleasant was the company headquarters, the machines were manufactured by Brown & Sharp Co. of Providence, Rhode Island. Many other makers employed this same style, which persisted into the twentieth century.

HENDRICKS (figure 2-124): The original of the SEWING SHEARS machines, the Hendricks sews a simple chain stitch. Constructed of silver-plated brass, the Hendricks is one of the FIGURAL machines because of its very strong resemblance to a pair of scissors. The machine was made by the Nettleton and Raymond Co. of Bristol, Connecticut, for a brief period during the late 1850s. As is typical of figurals, the Hendricks is highly desirable and is valued beyond what rarity alone might warrant.

HODGKIN'S (figure 2-231): This unusual PAW FOOT type features a wheel cloth feed, which is a strange mechanism to find on a small hand-operated machine. The device was patented in 1861 by Christopher Hodgkins, but the actual manufacturer for the machine is unknown. A version without the feet was also produced (figure 2-232).

HOLLY (figure 2-125): This machine was made by Birdsell Holly of Lockport, New York. Holly's sewing machine was based upon a patent that allowed the head to swivel back without disengaging the drive belt. Underneath the machine is painted, "Giles and Millege Japanners, Lockport, New York." This refers to the company that put the finish on the head. This model was manufactured from about 1861 to 1863 in a factory that was probably in Lockport. It is unlikely that many of these extremely unusual two-thread chain stitch machines were made.

HOME SHUTTLE (figure 2-126): This machine is also known as GOLD MEDAL. It sews a shuttle lockstitch and was sold as a hand-operated machine, but could be mounted on a treadle stand (figure 2-127). At least 50,000 of these were made at a factory in Orange, Massachusetts, by Johnson, Clark & Co. during the 1870s. As was typical for many of the larger companies, Johnson, Clark & Co. had offices in several major cities, namely Boston, New York, Pittsburgh, Chicago, and St. Louis. The machine evolved into the model shown in figure 2-129 and eventually into the very popular NEW HOME sewing machine, which became the company name in 1882. New Home sewing machines continue to be manufactured today.

HOOK (figure 2-130): Manufactured for a short period around 1860, this small machine is barely 2" high. Probably no more than a couple of thousand were made.

HORSE SEWING MACHINE: See ORMOND, W. G. WILSON.

HOUSEHOLD (figure 2-131): Although this machine appears to have been manufactured as early as 1873, its overall form has the appearance of later machines. At least 100,000 of these shuttle lockstitch treadle machines were sold by the Providence Tool Co. of Providence, Rhode Island. The low value is due to the fact that this machine has an ordinary appearance and is rather common.

Figure 2-120. Hancock (R/6), circa 1868.

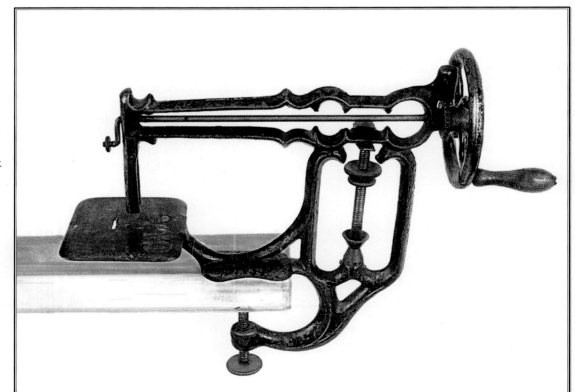

Figure 2-121. Hancock (R/6), circa 1868.

Sewing Machine Manufacturers from 1850 to 1880

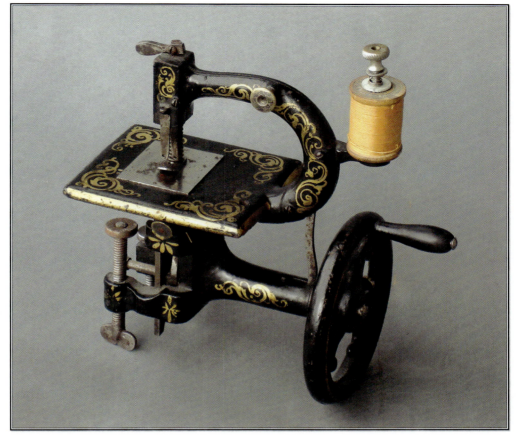

Figure 2-122. Hardie (R/7), circa 1862.

Figure 2-123. Heberling (O/5), circa 1885.

Sewing Machine Manufacturers from 1850 to 1880

Figure 2-124. Hendricks (R/7), circa 1858.

Figure 2-125. Holly (X/10). The stand is made of walnut and reflects a furniture style from the 1840s, but the machine was made in 1862.

Figure 2-126. Home Shuttle (O/5), circa 1870. The hand-operated model.

Sewing Machine Manufacturers from 1850 to 1880

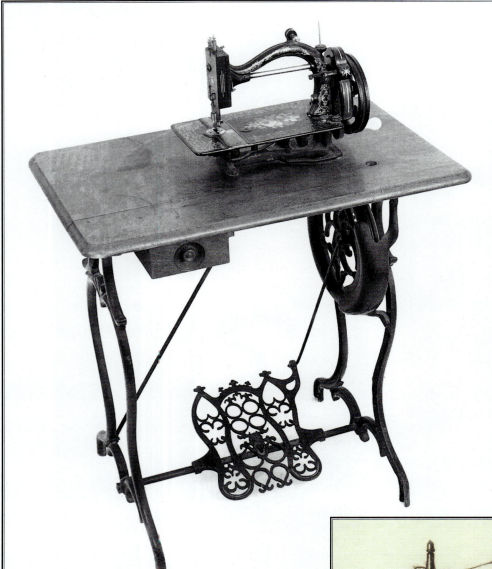

Figure 2-127. Home Shuttle (O/5). This machine could be hand operated and was sold both with and without the treadle stand. Several variants of the head exist.

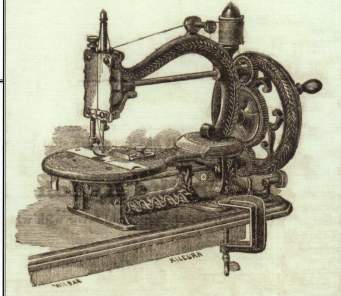

Figure 2-128. Home Shuttle (O/4). This hand-operated version is more typically found on a treadle stand similar to that in figure 2-127.

Figure 2-129. Home Shuttle (R/4), circa 1875. This was the final model before the New Home was introduced.

Figure 2-130. Hook (R/7), circa 1859. The arm of this machine is only 2" high.

Sewing Machine Manufacturers from 1850 to 1880

Figure 2-131. Household (F/2), circa 1875.

HOWE, A. B. (figures 2-132, 2-133, 2-134): These machines were manufactured in New York by A. B. Howe (Elias's brother) and B. P. Howe (Elias's nephew). Around 100,000 were made from 1855 to after 1870. Examples made before 1865 are quite rare.

HOWE (STOCKWELL BROTHERS): The Stockwell Brothers (Elias's sons-in-law) built machines at the Bridgeport, Connecticut, factory that was opened by Elias Howe in 1865 (figures 2-135 and 2-136). They are usually called simply "Elias Howe Machines," though he had little to do with the manufacture, since he died in 1867. A variety of types of treadle stands and cabinets were made for these machines (figures 2-137 through 2-139). Some have mother-of-pearl inlaid heads and closed cabinets; others are much simpler. In all cases, the machine itself sports a brass medallion depicting the head of Elias Howe, "Inventor and Maker." One type also features the medallion of Elias Howe on the wooden box cover. Regardless of the appearance, Howe machines are almost always found as treadle models. The style evolved during the 1880s into that shown in figure 2-141; here the illustration is taken directly from a photograph in a dealer's sample book of that period. About a million Howe machines were made; this includes several models that were designed for specific manufacturing applications (figures 2-140 and 2-142).

HUNT & WEBSTER: Also known as the Hunt, Webster & Co. sewing machine, approximately 1,500 of these lockstitch treadle machines were made from 1853 to about 1858. The machine is nearly identical to the later LADD & WEBSTER, differing mainly in the name.

INDEPENDENT (figure 2-143): Also known as the Independent Noiseless, this machine sews a single-thread chain stitch. Probably one or two thousand were made during the 1870s, by a company based in Binghamton, New York. A more precise count is difficult to determine, as serial numbers were not stamped on any of the examples that have turned up so far. All appear to have been manufactured for use with a treadle stand.

JAMESON'S AUTOMATIC (R/4): This machine is identical to the F & W AUTOMATIC.

JENNIE JUNE: This machine is probably more common than it would appear from the few numbers that have turned

Figure 2-132. Howe (R/8), circa 1863. This was an early model of the A. B. Howe machine. Its serial number is 4638.

Figure 2-133. Comparison of two early A. B. Howe models. When viewed from above, it is hard to tell that the machine on the right is actually a Howe, but the mechanisms underneath both machines are practically identical.

up, for many were made during the 1880s, and they were widely advertised. According to Cooper, the company was based first in Chicago and later in Belvidere, Illinois.

JOHNSON (figure 2-144): Not to be confused with the Johnson, Clark & Co., this machine was made by Emery, Houghton & Company of Boston for nine years, starting in 1856. The machine superficially resembles the early WHEELER & WILSON, but it is smaller.

KEYSTONE (figure 2-145): Using serial numbers as a guide, one would conclude that at least 10,000 of these shuttle lockstitch machines were made in the early 1870s. However, as has been stated before, serial numbers cannot always be relied upon, and other sources (see appendix A) indicate that approximately 3,000 were made. This lower number is also suggested by the fact that very few examples have turned up.

KRUSE (F/3): This WILLCOX & GIBBS clone was made in New York during the 1880s and later. A number of companies made machines that were identical to the Willcox & Gibbs.

LADD & WEBSTER or **LADD, WEBSTER & CO.** (figure 2-146): Production began on these machines in 1858 and ended about eight years later, after more than 5,000 had been sold. Made in Boston, the Ladd & Webster was a treadle-powered shuttle lockstitch machine; its predecessor, the HUNT & WEBSTER, was one of the first machines licensed under Howe's patent and was made as early as 1853.

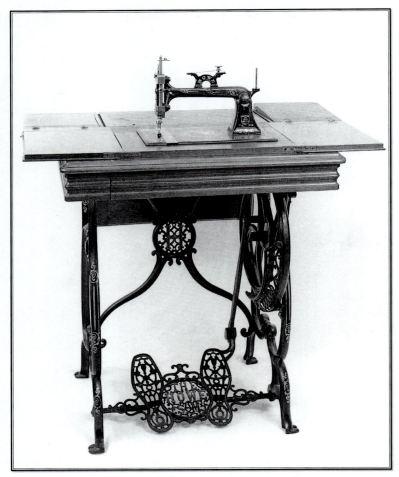

Figure 2-134. A. B Howe (F/4), circa 1870.

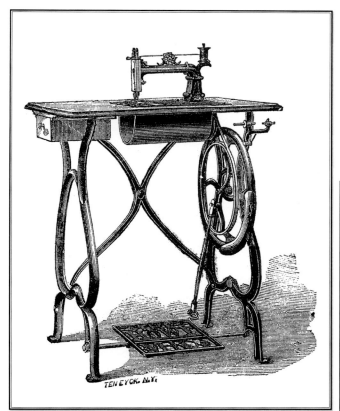

Figure 2-135. Howe (Stockwell Brothers, A/2), circa 1870. This is the most typical treadle stand.

Figure 2-136. Howe (Stockwell Brothers, O/3), showing the head, which in this case has been highly decorated and inlaid with mother-of-pearl.

Figure 2-137. Howe (Stockwell Brothers, F/2). This stand had a cover that unfolded to create more work area.

Figure 2-138. Howe (Stockwell Brothers, O/5), one of several cabinet styles.

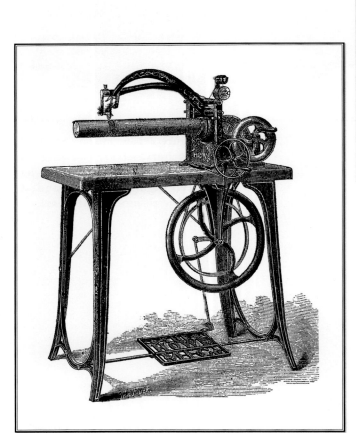

Figure 2-139. Howe (Stockwell Brothers, U/7) with an unusual spool-turned cabinet. The illustration is from an 1870 catalog produced for the European market.

Figure 2-140. Howe (Stockwell Brothers) leather machine (U/6). From the same catalog as figure 2-139.

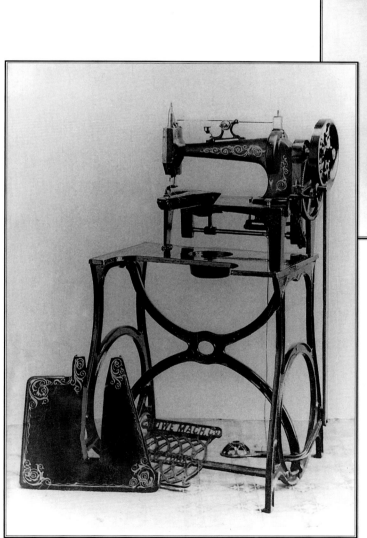

Figure 2-141. Howe (Stockwell Brothers, U/3). This is the last style produced for home use. The photo is taken from a dealer sample booklet from about 1880.

Figure 2-142. Howe (Stockwell Brothers) leather machine (R/4). From the same booklet as figure 2-141.

Sewing Machine Manufacturers from 1850 to 1880

Figure 2-143. Independent (R/7), circa 1875.

Sewing Machine Manufacturers from 1850 to 1880

Figure 2-144. Johnson (R/8), circa 1858. The machine is only 7" long.

LAKE (figure 2-147): This machine is similar to the HANCOCK machines in design and function. Although it appears about as often as the HANCOCK varieties, there is no mention of it in Cooper, and its place of manufacture is not known at this time.

LANDFEAR (figures 2-148, 2-149): Made for a very short time starting in 1857, the Landfear machine sews a single-thread chain stitch and was produced as both a hand-operated and a treadle machine. Although the sewing mechanism is identical on both varieties, there is an obvious major difference in design, which is unusual, as simple modification of a head for treadle mounting was the rule. As was typical, the small hand-operated version is designed to be clamped to a table for use. Landfear machines were manufactured by Parkers, Snow, Brooks & Co. of West Meriden, Connecticut, and are very desirable, whether in treadle or hand-operated form.

LATHROP (figures 2-150, 2-151): The Lathrop was made for a very short period during the 1870s and sports an unusual mechanism for producing the lockstitch. An entire spool of thread is mounted on a rather skeletal shuttle. To form the stitch, the ensemble is pushed into and then pulled through a large loop drawn out from the upper thread by a rather involved mechanism. This entire operation is a delightful curiosity to behold. Unfortunately, very few of these machines were made; the example illustrated has a serial number of 12 and the only other examples known have serial numbers of 1 and 31. These are true serial numbers — the cloth plate of the illustrated machine has been stamped "No. 12." Using the serial numbers statistically as a guide, one would estimate logically that only 100 or so were made. However, it is difficult to believe that the factory did not produce more machines, and 1,000 would be more reasonable estimate. The place of manufacture is unknown — even the instruction book does not say — but the example pictured here was found in the state of New York.

Figure 2-145. Keystone (R/7), circa 1873. The box cover unfolds to produce a table surface.

Sewing Machine Manufacturers from 1850 to 1880

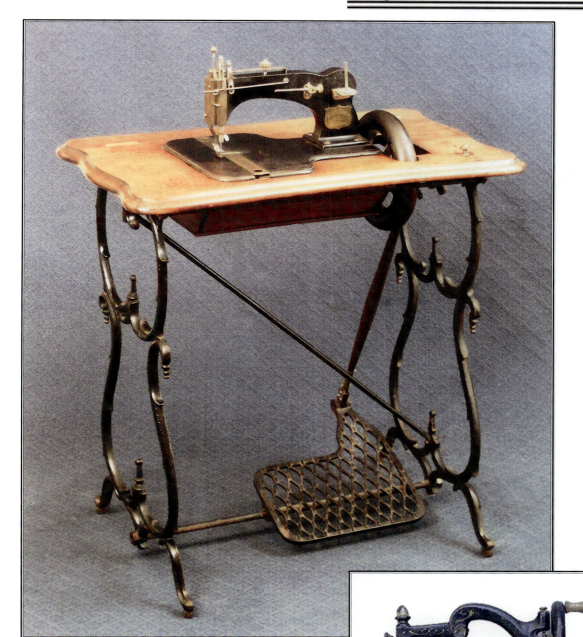

Figure 2-146. Ladd & Webster (R/8), circa 1860.

Figure 2-147. Lake's Patent Sewing Machine (R/6), circa 1870. This machine is quite similar in operation to the various HANCOCK varieties (see figures 2-120 and 2-121).

LEAVITT (figures 2-152, 2-153): Although this machine is very unusual looking, its mechanism sews an ordinary shuttle lockstitch. About 10,000 were made from 1855 to 1870, and all examples known are treadle-powered except the early industrial model, which is similar in appearance to the BATTELLE. The Boston-based Leavitt Company also manufactured a machine similar to the GREENMAN & TRUE, which is much scarcer than the later variety shown here. The Leavitt is one of the more easily found of the highly desirable early rare treadle machines. This does not imply that the Leavitt turns up often.

LESTER: The Lester machine shown in figure 2-154 sews a shuttle lockstitch and was made around 1860. The Lester Manufacturing Co. of Richmond, Virginia, also made an ELLIPTIC machine for a short time during 1860.

LITTLE GIANT (figure 2-220): One of several PAW-FOOT machines, this model may have been manufactured by SHAW & CLARK. Except for the original label underneath the machine, there is little to distinguish the Little Giant from other PAW FOOT type machines.

LITTLE MONITOR (figures 2-155, 2-156): This machine was made for a short period during the 1870s by G. L. Dulaney & Co., at a factory in Rhinebeck, New York, although the company sold its product from New York City headquarters. It is a shuttle lockstitch machine with an unusual hard rubber shuttle that can hold an entire spool of thread. It was more than likely made exclusively for treadle operation, for the working mechanism protrudes a considerable distance below the machine. The company probably produced no more than 2,000 machines, and it went out of business around 1875.

LITTLE WORKER (figure 2-157): This small hand-operated machine was produced in considerable numbers around the turn of the century by the NEW HOME Sewing Machine Company.

Figure 2-148. Landfear (R/8), circa 1859. This small machine could be clamped to a table.

Figure 2-149. Landfear (X/9), circa 1859. Although the machines in figures 2-148 and 2-149 differ considerably in appearance, the mechanism is the same.

Figure 2-150. Lathrop (X/9), circa 1873. It is probable that very few of these machines were made. The mechanism is quite complicated.

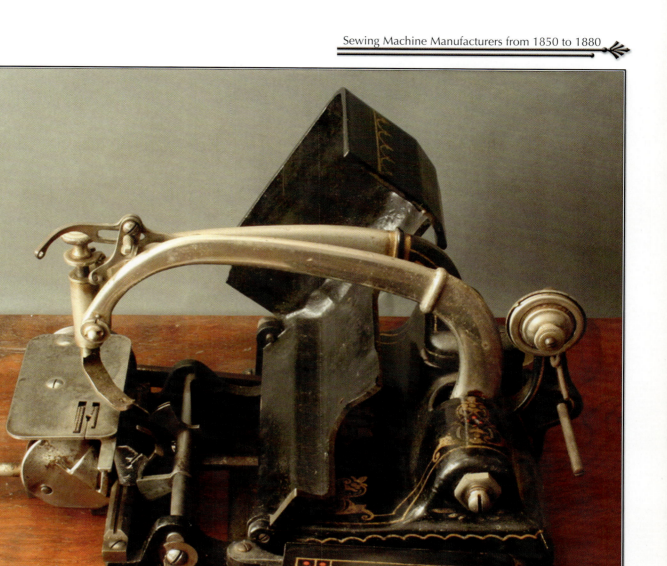

Figure 2-151. Detail of the Lathrop machine. The mechanism is quite complicated. There were two hinged portions to the sewing surface, which opened up and exposed the workings inside.

Figure 2-152. Leavitt (R/7), circa 1870. Another model is shown in figure 2-100.

Figure 2-153. Detail of the Leavitt head, shown from behind. In spite of its bizarre appearance, the Leavitt sews an ordinary lockstitch.

Sewing Machine Manufacturers from 1850 to 1880

Figure 2-154. Lester (X/8), circa 1858.

MACK (figure 2-158): This shuttle lockstitch machine was produced during the 1860s and is the first known model that featured the ahead-of-its-time high arm. The familiar appearance of this machine attests to its superior design, which had been adopted by practically every maker by 1885. The Mack sewing machine evolved into the DOMESTIC, which was one of the most successful models of the last quarter of the nineteenth century.

MADAME DEMOREST (figures 2-159, 2-160, 2-161): Highly ornamented and compact in size, the Madame Demorest employs a running-stitch mechanism, requiring much interaction on the part of an operator. Despite its drawbacks, and because it was so inexpensive, it was commercially successful during the 1860s; thus, imitations were made by several other companies (see FAMILY GEM and GOLD MEDAL). There are no serial numbers stamped on these machines; hence, it is unknown exactly how many were manufactured, but 3,000 – 5,000 would be a reasonable estimate. When in mint condition, the steel body found on most machines is covered entirely by gilt (although a black and gilt model was also made, and was sold in a smaller, rectangular cardboard box). On the illustrated box is written, "Mme. Demorest's 5 dollar first premium running stitch sewing machine, Emporium of Fashions, 473 Broadway, New York." Machines like the Madame Demorest that are small and ornamental tend to have a premium value today.

Sewing Machine Manufacturers from 1850 to 1880

Figure 2-155. Little Monitor (R/8), circa 1870.

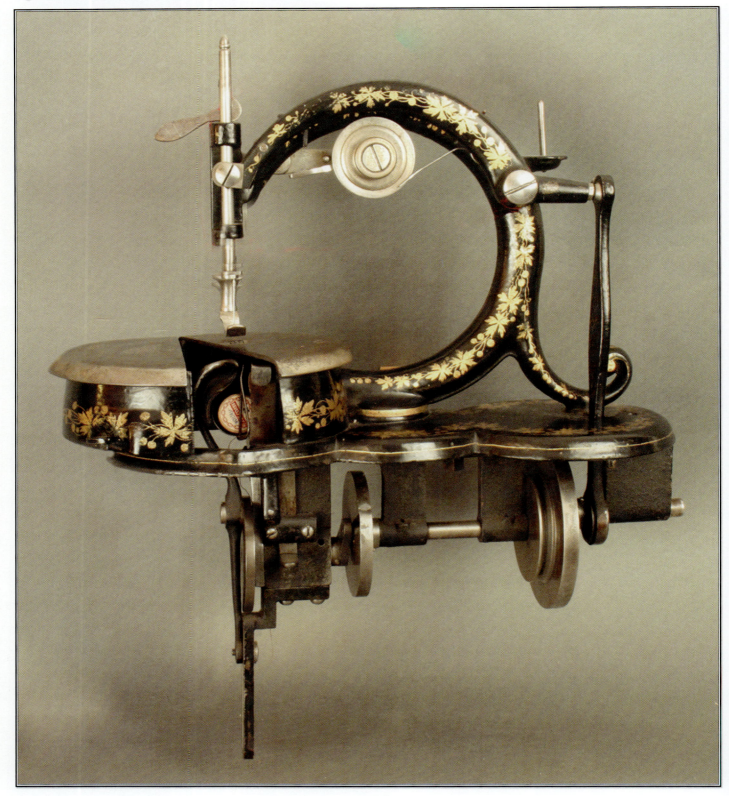

Figure 2-156. Mechanism of the Little Monitor. The machine extends almost as far underneath the table as it does above.

MANHATTAN (figures 2-162, 2-163, 2-164): Made in New York, the Manhattan is a treadle-powered machine that produces a two thread chain stitch and, like the earlier HOLLY machine, has the unusual ability to tilt up without disengaging the belt. About 3,000 to 5,000 were made during the 1870s, and there were several models from which to choose, although the head was similar for all.

McLEAN & HOOPER (figures 2-165 through 2-168): Also known as the CENTENNIAL machine, this name probably can be traced to some models that have "Centennial Sewing Machine" stamped on a large brass medallion instead of the usual "McLean and Hooper Sewing Machine." Since the Centennial medallion turns up infrequently, it is likely that this version was made as a special promotion during the Centennial year of 1876. About 10,000 McLean and Hooper machines were made during the 1870s by B. W. Lacy & Co. of Philadelphia, and although the machine seems to have been designed solely for treadle power, many heads are found without their stands. The stand was probably discarded, while the head was saved because of its diminutive size and attractive decorations — also because you could place it flat on a table. Note that the head of a man is cast into the machine on the back opposite the medallion, perhaps Mr. McLean or Mr. Hooper.

MEDALLION: See FRANKLIN

MONITOR: The Monitor is a PAW FOOT machine made by SHAW & CLARK during the early 1860s. Sometimes the term Monitor-type is used to describe any of several varieties of Paw Foot machines. There is no relation between Monitor machines and the LITTLE MONITOR.

MURPHY (figure 2-169): Some might mistake this machine for a toy, but the inventor, Edward Murphy, claimed in his May 2, 1876, patent that his aim was "to construct a sewing machine which can be manufactured at a greatly reduced cost and at the same time be durable and effective in use..."

NATIONAL (A/2): The National sewing machine, a WILLCOX & GIBBS clone (see the machine of figure 2-336), was the successor to the ELDREDGE AUTOMATIC. Large numbers were produced from the 1890s on into the twentieth century by the National Sewing Machine Co., the successor to the Eldredge company of Belvidere, Illinois.

NATIONAL WAX THREAD SEWING MACHINE (figure 2-170): This huge machine weighs more than 100 pounds and is 18" high. It was designed for heavy-duty use — apparently the thought was that a heavy-duty machine had to be heavy. As has been pointed out (see BRADFORD & BARBER

Figure 2-157. Little Worker (O/3), circa 1890.

and BATELLE), most heavy-duty machines of the era were similarly large. This example is actually a patent model (see appendix C); the flywheel was broken off intentionally as it was not considered necessary and the submitter wanted to cut down on the weight! It was common for inventors to submit patents on machines already in production.

NE PLUS ULTRA (figures 2-171, 2-172): This highly desirable chain stitch treadle machine was made for only a short time starting around 1857, by the O. L. Reynolds Co. of Dover, New Hampshire. Although the machine was produced as a hand-operated model, at least some treadle versions were made. The illustrated example has an unusually wide foot pedal, two pitman rods, and two flywheels. Perhaps the maker thought two would perform better than one, or maybe these features were emphasized in the advertising for this model. Total production of both hand and treadle models was probably limited to a few hundred machines.

NETTLETON & RAYMOND (figures 2-173 through 2-176): This Brattleboro, Vermont, company made machines of both treadle and hand-operated varieties. Both machines have handles on the flywheel and employ a rather crude mechanism that sews a two-thread chain stitch. Only a very few thousand of these machines were made during the late 1850s. An almost identical machine went under the name SCOVEL AND GODELL.

Figure 2-158. Mack (R/4). This machine was probably the forerunner of the modern high arm machines that dominated the market starting around 1880. The Mack, however, was made during the mid-1860s.

Figure 2-159. Madame Demorest (O/6), circa 1865. This machine sews a running stitch.

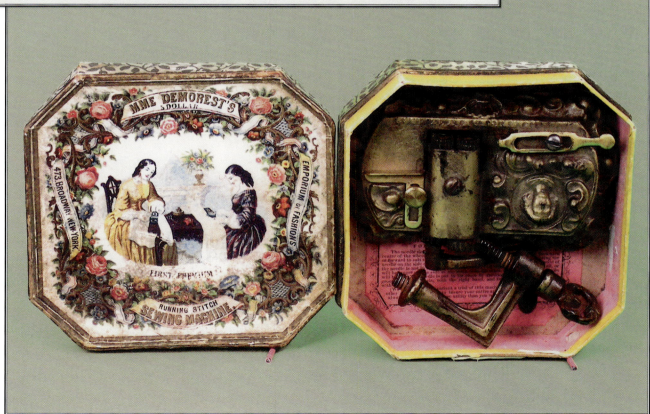

Figure 2-160. Madame Demorest (O/7), showing the original box.

Sewing Machine Manufacturers from 1850 to 1880

Figure 2-161. Madame Demorest (R/6), circa 1865, the gold and black model.

Figure 2-162. Manhattan (R/8), circa 1870.

Figure 2-163. Note how the Manhattan of figure 2-162 tilts to allow servicing.

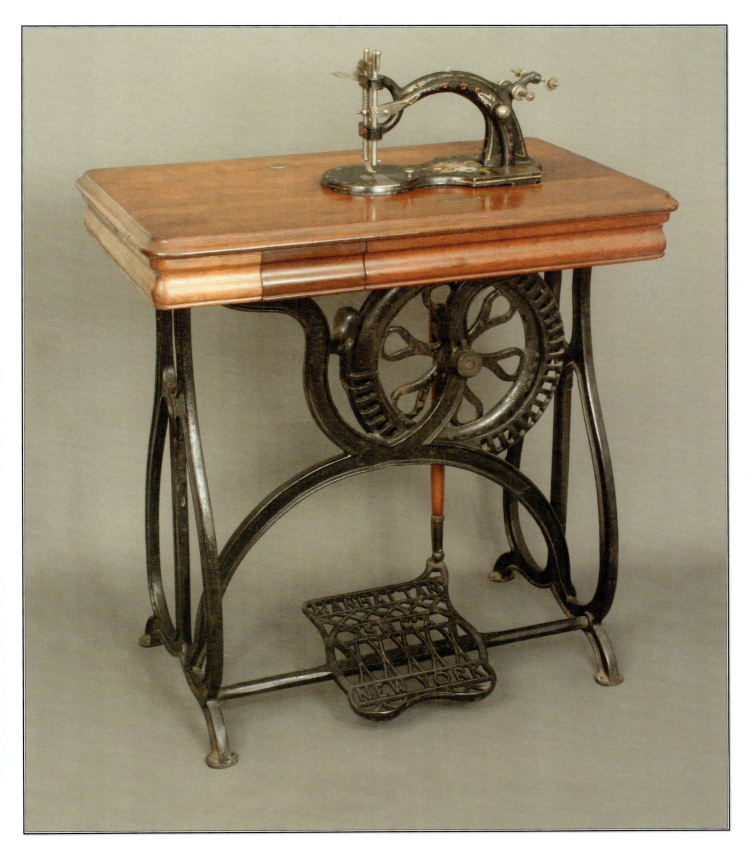

Sewing Machine Manufacturers from 1850 to 1880

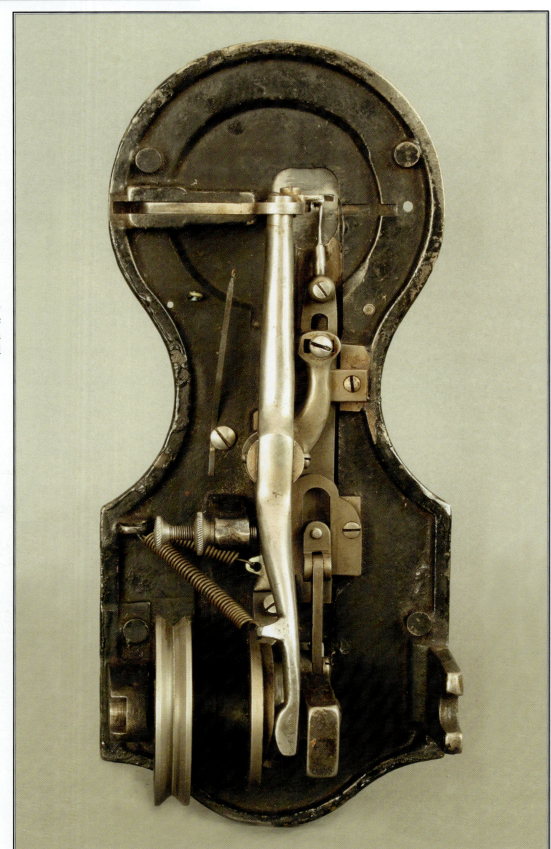

Figure 2-164. Mechanism of the Manhattan, which sews a two-thread chain stitch.

Sewing Machine Manufacturers from 1850 to 1880

Figure 2-165. McLean & Hooper (X/8), the first model. Probably only a few hundred were made.

Figure 2-166. McLean & Hooper (R/6), circa 1875, typical model. This machine is embossed on the back with the head of a man.

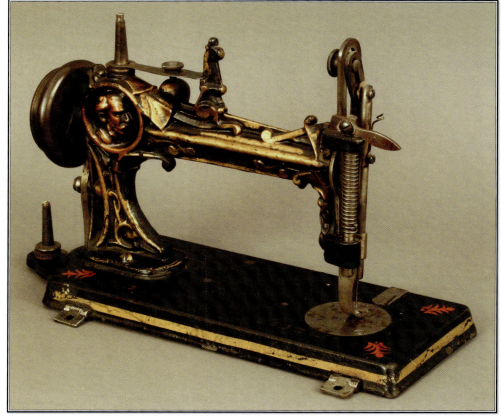

Figure 2-167. McLean & Hooper (R/7). The foot treadle for these machines is similar to those produced by the Grover and Baker company.

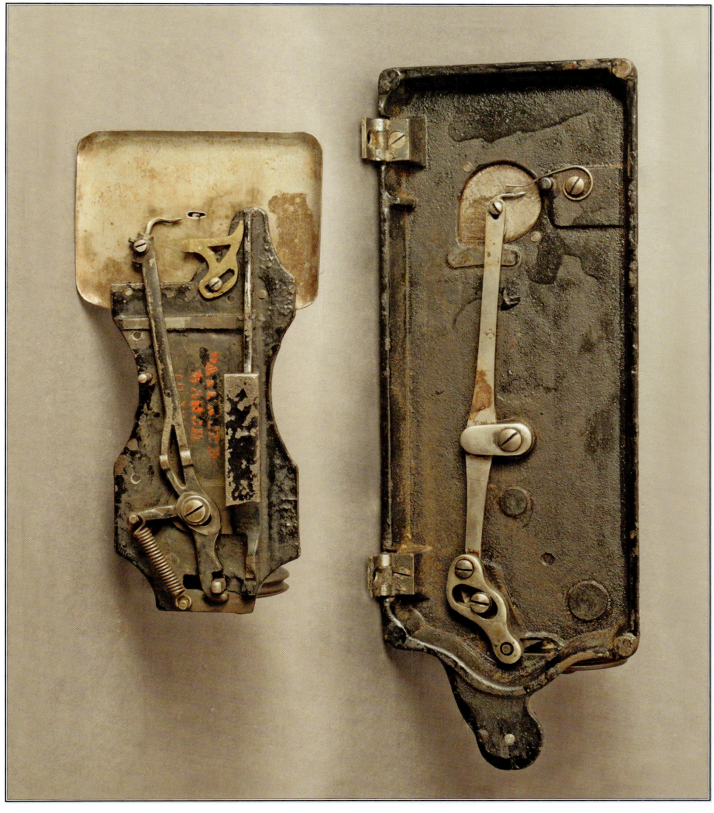

Figure 2-168. Mechanism of the two McLean & Hooper models. Although somewhat different in appearance, each functions in the same manner and sews a two-thread chain stitch. Note that the later version (right) is somewhat simpler.

Sewing Machine Manufacturers from 1850 to 1880

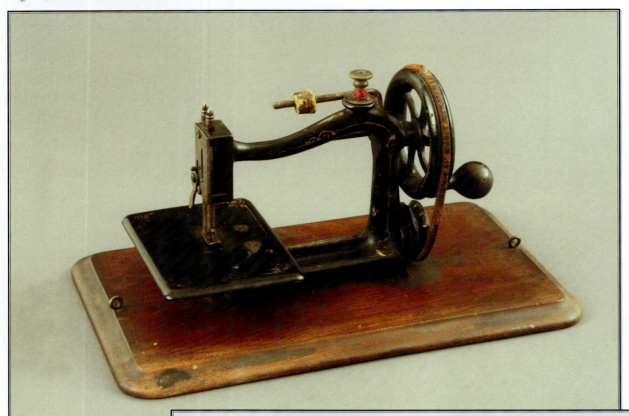

Figure 2-169. Murphy (R/6), circa 1876. This small machine was not considered a toy.

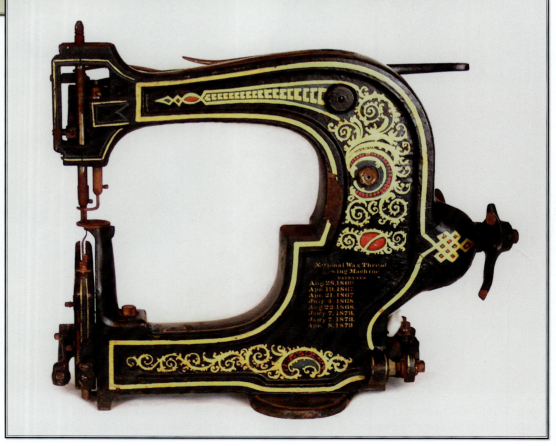

Figure 2-170. National Wax Thread sewing machine (X/6), circa 1875. This machine is more than 18" tall and was designed for heavy-duty sewing.

Figure 2-171. Ne Plus Ultra (X/10), circa 1857. This machine is highly decorated with mother-of-pearl. One can only guess what the designers were thinking when they supplied the machine with two flywheels and two pitman rods.

Figure 2-172. Ne Plus Ultra (X/9). Although this view depicts the flywheel and handle at the front, one can infer that the machine was operated with the handle at the right (see figure 2-171).

Figure 2-173. Nettleton and Raymond (R/8) treadle machine, circa 1859. This particular example was decorated with false wood grain. The decoration is original and the top is constructed from basswood instead of walnut.

Figure 2-174. Detail of the machine in figure 2-173.

Figure 2-175. Nettleton and Raymond (R/7).

Figure 2-176. Mechanisms of the two Nettleton and Raymond models. They are quite similar in appearance, and each sews a two-thread chain stitch.

Sewing Machine Manufacturers from 1850 to 1880

Figure 2-177. New England type (F/3). Machines in this general category were made during the 1860s and 1870s.

Figure 2-178. New England type (F/3). This is a shortened version of the machine in figure 2-177.

NEW ENGLAND (figures 2-177 through 2-206): The name New England collectively refers to many machines made during the 1860s and 1870s that look quite similar, but which were made by a variety of companies and sold as "COMMON SENSE" or "FAMILY" sewing machines. All produce a single-thread chain stitch utilizing Charles Raymond's 1861 patent for a reciprocating hook. The various companies engaged in the manufacture of these machines are given in Cooper as Nettleton & Raymond of Brattleboro, Vermont, Grout & White of Orange, Massachusetts, Clark & Barker of Orange, Massachusetts, Wm. Grout of Winchendon, Massachusetts, J. G. Folsom of Winchendon, Massachusetts, and A. F. Johnson of Orange, Massachusetts.

The rarity and value range from A/3 to R/6 and are difficult to assign with great precision, for serial numbers were not used, and it is impossible to determine with accuracy how many of each species were made. The illustrations are more-or-less arranged showing the most typical (and most common) machines first. Many more types and minor variations have not been illustrated, and still more remain to be discovered.

NEW HOME: See HOME SHUTTLE.

NOVELTY: The needle-from-below machine shown in figure 2-22 was advertised as the BARTLETT NOVELTY during the late 1860s. An unrelated Novelty Sewing Machine was advertised during the same period and is shown in figures 2-208 through 2-210. A few thousand of each were made.

ORMOND: The machine illustrated is better known as the HORSE SEWING MACHINE (figures 2-211 and 2-346), although a diamond-shaped brass plate imbedded in the table is stamped, "From Ormond Manufacturing Company 41 N. Gay Street, Baltimore, Md.," and the horse is actually not a part of the working mechanism. The machine itself is a W. G. WILSON shuttle lockstitch machine. This particular example may have been specially commissioned for a Masonic lodge, for there are Masonic emblems throughout the painted and inlaid designs. This machine is obviously highly ornamental; the head is covered with mother-of-pearl, and the cabinet construction has been executed with fine attention to detail. The massive size is quite imposing — 48" wide by 22" deep — and reflects the fact that a sewing machine, as a symbol of modernity and prosperity, deserved a position of honor in any parlor. As was mentioned, the particular designs found on this machine indicate a special commission, but the dramatic horse figure is not unique; at least one other box cover from an almost identical machine survives today.

PARHAM: Mr. Charles Parham was involved with sewing machines at least as early as 1854, having received a patent then (figure 2-212). Much later, the Philadelphia-based Parham Sewing Machine Company manufactured the machine shown in figure 2-213. This later machine appears to have been made from 1869 to 1871. On the machine is a silver-plated round medallion that is inscribed, "THE PARHAM S. M. CO/INCORPORATED 1868 Pa. U.S.A." Both the earlier and the later machines were fairly large, weighing more than 20 pounds each.

PARKER (figures 2-214 through 2-217): The company was based in Meriden, Connecticut, and produced machines from around 1859 until after 1867. Probably fewer than 5,000 were made.

PAW FOOT MACHINES (figures 2-218 through 2-234): These machines are common, yet every collector tries to obtain as many of this type as possible, because they are cute and many minor variations exist. As is the case with the NEW ENGLAND sewing machines, serial numbers are seldom present, but occasionally a maker's name appears on the cloth plate or on a paper label that has been affixed to the machine. Many varieties other than those illustrated will undoubtedly turn up.

PEIRCE & RUDDICK (figure 2-235): Circa 1863. Little is known about this company, but the two-thread chain stitch mechanism appears typical of mechanisms manufactured in the mid-1860s. Embossed on the cloth plate is "Peirce & Ruddick/May 29 1860/Boston Mass." Very few of these machines were made — probably a couple of thousand or less.

PLANER AND KAYSER (figures 2-236, 2-237): This shuttle lockstitch machine was the predecessor to the AETNA and was apparently made strictly for treadle operation. About 10,000 were manufactured during the mid-1860s, but the design was clearly copied from the SINGER LETTER A of five years earlier. Written in gold on the arm of the machine is "Planer & Kayser/84 Bowery, New York."

Figure 2-179. New England type (F/3).

Figure 2-180. New England type (R/4).

Figure 2-181. New England type (R/4).

Figure 2-182. New England type (F/3). Slightly different versions of this machine have been found. This is the case for many of the New England types.

Figure 2-183. New England type (O/3). This machine differs slightly from the machine in figure 2-182.

Sewing Machine Manufacturers from 1850 to 1880

Figure 2-184. New England type. Although probably not made in the U. S., this machine turns up occasionally; hence it is included here. In England, where it is known as the Weir, it is very common. It is distinguished from other types by the double curl on the lower part of the iron arm.

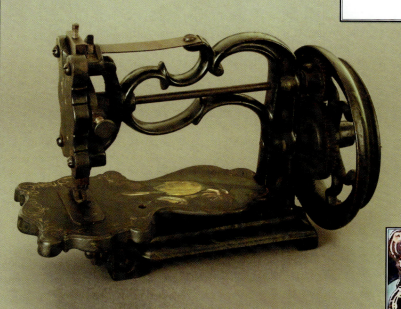

Figure 2-185. New England type (F/3). The body of this machine and the body of the machine in figure 2-177 are identical. The needle bar cover and cloth plate are different. Other New England types also exhibit this characteristic.

Figure 2-186. A sample of the hand-painted designs from the front plates of typical New England–type machines.

Sewing Machine Manufacturers from 1850 to 1880

Figure 2-187. New England type (F/3).

Figure 2-188. New England type (O/4).

Figure 2-189. New England type (O/4; R/6 with mother-of-pearl). This example, another version of a Folsom machine, is very fancy, with mother-of-pearl and some silver-plated parts — unusual on a New England type machine.

Figure 2-190. New England type (O/4).

Sewing Machine Manufacturers from 1850 to 1880

Figure 2-191. Grant Brothers (O/4), circa 1870. The true Grant Brothers machine feeds cloth with a four-motion feed, not the upper feed that is typical of the New England varieties. This machine is also known as the Erie or Universal Underfeed sewing machine.

Figure 2-192. New England type (R/4). Similar to Grant Brothers, but features an upper feed mechanism, like most of the New England varieties.

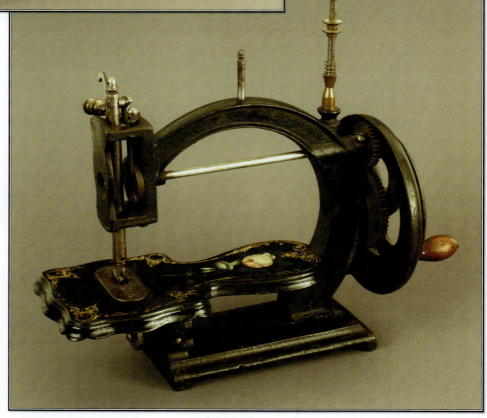

Figure 2-193. New England type (O/4).

Figure 2-194. New England type (R/4). This machine has a top part that is identical to the "Shaw" machine of figure 2-226. Moreover, the spring at the top has stamped on it the date of Shaw's patent, Dec. 16, 1862. Although this machine could possibly be called a Shaw machine, its underneath mechanism differs from that described in his patent papers, being more typical of the New England type. Interestingly, the examples examined so far, like those of figure 2-226, sport a two- or three-digit number painted underneath; hence, both models were likely made by the same company.

Sewing Machine Manufacturers from 1850 to 1880

Figure 2-195. New England type (R/4).

Figure 2-196. New England type (O or R/4).

Figure 2-197. New England type (O/4).

Figure 2-198. New England type (O/4).

Sewing Machine Manufacturers from 1850 to 1880

Figure 2-199. The New England Snake machine (O/5).

Figure 2-200. Close-up of the snake of figure 2-199. He's got a tight grip on the presser foot spring.

Sewing Machine Manufacturers from 1850 to 1880

Figure 2-201. New England type (O/6).

Figure 2-202. New England type (R/6).

Figure 2-203. Thompson (R/5), circa 1870. Unlike most other New England types, this machine utilizes a four-motion feed.

Figure 2-204. New England type (R/6).

Sewing Machine Manufacturers from 1850 to 1880

Figure 2-205. New England type (U/6).

Figure 2-206. New England type (R/6).

Figure 2-207. Mechanism employed by almost all New England varieties. Next to the WILLCOX AND GIBBS revolving hook, this mechanism was the most common method of producing a single-thread chain stitch (see figure 2-1).

Figure 2-208. Novelty (R/6), circa 1868.

Figure 2-209. Novelty (O/6), circa 1868.

Figure 2-210. Novelty (O/6), circa 1868.

Figure 2-211. Ormond (X10), also known as the Horse, circa 1877. The machine head is actually a W. G. Wilson (see figure 2-346). The table surface is four feet across.

Figure 2-212. Parham (X/9), circa 1854.

Figure 2-213. Parham (R/6). 1869.

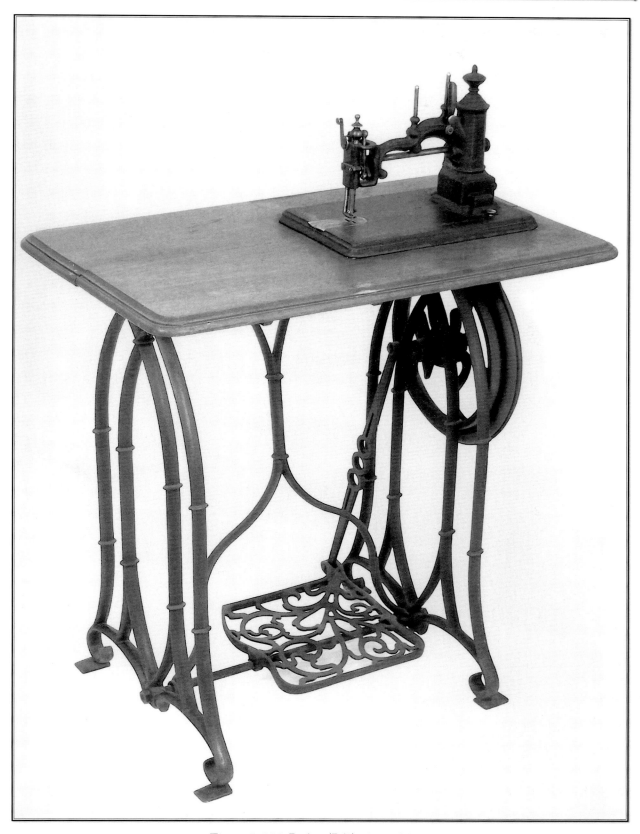

Figure 2-214. Parker (R/8), circa 1860.

Sewing Machine Manufacturers from 1850 to 1880

Figure 2-215. Parker(?) (R/7), circa 1860.

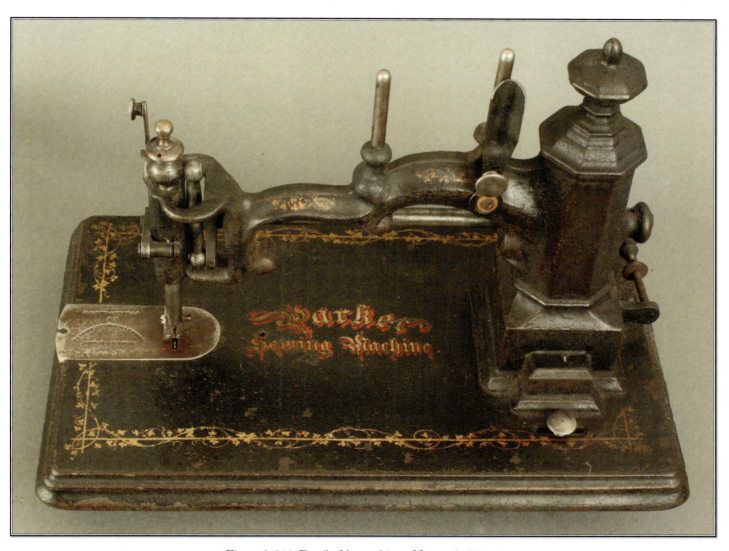

Figure 2-216. Detail of the machine of figure 2-214.

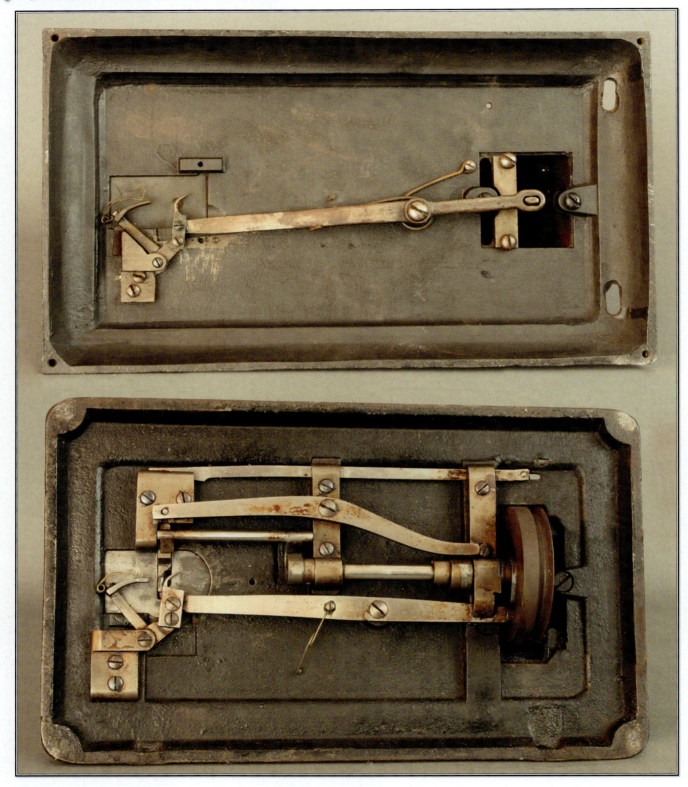

Figure 2-217. Mechanisms for both Parker models (figures 2-215 and 2-216). Each machine sews a two-thread chain stitch, and both mechanisms are quite similar. It is likely that the version depicted in figure 2-215 is a later model of the Parker, as the mechanism is somewhat simpler. Its identity is not absolutely certain, however.

Figure 2-218. Paw Foot type (R/5), Folsom. This machine more typically appears as shown in figure 2-88. Paw Foot–type machines were made from the early 1860s to the early 1870s.

Figure 2-219. Paw Foot type (R/5). The finial atop the "fire hydrant" takes on many forms for these machines. This "acorn" version appears infrequently.

Sewing Machine Manufacturers from 1850 to 1880

Figure 2-220. Paw Foot type (O/5). According to the paper label attached to the machine, and to the accompanying instruction booklet, this machine was produced by the Little Giant Sewing Machine Co. of Toledo, Ohio. Cooper gives the name as Monitor, and the maker as Shaw & Clark. It is reasonable that Shaw & Clark was the actual manufacturer.

Figure 2-221. Paw Foot type (O/5). This is the direct drive (i.e., no gears) version of the machine depicted in figure 2-220.

178

Figure 2-222. Paw Foot type (O/5), Wilson. Sometimes the name is not present, but these are usually marked with "Ketchum's Patent, April 28, 1863."

Figure 2-223. Paw Foot type (O/5). Probably made by Shaw & Clark.

Sewing Machine Manufacturers from 1850 to 1880

Figure 2-224. Empire (O/5). This example has been repainted.

Figure 2-225. Paw Foot type (R/5). There are many minor variations of the paw foot style. This one is infrequently found.

Figure 2-226. Paw Foot type (R/5), circa 1863. This machine could be called "Shaw's Patent Sewing Machine," for the patent date of Dec. 16, 1862, appears on the flat spring on top of the machine. The crude two-thread chain stitch mechanism underneath is described in his patent application, though no patent is claimed for it. His claim deals only with the spring and the cloth feed mechanism on the top side of the machine. All examples found so far have a two- or three-digit number painted in one or two places under the machine. This is probably not a serial number, due to the quantity (albeit small) of these machines that has turned up. For another "Shaw" machine, see figure 2-194.

Figure 2-227. Paw Foot type (R/6). No identifying marks. This may be a variant of the Granite State sewing machine (see text).

Figure 2-228. Paw Foot type (R/6), Atwater, circa 1865. Another version was mounted on a treadle stand (see figure 2-14).

Sewing Machine Manufacturers from 1850 to 1880

Figure 2-229. Paw Foot type (O/5). Marked "Goodspeed & Wyman, Winchendon, Mass."

Figure 2-230. Paw Foot type (R/6). No identifying marks. This machine is somewhat smaller than the others.

Figure 2-231. Paw Foot type (X/7). Hodgkin's patent sewing machine, circa 1862. This machine has a very unusual mechanism. The feed is a round toothed wheel, a device usually found only upon certain earlier treadle machines. The reciprocating hook that forms the chain stitch tends to collide with the needle if the machine is operated backwards.

Figure 2-232. Hodgkin's patent sewing machine (U/6), a version encountered less frequently than the machine of figure 2-231.

Sewing Machine Manufacturers from 1850 to 1880

Figure 2-233. Paw Foot type (R/6), the Granite State sewing machine. Despite the atypical appearance, the machine sews the usual single-thread chain stitch, employing the ordinary reciprocating hook at the end of a long shaft.

POCKET: The Pocket "sewing machine" (figures 2-238 and 2-239) turns like an eggbeater and was alleged to be a sewing machine, though it couldn't have sewn much. It was advertised during the late 1860s by the FINKLE & LYON company, and, although small enough to fit in a pocket, not too many have turned up.

POND (figure 2-240): Little is known about the actual manufacturer of this shuttle lockstitch machine, except that other nearly identical models sport different names printed in gilt on the side of the arm. These are heavy-duty models from the 1860s that mimic somewhat the earlier SINGER #1.

PRATT (figure 2-241): Also known as the Lady's Companion, fewer than 2,000 were made by a Boston company during the latter part of the 1850s. This type of stand appears very infrequently in America, but is fairly common for European makers. Stands somewhat similar to this design were occasionally sold in order to mount hand-operated machines so that they could be powered by foot.

QUAKER CITY (figures 2-242 through 2-244): This machine employs an 1858 patent of W. P. UHLINGER, and the foot pedal of some stands is stamped "W P U & Co. Phila Pa." Although it could be called the Uhlinger sewing machine, it has become popularly known as the Quaker City. Fewer than 2,000 were made, and for only a short period of time around 1860, yet a variety of stands and two machine models have been discovered. One generally finds that machines of such limited production have one standard treadle base, but the Quaker City has at least three. All examples are powered

Figure 2-234. Paw Foot type (R/6). This machine has no identifying marks. Perhaps calling it a "paw foot" type is a stretch, but the machine is clearly similar to one of that genre.

Figure 2-235. Peirce & Ruddick (R/7), circa 1862.

Figure 2-236. Planer and Kayser (R/6), circa 1866. This is the predecessor to the Aetna. The box cover unfolds to create a table surface.

Sewing Machine Manufacturers from 1850 to 1880

Figure 2-237. Detail of the Planer and Kayser head. The writing on the side says, "Planer and Kayser, 84 Bowery New York." Compare this machine with the Aetna of figure 2-3. Although the Aetna is 1" longer, the two machines are otherwise very similar.

by treadle and sew (subject to their own whims) a crudely mechanized two-thread chain stitch.

REESE (figures 2-245, 2-246): The Reese, made for treadle use, sews a lockstitch with a stationary bobbin. No more than a few thousand were made during the early 1870s.

REMINGTON (figures 2-247 through 2-249): The Remington descended from the EMPIRE and was one of the more popular machines of the 1870s and 1880s. Although a hand-operated version shows up occasionally, most examples were designed for use on a treadle base, and all sew a lockstitch. About 75,000 machines were manufactured by the Remington company, which was first based in Philadelphia and then moved to Illion, New York. By the 1880s, the models took on a more modern look, resembling most of the other machines of that period. Many people will recognize the name as that of a gun manufacturer; in fact the same company produced both the gun and the sewing machine. If you are lucky enough to obtain the little silverplated R-shaped attachments, you might encounter some that are embossed, "The sewing machine like the rifle gun, that beats the world is the Remington."

RIVAL (figure 2-250): Little is known about this machine, which sews a two-thread chain stitch.

ROBINSON AND ROPER (figure 2-251): At least three different designs have turned up. The version illustrated here does not look like either of the machines shown in Cooper, which indicates that the machine was made by the Howard and Davis Manufacturing Company of Boston. The machine did not achieve much success and was only manufactured for about two or three years, with production ceasing around 1856.

SCOVEL & GODELL (figure 2-252): This machine is identical in appearance and operation to the treadle version of the NETTLETON & RAYMOND. The name Scovel and Godell appears on the needle bar cover along with a serial number. If one is to use the serial number as a guide, about 2,000 – 3,000 machines were made, although it is possible that the number may refer to the overall Nettleton and Raymond series itself.

THE SEAMSTRESS FRIEND (figures 2-253, 2-254): Probably circa 1865. Little is known about this magnificent machine. It is quite large (15" by 13") and heavy; thus, it has the distinction of being the largest known FIGURAL sewing machine; it is highly embossed with many seemingly unrelated motifs — an anchor, a bunch of grapes, an American eagle, and much more. It is made of brass, except for some mechanism parts and the flywheel, which are iron. Perhaps it was a specialty item designed for use on a ship.

SECOR (figures 2-255, 2-256): Manufactured by the Secor Machine Co. of Bridgeport, Connecticut, during the 1870s, the 10,000 or so produced appear to have been made exclusively for treadle operation and are mounted on stands like the rather ornate one shown. Variants have been found with minor differences in the table top, but the iron legs are always the same. The Secor machine sews a shuttle lockstitch, but the company also produced the entirely different FAIRY machine.

SEWING SHEARS: See HENDRICKS, AMERICAN HAND, GOODBODY.

SHAW & CLARK (figures 2-257 through 2-263): There were a total of 20,000 – 30,000 of these hand-operated models produced by this Biddeford, Maine, company during the 1860s, representing at least seven different varieties. The Shaw & Clark machine is quite popular as a collectible, therefore several types have been illustrated. The most common, shown in figure 2-257, is called the "closed-pillar" type. Similar to the closed pillar is the "open-pillar" machine (figure 2-258). This type appears to have been an early model, as the serial numbers are lower than those found on closed-pillar machines. Shown in figure 2-259 is the "skinny-pillar" type. These have low serial numbers and would therefore also be among the earlier models made by the company. When examining these machines, you will notice that the open- and skinny-pillar machines have a very wide needle bar as opposed to the smaller round mechanism of the varieties that have higher serial numbers. As more machines were produced, the company probably learned to economize on the amount of metal used in production, or perhaps the smaller round needle bar gave the machine a streamlined look. The open-pillar type probably evolved into the closed-pillar variety in an effort to give the machine more strength or to hide part of the mechanism, which was inside the pillar for the closed models. The stitch-forming mechanism for the open pillar design is the NEW ENGLAND–type looper; the closed pillar uses a simple reciprocating hook attached to a long shaft. The examples shown in figures 2-260 and 2-261 are the "fat-pillar" varieties, whose larger serial numbers indicate a later date, e.g., the latter half of the 1860s. The mechanism is the same as that found on the closed-pillar machine. The MONITOR-type Shaw & Clark is one of the most frequently found of all the varieties (see PAW FOOT figures 2-220 and 2-223), but seldom appears with the stamped "Shaw & Clark," as do other models. The running stitch variety sews a stitch similar to that of the MADAME DEMOREST and is one of the rarest (figure 2-262). The final model, though stamped with the company name, is not of the same type as the other Shaw & Clark machines illustrated. It is a later lockstitch machine and was made in 1867 after the company moved to Chicopee Falls, Massachusetts (figure 2-263). According to Cooper, the CHICOPEE sewing machine company may have evolved from the Shaw & Clark company.

Figure 2-238. Pocket "sewing machine" (R/4), circa 1868.

Figure 2-239. Pocket sewing machine variant (R/5), with a hollowed-out thread spool holder.

Figure 2-240. Pond (R/7), circa 1865.

Figure 2-241. Pratt (R/9), circa 1859. The stand retains its original dark green paint.

Figure 2-242. Quaker City (R/8), circa 1859.

Figure 2-243. Quaker City (X/8), circa 1860. This appears to have been a later model. The sewing mechanism is improved, being more typical of machines made after 1860.

Figure 2-244. Mechanisms for both Quaker City models. The machine of figure 2-243 is at the top.

Figure 2-245. Reese (R/7), circa 1872.

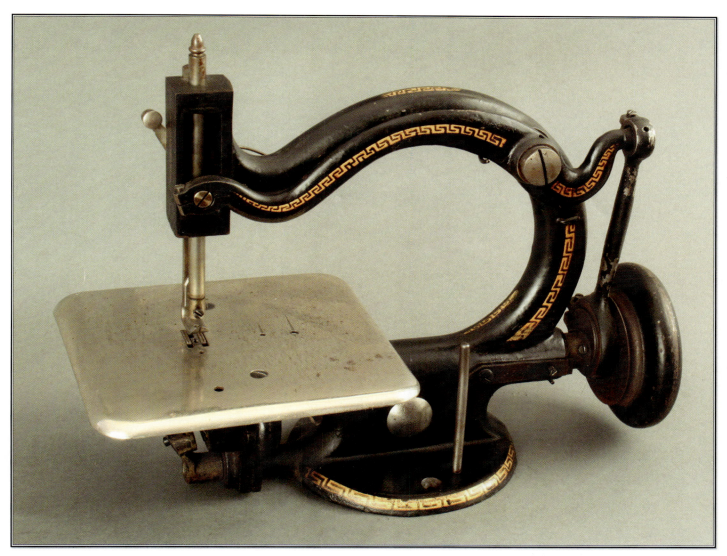

Figure 2-246. Detail of the Reese machine. (This is what you get when you mate a SECOR with a WILLCOX AND GIBBS.)

Sewing Machine Manufacturers from 1850 to 1880

Figure 2-247. Remington (O/4), circa 1875.

Figure 2-248. Remington (R/3), circa 1880, the hand-operated version.

Figure 2-249. Remington (R/5), circa 1875. The company made several different cabinet models.

Figure 2-250. Rival (U/7 or 8), circa 1865.

Figure 2-251. Robinson and Roper (U/9), 1855. This machine was manufactured, but possibly not in the form that is depicted here.

Figure 2-252. Scovell & Godell (R/8), circa 1859. This machine and its mechanism are identical to the Nettleton & Raymond. The only difference: the Scovell & Godell does not have the name "Nettleton & Raymond" embossed underneath (see figure 2-176).

Figure 2-253. The Seamstress Friend (X/9), probably from around 1865. This large fancy brass machine may have been used on a ship.

Figure 2-254. The Seamstress Friend back view.

Figure 2-255. Secor (R/7), circa 1875. There were several different Secor models, but the machine design was the same for all.

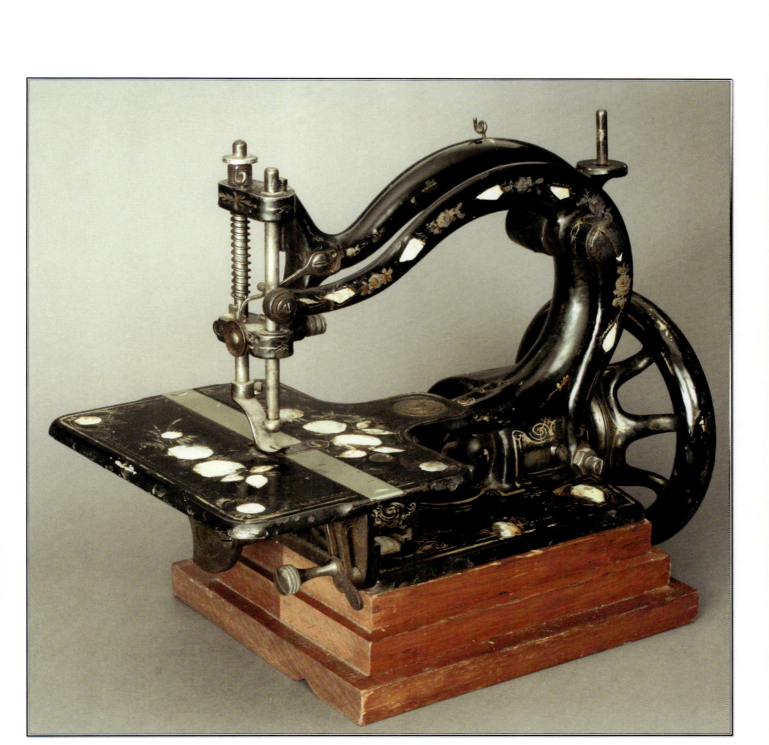

Figure 2-256. Detail of a Secor head that has been embellished with mother-of-pearl inlay.

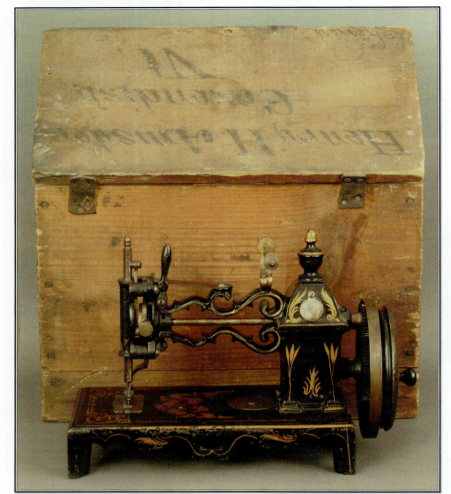

Figure 2-257. Shaw & Clark "closed pillar" (R/6, with box; O/5, without box), circa 1866.

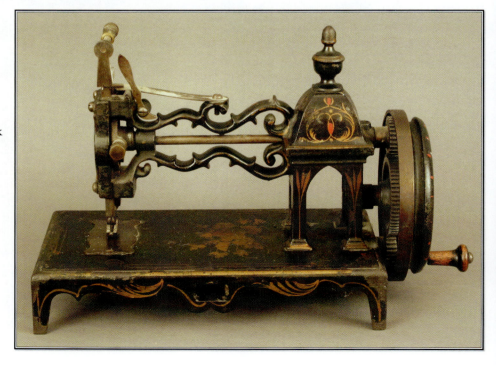

Figure 2-258. Shaw & Clark "open pillar" (R/7), circa 1864.

Figure 2-259. Shaw & Clark "skinny pillar" (R/7), circa 1864.

Figure 2-260. Shaw & Clark "fat pillar" (O/6), circa 1866. This model could be operated by hand or mounted on a treadle stand, as could many models.

Figure 2-261. Shaw & Clark (R/7), designed exclusively for treadle operation.

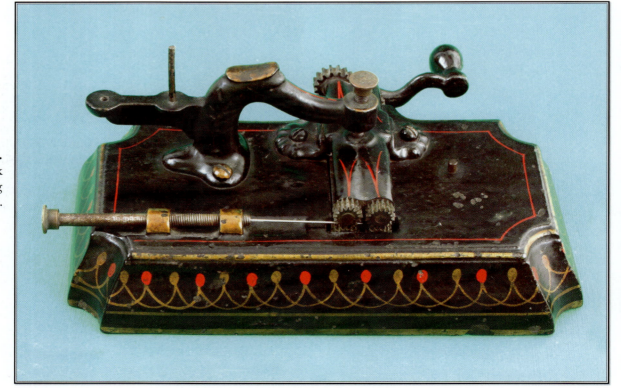

Figure 2-262. Shaw & Clark (X/8) running stitch machine.

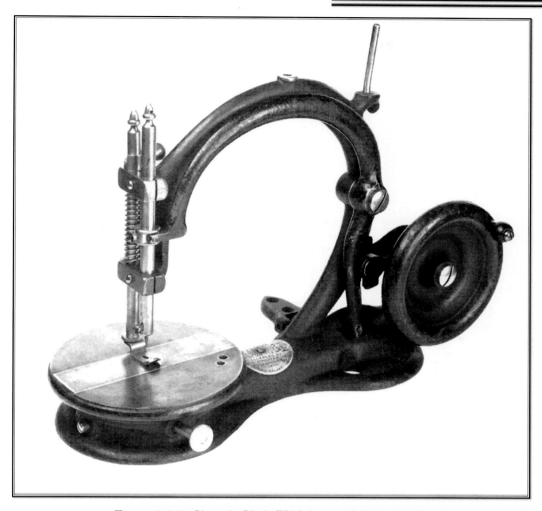

Figure 2-263. Shaw & Clark (X/8), last model, circa 1868.

SHAW'S PATENT SEWING MACHINE: See figures 2-194 and 2-226.

SIMPLICITY (figure 2-264): Circa 1880. Little is known about this unusual machine, except that it was probably not a toy. Typical toy treadle machines are about 22" – 23" high (as measured to the sewing surface). Regular treadle machines are 28" – 30", and the Simplicity is 29" to the sewing surface. Hence a small child would need to stand while sewing. Made of cast iron, it is nevertheless very light and can be easily carried around by hooking one finger of one hand around the arm of the tiny machine, which by the way sews a single-thread chain stitch with a WILLCOX & GIBBS–type rotary hook.

SINGER: The Singer NUMBER ONE, shown in figures 2-265 through 2-267, could be mounted on a treadle stand or operated by hand. Approximately 10,000 of these heavy shuttle lockstitch machines were made from 1851 to about 1860. Despite the relatively large number produced, this machine is quite valuable because of its historical significance and because, due to its large size, most were scrapped rather than saved. The commercial success that this machine enjoyed is doubtless due more to successful marketing strategy than to the inherent qualities of the machine, as it is quite noisy and bulky.

The Singer NUMBER TWO machine (figure 2-268), which replaced the No. 1 and strongly resembles it in design, was produced in this and other similar styles from the early 1860s through the early 1900s. The No. 2 is very heavy and bulky, and although it does not appear too frequently, its value is not great because of its size and the large number made (probably over 100,000).

The TURTLEBACK was the first home machine that Singer introduced and is one of the most highly sought-after machines today (figures 2-269 through 2-271). Produced for a very short time, from 1858 to 1861, approximately 1,500 were made. The Turtleback was not a great success, as the mechanism was too frail to be of much use on a variety of fabrics; hence not many were sold.

The Turtleback was quickly replaced by the popular Singer LETTER A (figures 2-272 and 2-273), which was made from

Sewing Machine Manufacturers from 1850 to 1880

Figure 2-264. Simplicity sewing machine (X/9), circa 1880.

1858 to 1865, but which is found only occasionally today. One reason why the Letter A and the Turtleback survive in such relatively small numbers is because of Singer's sales policy. Machines could be purchased on a payment plan, and old machines could be traded in for a discount. Since Singer did not deal in used machines, any old Singer machine the company accepted in trade was broken up and melted down. The Turtleback stand was made completely of metal and was very heavy; hence, it was a prime candidate for meltdown. Approximately 75,000 Letter A machines were manufactured, some with a metal table and stand (the ones most frequently found), others with a wooden table, or with a mother-of-pearl head and a folding wooden box cover. A deluxe cabinet model, with a style similar to that of the machine in figure 2-271, was also made (figure 2-273).

One interesting feature of most early Singer machines, up to and including the Letter A, is a dual set of serial numbers appearing on the underside of the cloth plate. The two serial numbers differ from each other by exactly 4,000. In addition, the Letter A has a third number scratched by hand under each cloth plate and stamped at the top of the needle bar. This number is always considerably less than the overall serial numbers, but the last three digits are identical in all three numbers. Probably this number represents the actual quantity of Letter A machines produced as opposed to the total of all Singer machines. At any rate, there seems to be a linear relationship between the true serial number and the scratched-in number.

In 1865, the company introduced the NEW FAMILY machine (figures 2-274 and 2-275). The Singer New Family was the most widely copied machine of its day. Millions of similar machines were made by several other manufacturers from 1875 to about 1920. The machine was an enormous success for the Singer company, which sold more than 4,000,000 before changing the model in the early 1880s (figure 2-276). All models sew a shuttle lockstitch, but there were a wide variety of cabinet choices for the customer, including hand-operated versions. The fanciest styles were full cabinet models utilizing heads covered with mother-of-pearl (figure 2-275).

The later AUTOMATIC (figure 2-277) was the Singer company's version of the WILLCOX & GIBBS mechanism. This machine was made for about 40 years, starting around 1890, and was usually placed upon a rather ordinary treadle

Figure 2-265. Singer Number One (R/8), 1858, on its original shipping crate, which was also used to provide foot power. A misguided decorator painted the machine red.

stand. A very interesting cabinet for this machine appeared in 1900, possibly to celebrate the new century. Here the metal parts of the treadle stand were made entirely of brass, including the large flywheel and the foot pedal (figures 2-278 and 2-279).

As one would expect with such a successful company, Singer had offices in virtually every major city throughout the country. The main corporate headquarters moved from Boston to New York, and then to Elizabeth, New Jersey, where a large manufacturing facility was built. After the turn of the twentieth century, Singer bought the Wheeler & Wilson Co. and utilized its old facilities in Bridgeport, Connecticut, to continue to build old style WHEELER & WILSON machines with the Singer name on them (figure 2-281). Of course, most of the twentieth century Singer machines resembled those illustrated in figures 2-280 and 2-282.

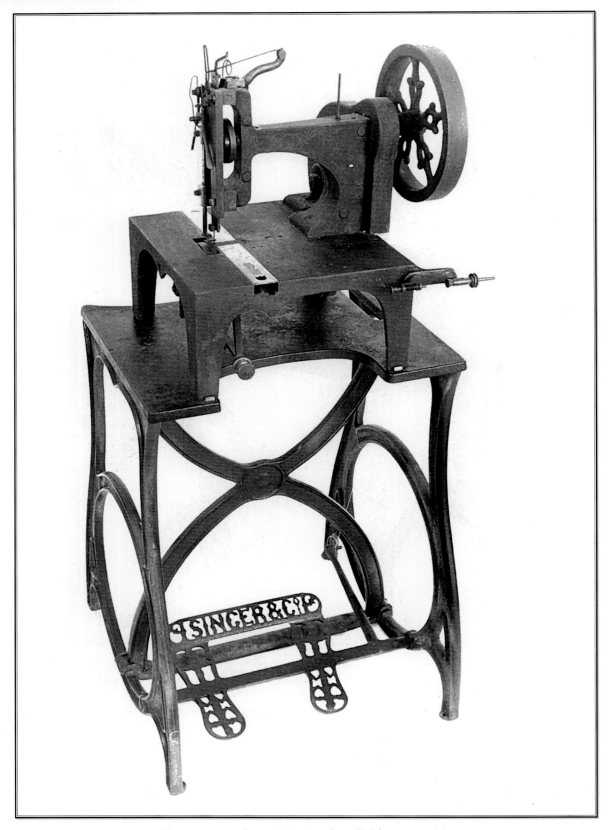

Figure 2-266. Singer Number One (R/8), circa 1855.

Sewing Machine Manufacturers from 1850 to 1880

Figure 2-267. Singer Number One (X/8). This stand variation is very seldom encountered.

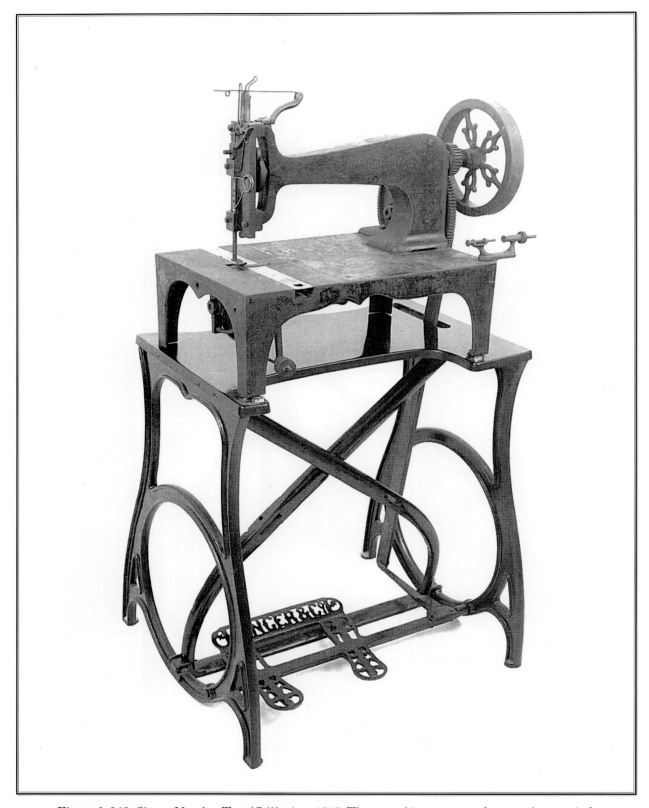

Figure 2-268. Singer Number Two (O/3), circa 1862. These machines were made over a long period.

Figure 2-269. Singer Turtleback (R/9), circa 1858.

Figure 2-270. Singer Turtleback (X/10). The head is black and the stand, originally a shade of green, has faded to a greenish brown.

Sewing Machine Manufacturers from 1850 to 1880

Figure 2-271. Singer Turtleback (X/10), cabinet model. The top is cast iron and the sides are wood. The painting is original.

Figure 2-272. Singer Letter A with mother-of-pearl inlay (R/7), circa 1861. The usual model (O/5) has a small iron table surface instead of the unfolding cover shown here.

Figure 2-273. Singer Letter A (X/8) on a stand similar to that in figure 2-271, except the cabinet was made of walnut and hence was not painted.

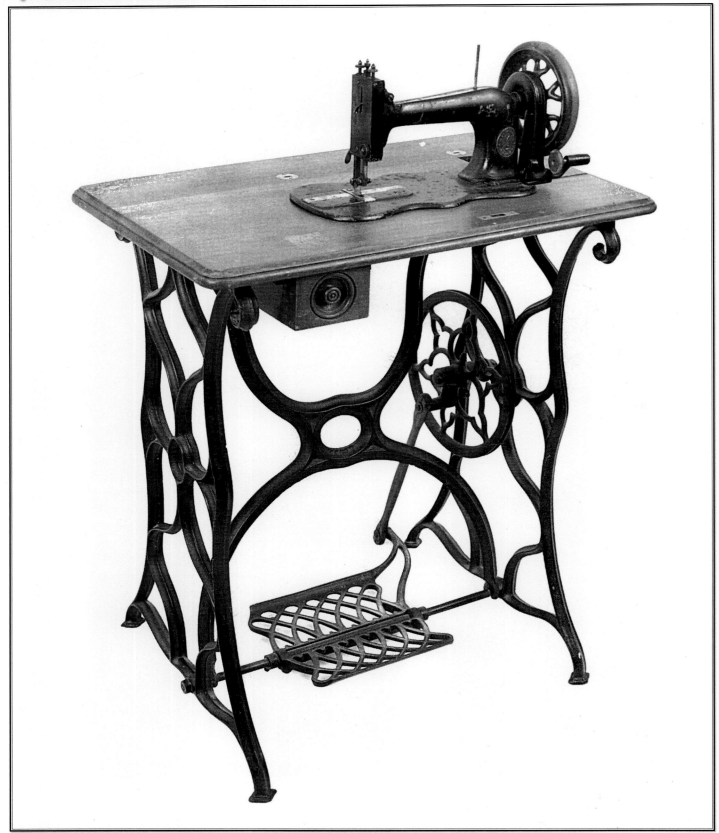

Figure 2-274. Singer New Family (A/2), circa 1870.

Figure 2-275. Singer New Family (O/6, in cabinet with very fancy head), circa 1865. The machine is almost entirely covered with mother-of-pearl, which is typical for full cabinet models. In many such models, the gilt has worn off due to use of the machines, leaving behind just the mother-of-pearl. This particular head is extremely decorated — the inset shows the etched design that appears on the sliding shuttle covers. Note also the foot pedals, which operate independently. This is the "Halls Patent" foot pedal, which was utilized by several different manufacturers from time to time.

Figure 2-276. Singer (F/1 without motor, which is extremely rare), circa 1885. This machine normally has the typical flywheel (see figure 2-280). But in this case, the flywheel has been replaced by a Diehl electric motor. This is a rare early example of an electrified sewing machine. (See figures D-7 and C-12 for even earlier examples.)

Figure 2-277. Singer Automatic (A/1), circa 1890. This was the Singer version of a Willcox & Gibbs.

Figure 2-278. Singer Automatic (R/6), 1900. Here, the metal parts of the stand are all brass, and the wood is dark mahogany. This was not a typical stand for the period. See figure D-50 for a more usual stand (A/2) for this machine.

Sewing Machine Manufacturers from 1850 to 1880

Figure 2-279. Singer Automatic, showing the closed cabinet.

Figure 2-280. Singer (A/1), circa 1900.

Figure 2-281. Singer (U/3), circa 1910. This example was actually a Wheeler & Wilson #9 machine (see figure 2-329). After Singer bought the Wheeler & Wilson company in 1905, it continued to sell machines under the Wheeler & Wilson name for a few years. Around 1910, it started putting its own name on many of the Wheeler & Wilson models. It is unknown how long the Singer version of the #9 machine was produced, but it differs from other Singer models of the period in that it utilizes Wilson's stationary bobbin instead of a shuttle. Few of these machines have turned up.

Figure 2-282. Singer (A/1), hand-operated portable, circa 1910.

SMITH, E. H. (figure 2-283): Little is known about this machine, which appears to have been made during the early 1860s. The example pictured sews a shuttle lockstitch and was designed for treadle installation.

SMITH, WILLIAM (figure 2-284): The Smith sewing machine is unusual in that the head and the table are one unit. This machine, which sews a shuttle lockstitch, was made for a short period in the 1870s and appears to have been a crude copy of the SINGER No. 2.

SPRINGSTEEN (figures 2-285, 2-286): Circa 1870. Here is another company that requires more investigation. At the time of this publication, the illustrated machine is the only example known. Stamped on top of one of the sliding shuttle covers is "B.C. SPRINGSTEEN / OWEGO, N.Y." Under both shuttle covers and on the machine is "107," which could be a serial number, but cannot be necessarily regarded as such, since it is not in plain view on any surface.

SQUIRREL (figure 2-287): The Squirrel is an elusive FIGURAL machine first illustrated in Grace Cooper's book. As neither a machine nor an advertisement has been discovered, it is unlikely that a working mechanism was ever commercially produced. Figure 2-288 shows the patent model (see appendix C), which is merely a wood cutout for a design patent received in 1859 by S. B. Ellithrop.

STEBBINS (figures 2-289, 2-290): According to a 1991 newspaper article, Mr. Carlos Stebbins, of Pike, New York, first produced sewing machines between 1861 and 1863. Only a few examples of this first model were made. He then supposedly ceased making sewing machines at the onset of the Civil War, then resumed at a later date with a slightly different model.

The sliding brass shuttle covers are crudely embossed by hand, in cursive, with the patent dates and with Mr. Stebbins' name. Thus, one would suspect that whatever the production schedule, few machines were made. The machine sews an ordinary shuttle lockstitch, but the cloth moves from front to back, toward the arm, and hence might tend to bunch up. Nevertheless, the Stebbins machine apparently could handle wider pieces of cloth than could be accommodated by a more typical arm arrangement.

Figure 2-283. Smith, E. H. (X/7), circa 1860.

STEVENS (figure 2-291): Little is known about this maker except that obviously several models were made. Manufacture took place during the 1860s, but it is unknown for how long.

STRANGE & HUNTLEY (figure 2-292): Circa 1860. The illustration depicts a rather fancy treadle machine that unfortunately has not turned up yet. It was supposed to have been made in Tauton, Mass.

TAGGART & FARR (figures 2-293, 2-294): About 1,000 Taggart & Farr sewing machines were made for a short period starting in 1858. The machine sews a two-thread chain stitch and was designed for treadle use. The company was based in Philadelphia.

THOMPSON (figure 2-203): This machine is stamped "Thompson, D. A. Abbott, Patented Jan. 22 1856, Dec. 9 1856, Dec. 12 1865." It may be the same machine listed by Cooper as being made by the C. F. Thompson Co. in 1871. The machine has a mechanism typical of most NEW ENGLAND machines, but it is significantly different in appearance.

THOMSON (figures 2-295 through 2-297): This machine is quite rare; no identification is given on the single machine that has turned up, other than the name "Thomson Patent" painted on the arm and "J Thomson/Patented/June 29, 1858/Feb 7, 1860" on the cloth plate. The mechanism is extremely complicated for what the machine does, which is sew an ordinary double-thread chain stitch. It is doubtful that many were made.

TRIUNE (figure 2-298): Probably no more than a few thousand Triune sewing machines were made by the Philadelphia Sewing Machine Co. during the early part of the 1870s. It is treadle powered and sews a lockstitch using a peculiar looking stationary shuttle-like bobbin enclosure. The reason for the quick demise of this machine can probably be explained by the fact that the bobbin is rather difficult to remove for rethreading.

UHLINGER: See QUAKER CITY.
UNION: See ELLIPTIC.

Figure 2-284. Smith, William (X/8), circa 1870.

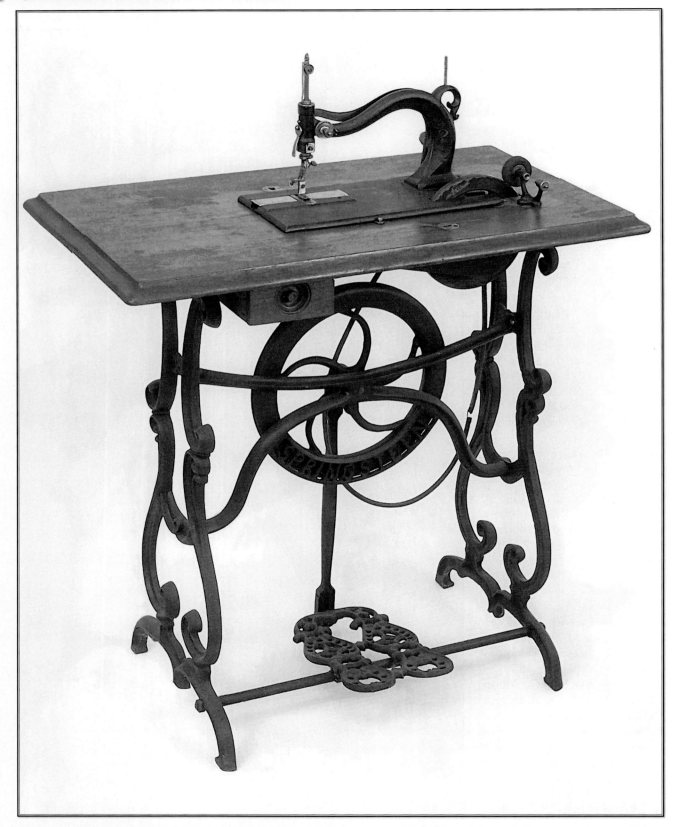

Figure 2-285. Springsteen (X/8), circa 1870. This appears to be a later adaptation of the early Leavitt mechanism (figure 2-100).

Figure 2-286. Mechanism for the Springsteen machine of figure 2-285. Compare this with figure 2-102. Except for the conversion to a four-motion feed, the Springsteen has a mechanism quite similar to the earlier Greenman & True.

Figure 2-287. Squirrel, as drawn for a publicity article, 1857. This machine was probably never manufactured.

Figure 2-288. Squirrel patent model (see appendix C), 1859.

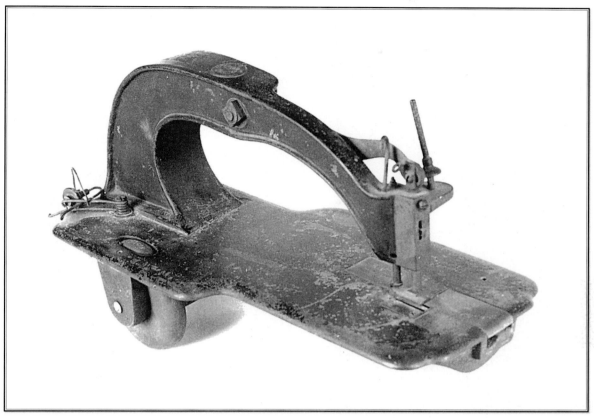

Figure 2-289. Stebbins (X/8), circa 1862. This is the earlier version of the head. The treadle stand is rather ordinary.

UNIVERSAL (figure 2-299): Both shuttle lockstitch and reciprocating-hook chain stitch machines were produced under this name during the mid-1870s. The model illustrated sews a shuttle lockstitch; the chain stitch model is identical in appearance to the GRANT BROTHERS sewing machine and was also sold under the name ERIE. No name appears on the machine illustrated here.

VICTOR (figure 2-300): The Victor is the descendant of the FINKLE & LYON and was designed for treadle use. About 75,000 – 100,000 shuttle lockstitch machines were made from 1872 to 1888 by the Victor Sewing Machine Company, whose headquarters and factory were in Middletown, Connecticut.

WANNAMAKER (O/3): This machine was one of many later varieties that copied the WILLCOX & GIBBS mechanism almost exactly. It was manufactured by a Philadelphia company.

WARDWELL (figures 2-301 and 2-302). This very unusual machine could be oriented in any direction upon its treadle stand by rotating the head, which was mounted on a circular piece of wood separate from the rest of the table. As if this wasn't enough, the sewing machanism was very unusual (see figure 2-302). About 1,500 were made by this St. Louis–based company during the mid-1870s.

WASHINGTON (figure 2-303): Little is known about this machine, which sews a two-thread chain stitch. According to the illustrated advertisement, the Boston-based company produced machines throughout the 1860s. It is almost certain that fewer than 5,000 were manufactured.

WATSON (figures 2-304 through 2-307): The Watson machine frequently sports a brass plate stamped, "William C. Watson's patent Nov. 25, 1856." This is one of the most frequently found of the pre-1860 sewing machines; however, it is by no means common. It features an unusual and rather primitive mechanism for sewing a single-thread chain stitch. The base is similar to the hand-operated NETTLETON & RAYMOND and FETTER & JONES. Another machine (figure 2-306) appears to be a two-thread version of the Watson, but the manufacturer's name is not present on the machine. The Watson Company was based in Bristol, Connecticut.

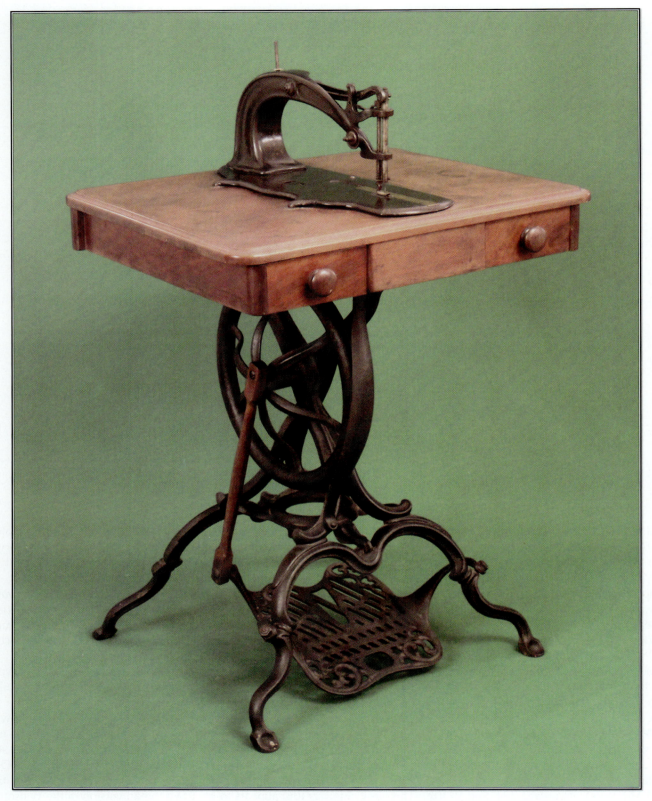

Figure 2-290. Stebbins (X/9), circa 1868. The later model was mounted upon an unusual stand.

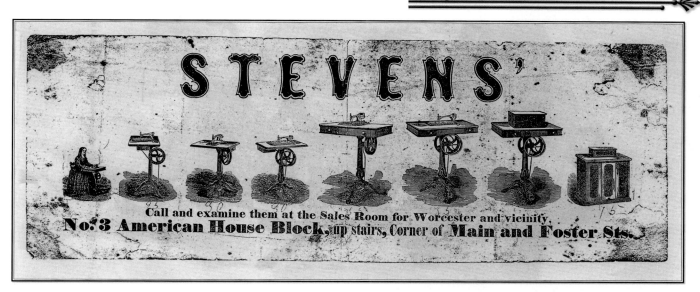

Figure 2-291. Stevens (U/8 or U/9) from an advertising pamphlet, circa 1865.

Figure 2-292. Strange & Huntley (U/9), circa 1860.

Figure 2-293. Taggart & Farr (X/8), circa 1858.

Figure 2-294. Mechanism for the Taggart and Farr.

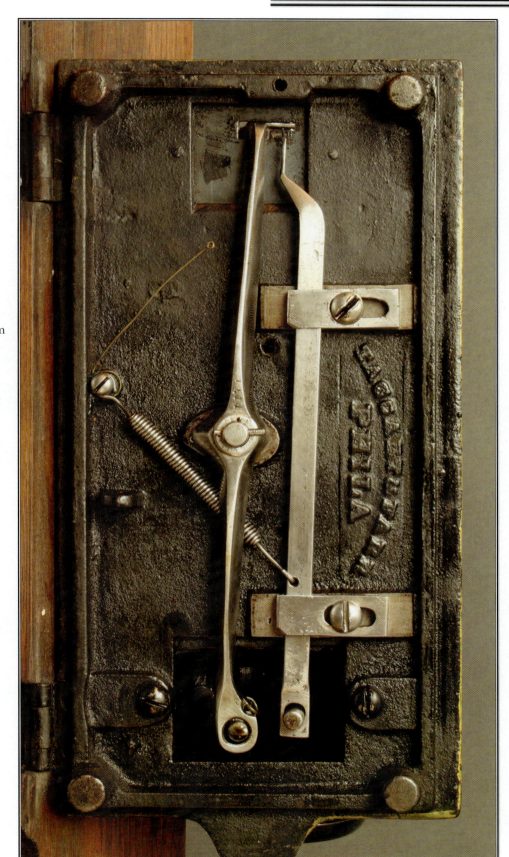

Figure 2-295. Thomson (X/9), circa 1860.

Sewing Machine Manufacturers from 1850 to 1880

Figure 2-296. Detail of the Thomson machine.

Figure 2-297. Mechanism for the Thomson machine, which sews a two-thread chain stitch. Note its rather extreme complexity (see for example figure 2-168). It is little wonder that the maker did not remain in business very long.

Figure 2-298. Triune (R/6), circa 1870.

Figure 2-299. Universal (O/5), circa 1875.

Figure 2-300. Victor (O/3), circa 1875.

Sewing Machine Manufacturers from 1850 to 1880

Figure 2-301. Wardwell (R/8), circa 1875. The head could be rotated on the circular table to allow sewing in any chosen direction.

Sewing Machine Manufacturers from 1850 to 1880

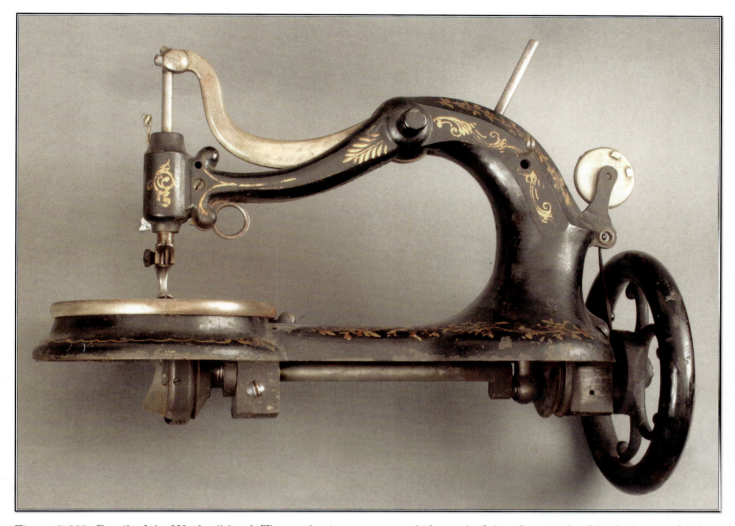

Figure 2-302. Detail of the Wardwell head. The mechanism was unusual. A spool of thread was utilized both above and below; hence no bobbin. The take-up lever, near the needle bar on most machines, was next to the flywheel (see the lever with the tiny hole in the end that shows through a hole directly above and to the left of the flywheel).

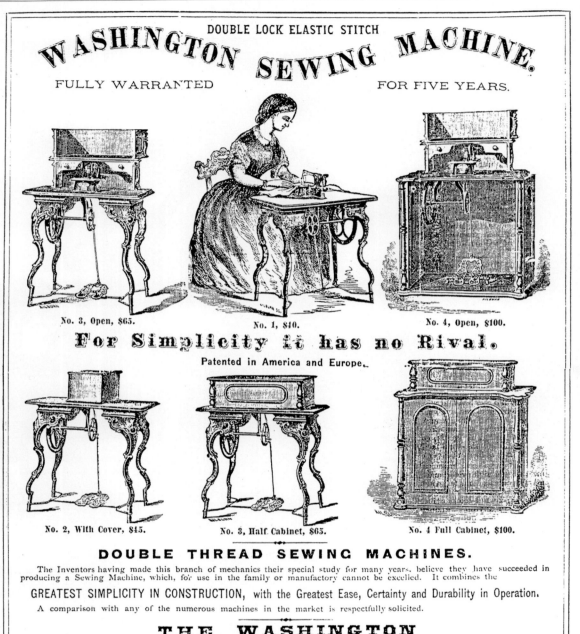

Figure 2-303. Washington (U/8), as illustrated in a promotional pamphlet, 1867.

Figure 2-304. Watson (O/7), circa 1860. Note the patriotic emblem, which is not typical.

Figure 2-305. More typically, the Watson sports a small brass emblem across the arm that says, "Wm C. Watson's Patent, Nov. 25th 1856."

Figure 2-306. Watson (R/7), circa 1860. Though the manufacturer remains inconclusive, this is a two-thread chain stitch version of the Watson machine of figures 2-304 and 2-305, which sew a single-thread chain stitch.

WEED: The earliest models were made before 1860 at a factory in Nashua, New Hampshire. In 1865, the company moved its operation to Hartford, Connecticut, and remained in business there until about 1900, becoming one of the most successful makers during the 1870s and 1880s. All models produced seem to have been designed for treadle use and sew the usual shuttle lockstitch. The models from the early 1860s and before (figures 2-308 and 2-309) are hard to find and command a premium price, whereas the machines that were made a decade or more later are rather common. The most typical model was known as the Family Favorite and was made during the 1870s. Even on a well-worn example, one can generally still find traces of the letters *F F* on the bed of the machine. Figure 2-310 shows a mid-1870 model; figure 2-311, a somewhat later version. The company also made larger machines designed for manufacturing use. The iron stands for most Weed models, as well as for the WHITNEY machine, are very similar. (Mr. Whitney was at one time associated with the Weed company). All told, the company had made around 300,000 machines by 1880, but the pre-1865 versions probably numbered fewer than 6,000.

WEST AND WILLSON (figures 2-312 through 2-315): The West & Willson Co. of Elyria, Ohio, manufactured a treadle machine that utilized a two-thread chain stitch. About 2,000 were made during the late 1850s and early 1860s.

WESTERN ELECTRIC (O/3): This later machine copied the mechanism of the WILLCOX & GIBBS exactly. Like other Willcox & Gibbs clones, it has a rather low value.

WHEELER & WILSON: Wheeler & Wilson was one of the most successful companies of the nineteenth century and was one of the original three members of the Sewing Machine Combination (the others were SINGER and GROVER & BAKER). Family machines produced by the company showed a gradual change in outward appearance as time progressed,

Sewing Machine Manufacturers from 1850 to 1880

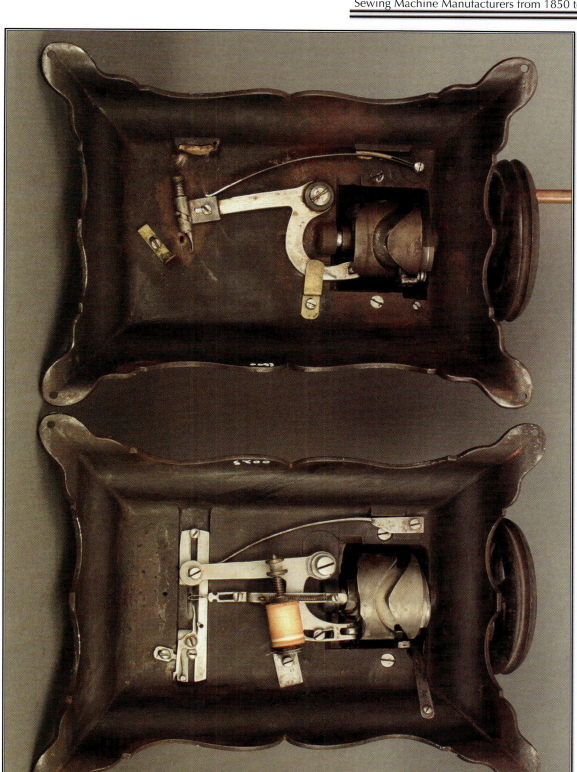

Figure 2-307. Mechanism for the Watson machines of figures 2-304 (top) and 2-306 (bottom). Both machines appear to have been made in the same factory. The top machine sews a single-thread chain stitch; the machine at the bottom, a two-thread chain stitch.

but they all used Wilson's stationary bobbin to form a lockstitch. The earliest model, shown in figure 2-316, was made from 1851 to 1856, with a production run of no more than 3,000 to 4,000. These machines are stamped "A. B. Wilson, Watertown, Connecticut." The machine shown in figure 2-317 was made in 1854. It is a large machine produced in very limited numbers, measuring over 14" in length, but otherwise similar to other Wheeler & Wilson heads and utilizing the same type bobbin. One cannot imagine why such a machine was produced, but the fact that it was made at all indicates that even at this early stage, the company was providing the public with different models to choose from.

Figures 2-319, 2-320, 2-323, and 2-324 show the most commonly found models made for home use. This machine was produced in huge quantities from 1856 through 1875 by the Wheeler & Wilson Mfg. Co., from a large factory in Bridgeport, Connecticut, although many of the machines sport a brass medallion embossed "44 Union Square, New York." Probably over a million of this popular machine were made, and it is consequently one of the most frequently found today. The deluxe example in figure 2-325 has mother-of-pearl inlay on the head (see figure 2-319), bird's-eye maple drawers, and a rosewood outer surface. This model does not turn up often, but plain walnut cabinet models do.

Around 1876, the Wheeler & Wilson Company introduced the popular No. 8. Sold usually as a treadle machine, a portable model was also produced (figure 2-326). It should be noted that the company continued limited production of the earlier model well into the 1890s (figure 2-327). Another

Figure 2-308. Weed (R/7), circa 1862. This early model was for manufacturing use. It is decorated with mother-of-pearl, a feature usually restricted to machines designed for home use.

model produced, with several variations, during the 1875 – 1885 period is the No. 6 (figure 2-328). The last model made for home use was the No. 9 (figure 2-329), which was manufactured well into the twentieth century. In 1905, the Wheeler & Wilson Company was bought by the SINGER company, which nevertheless continued to sell Wheeler & Wilson machines for a while.

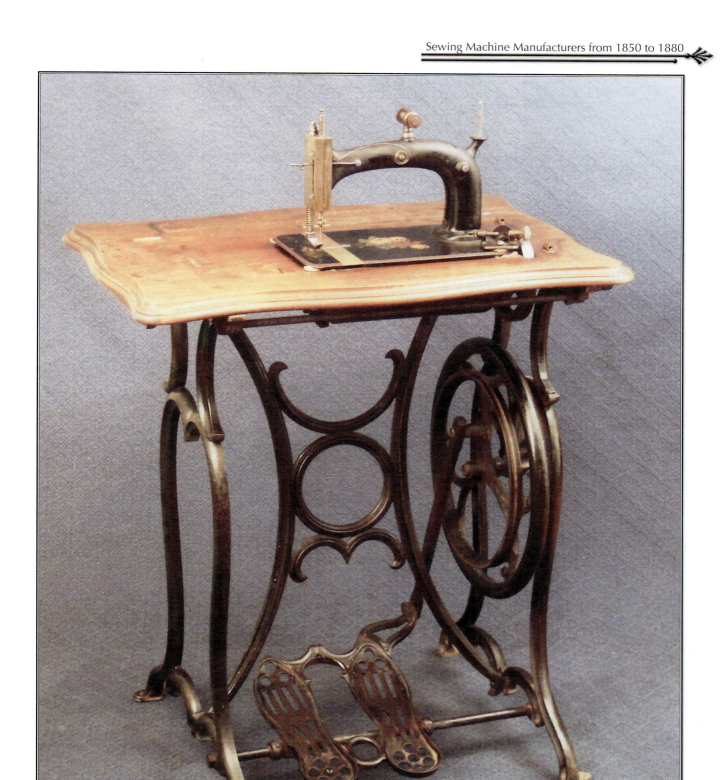

Figure 2-309. Weed (R/7), early model for home use, circa 1863.

Figure 2-310. Weed (F/3), Family Favorite model, circa 1873.

Figure 2-311. Weed (O/3), the later Family Favorite model, circa 1877. This model was exported to Europe.

Sewing Machine Manufacturers from 1850 to 1880

Figure 2-312. West & Willson (R/8), circa 1860.

Figure 2-313. Detail of the West & Willson head of figure 2-312. In England in 1861, George Whight received a patent for a machine that was based upon the (American) West & Willson. The resulting "Whight & Mann" machine, a rare entity in the United Kingdom, was copied from its American progenitor starting around 1861.

Sewing Machine Manufacturers from 1850 to 1880

Figure 2-314. West & Willson (R/8), circa 1860.

Sewing Machine Manufacturers from 1850 to 1880

Figure 2-315. Mechanism for the West & Willson machine.

Figure 2-316. Wheeler & Wilson (X/8), the earliest model, 1853.

Sewing Machine Manufacturers from 1850 to 1880

Figure 2-317. Wheeler & Wilson (X/8), early model for manufacturing use, 1854. This machine is over 14" long.

Figure 2-318. Wheeler & Wilson (U/4), 1856. The earlier cast embellishments (figures 2-316 and 2-317) have begun to settle down; they disappeared altogether in later versions.

Sewing Machine Manufacturers from 1850 to 1880

Figure 2-319. Wheeler & Wilson, wide head; fancy mother-of-pearl version, 1863 (O/4 with mother-of-pearl, F/2 without).

Figure 2-320. Wheeler & Wilson (A/1), the typical head, 1865 – 1875.

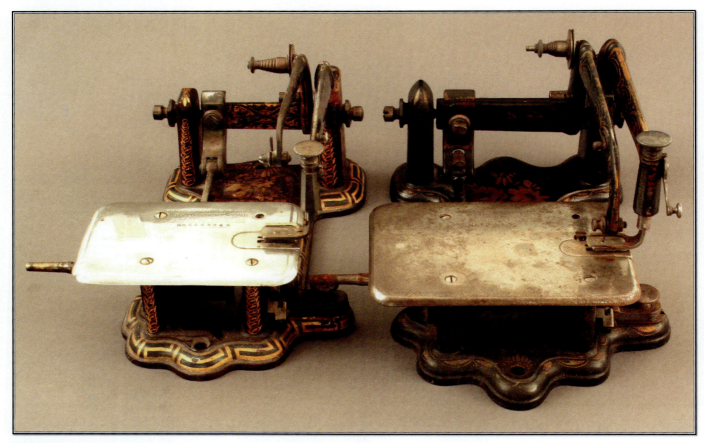

Figure 2-321. Wheeler & Wilson. A comparison of the typical machine (figure 2-320) and an unusual version that is about 15% smaller (see next figure).

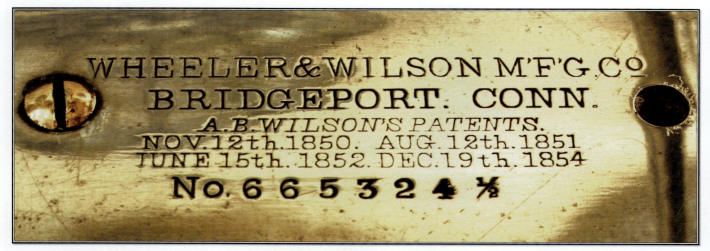

Figure 2-322. Note that the serial number of the machine at the left of figure 2-321 ends in "½"! It is unknown how many of these "half size" machines were made.

Figure 2-323. Wheeler & Wilson (A/2), a typical treadle model.

Figure 2-324. Wheeler & Wilson (A/2), a typical treadle model. The box cover is at the right.

Figure 2-325. Wheeler & Wilson (R/6). This deluxe cabinet model is rosewood and bird's-eye maple. Other, more ordinary cabinets (O/5) are made from walnut.

Figure 2-326. Wheeler & Wilson No. 8 (O/4), circa 1878. This is the portable version. The machine is more typically found on a treadle stand (F/3).

Figure 2-327. Wheeler & Wilson (O/2), circa 1890. The earlier models were produced well into the twentieth century.

Figure 2-328. Wheeler & Wilson (R/4), circa 1877. This is the No. 6 model.

Figure 2-329. Wheeler & Wilson (A/1), circa 1890. This is the very popular No. 9.

Sewing Machine Manufacturers from 1850 to 1880

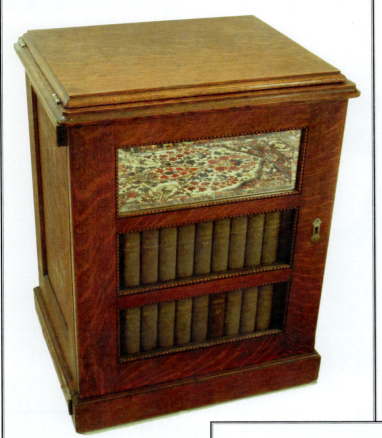

Figure 2-330. Wheeler & Wilson (R/6), circa 1890. This unusual cabinet contained faux books and a beveled glass mirror. The reflection in the mirror is of an Oriental rug that was on the floor.

Figure 2-331. The machine of figure 2-330, with the lid up.

WHITE: The White Sewing Machine Co. of Cleveland, Ohio, began production in 1876 and is still in business. The earliest model, shown in figure 2-332, was very modern looking for its time. About 100,000 of this particular type were made, and were it not so typical in appearance, it would probably command a higher price today. Later the company produced many models, including a chain stitch machine that was somewhat similar to the SINGER AUTOMATIC.

WHITNEY (figure 2-333): This machine rather resembles the WEED, which is not surprising, since Mr. Whitney was associated with the Weed company during its early days. Around 1872, Whitney formed his own company in Paterson, New Jersey, and began making lockstitch treadle machines whose iron stands were almost identical to those being made for Weed models. About 30,000 machines were manufactured over a period of about 10 years.

WILLCOX & GIBBS (figures 2-334 through 2-338): The Willcox & Gibbs is the bane of every sewing machine collector who asks antique dealers to search for machines. Early patent dates and a bizarre appearance lure the uninitiated with a false promise of rarity. Unfortunately for the collector, hundreds of thousands of these beautifully simple and quiet mechanisms were made, and thousands are still around. This machine exhibited very little change from 1857 until production ceased around 1940. The only major change in design was the thread holder and the tension. The earlier model, made until the mid-1870s, has a glass tension, and the thread holder is oriented in a typical vertical manner. Later machines all have the removable thread-holder placed at the odd angle shown, and a nickel-plated "automatic" tension. Many other companies made machines that employed this general type of tension, which simply held the thread fast during take-up until more was needed for the next stitch. The feature appears only on single-thread chain stitch machines; hence any machine that claims to be an "automatic" (e.g., F & W AUTOMATIC, KRUSE AUTOMATIC, SINGER AUTOMATIC, etc.) is referring to the tension device and uses Gibbs' patented revolving hook.

There are a great variety of forms for this machine: hand operated (figure 2-335), treadle stand, enclosed cabinet deluxe models, and, later, electric versions (figure 2-336). A fancy mother-of-pearl-inlaid Willcox & Gibbs machine in an enclosed cabinet would, of course, be much more valuable and desirable than more common varieties.

Every complete collection should have a Willcox & Gibbs or two, simply because of their historical significance. The rotating hook for forming a chain stitch was one of the most important sewing machine patents, ranking with the four-motion feed and other vital developments. The device was patented by J. E. A. Gibbs in 1857, and remains in use today on almost all single-thread chain stitch machines. It should be noted that although Willcox & Gibbs home or family machines utilize the revolving hook mechanism, the company also made specialized manufacturing machines that sewed other stitches. The New York–based Willcox & Gibbs Sewing Machine Co. remained in business until 1973, producing many industrial models.

WILLIAMS & ORVIS: This Boston-based company manufactured a rather small treadle-powered machine that had a great deal of gilt ornamentation, which, unfortunately, is frequently worn away. There are two models, both of which sew a two-thread chain stitch and are mounted on a treadle stand. No more than two or three thousand of the earlier model (figure 2-339) were made. The later model (figures 2-340 and 2-341) appears more often (though not in the form illustrated, a deluxe cabinet model); probably around 7,000 were produced. Sold during the early 1860s, the Williams & Orvis is unusual in that it is a friction-driven machine (see also FRANKLIN). The large flywheel mounted underneath, instead of being attached to the machine with a belt, presses against a rubber ring (figure 2-343) that is fastened directly to the outer circumference of the machine drive wheel, the shaft of which is stamped with the machine's serial number. Identification of this machine is sometimes hindered by the way the maker labeled it; the gilt lettering that should appear near the base of the arm has frequently been rubbed off through wear.

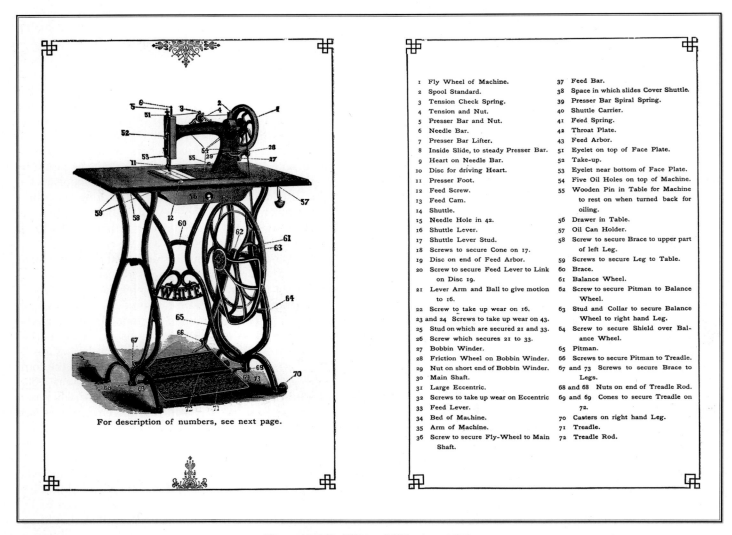

Figure 2-332. White (F/2), circa 1878.

Figure 2-333. Whitney (R/5), circa 1875.

Figure 2-334. Willcox & Gibbs (A/2), circa 1880. This is a typical treadle version.

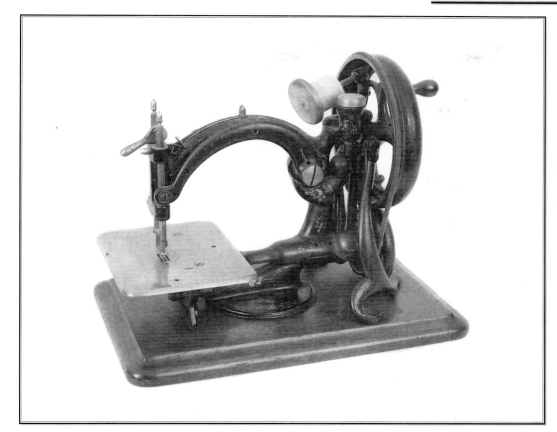

Figure 2-335. Willcox & Gibbs (O/3), circa 1880, a hand-operated model.

Figure 2-336. Willcox & Gibbs (A/1). Later (circa 1930), an electrified model was produced by mounting a machine on this iron base.

Sewing Machine Manufacturers from 1850 to 1880

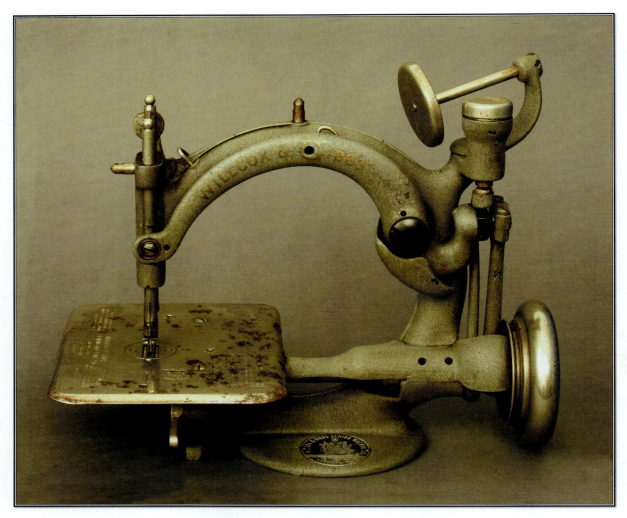

Figure 2-337. Willcox & Gibbs (R/4), an unusual greenish gray model.

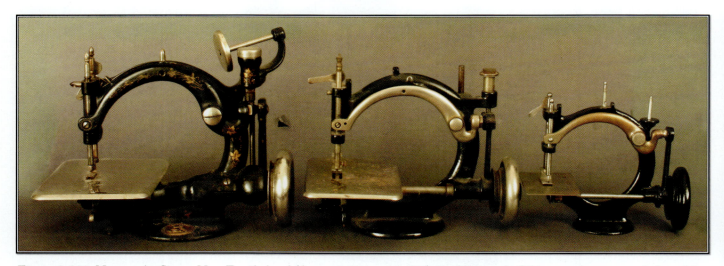

Figure 2-338. Next to the Singer New Family head (figures 2-274 and 2-275), the Willcox & Gibbs was the most copied machine of its time. Most copies were normal size, but the simplicity of mechanism rendered it useful for smaller machines (figure 2-350) and toys (figures 3-54, 3-55, 3-56). The machines illustrated here utilize the Willcox & Gibbs revolving hook (see figure 2-1).

Sewing Machine Manufacturers from 1850 to 1880

Figure 2-339. Williams & Orvis (R/8), circa 1860, the earlier model.

Figure 2-340. Williams & Orvis (X/9), circa 1862. This is the later model, in an elaborate cabinet. The head is decorated with mother-of-pearl. The most typical version (R/7) is on a stand identical to that in figure 2-339.

Figure 2-341. Williams & Orvis detail of the machine in figure 2-340.

Figure 2-342. Wilson (R/6), circa 1868. The needle bar is missing.

Sewing Machine Manufacturers from 1850 to 1880

Figure 2-343. The mechanism for both models of the Williams & Orvis was the same and is depicted here.

Figure 2-344. Wilson (F/3), circa 1875, the typical treadle model. This machine was discovered in a dump; hence the rather poor condition.

Figure 2-345. Wilson (F/2), head only.

WILSON, A. B.: See WHEELER & WILSON.

WILSON, W. G.: Initially based in Cleveland, this company produced an inexpensive PAW FOOT chain stitch model (figure 2-222) and the variety illustrated in figure 2-342, as well as the BUCKEYE sewing machine. Other similar models have been found with the W. G. Wilson name embossed on them instead of "Buckeye." Sometime during the 1870s, the company began to produce the shuttle lockstitch machine illustrated in figures 2-344 and 2-345, it frequently appearing in rather gaudy cabinets, such as the HORSE (figures 2-346 and 2-211). Although a few examples were made in Cleveland, most originated in Chicago, where the company moved around 1875. This company should not be confused with the Wheeler & Wilson Co. of Bridgeport, Connecticut.

WOODRUFF: At least two types of Woodruff machines were produced. The first is the AMERICAN EAGLE SEWING MACHINE (figure 2-347), which is one of the few FIGURAL machines made of cast iron. It is designed to be clamped onto a table, and it sews a shuttle lockstitch. The later version is the BIRD machine (figures 2-348 and 2-349). It shares the same mechanism as the earlier model and differs mainly in design. Both machines were made during the late 1850s.

XRAY (figure 2-350): Sometimes embossed "Larue Automatic," this machine resembles a somewhat scaled-down WILLCOX & GIBBS. Probably around 10,000 to 30,000 were made.

Figure 2-346. Wilson (X/10), circa 1877. This is the Horse machine with the cover removed (see Ormond, figure 2-211). The sliding plates that cover the shuttle are shown at the top — note the Masonic emblems.

Figure 2-347. Woodruff (X/10), circa 1858, the American Eagle model.

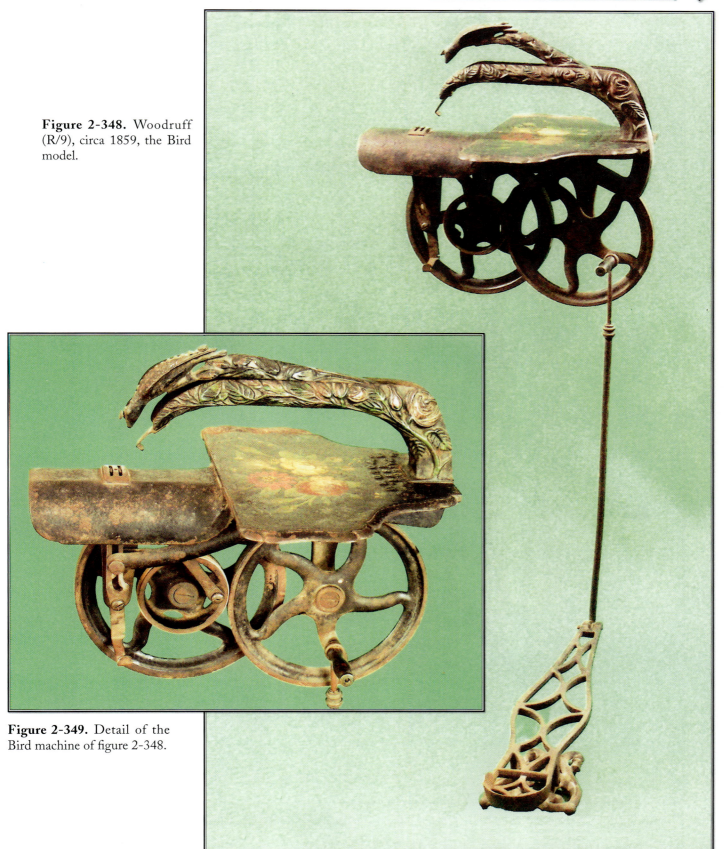

Figure 2-348. Woodruff (R/9), circa 1859, the Bird model.

Figure 2-349. Detail of the Bird machine of figure 2-348.

Figure 2-350. Xray (R/6), circa 1895. This machine is smaller than a Willcox & Gibbs, from which it was copied.

Early Toy Sewing Machines

During the growth years of the late nineteenth century, the sewing machine industry spawned several companion businesses that manufactured related items. There were companies that made attachments for sewing machines, motors for sewing machines (both electrical and mechanical), needles for sewing machines, etc. There were even music boxes (i.e. paper roll "organettes") that one could run by hooking up to the treadle belt, and fans that could be operated likewise.

It was only natural that manufacturers of full-size home sewing machines would turn their attention to the creation of machines for children. Perhaps this was done to bring up young ladies with the correct brand name solidly embossed on the impressionable mind. Certainly this was the Singer company's intention, for their child's machine emphasized the Singer name and even sported the same medallion trademark that appeared on its adult versions. Most of these little machines were well made; they were cast iron and utilized the WILLCOX & GIBBS revolving hook. Yet curiously, many manufacturers, when selling their little machines, frequently failed to place any brand identification (other than the model name itself; e.g., WEE, TRIUMPH) on the machine and occasionally even omitted the manufacturer from the instruction pamphlet. One possible explanation is that these machines were frequently sold not as toys, but as cheap machines that could be packed away for emergency repairs on vacations, or, as aptly put in the advertisements following:

"This is not merely a toy, or gotten up simply to sell. It is what every lady in the land should have, as many are not strong enough to run a foot power machine." (From an 1887 ad for the PANSY Sewing Machine.)

"The Sewing Machine for Summer Sewing. It is just the Machine to take to the seashore, country or mountains." (From the box of a SPENCER sewing machine, circa 1900.)

"For the grown up — it is a real, practical sewing machine in its simplest form and of a size easy to carry about and to pack. . . For the little girl — Any child above four years old can easily learn its use. . ." (From the back of The Singer Indian Puzzle, circa 1910, describing the attributes of the Singer model 20.)

Yet some manufacturers wanted to disclaim any possible dissatisfaction on the part of their customers by pointing out that, after all, these were only toys and one really could not expect them to sew either very well or very long. Note the interesting disclaimer on the box of the LITTLE HUSTLER:

"If this machine gets out of order, take it to the nearest Sewing Machine Repair Man where it can be adjusted at a reasonable price, thus saving yourself trouble and expense of returning it to manufacturers. This machine is not guaranteed, due to the fact that it is a toy and will be handled by inexperienced people."

Notwithstanding this confusion, it is helpful if today we classify these types of sewing machines as toys. The difficulty vanishes when we examine the later pressed-tin machines from the 1930 to 1950 period. These were clearly targeted toward little girls and, just as obviously, did not sew very well. The confusion persists, however, if we try to include early small machines; e.g., the tiny HOOK sewing machine was smaller than almost all toy sewing machine, but it is not a toy. Perhaps one way to clarify would be to point out that almost all machines that people nowadays call toys have all of the following characteristics. 1) They are little. 2) They sew a single-thread chain stitch and employ, for making the stitch, either a simple reciprocating hook or the WILLCOX & GIBBS revolving hook. 3) With few exceptions, they were made after 1880.

With this in mind, an attempt has been made to illustrate a selection of these machines covering the period from 1885 through 1950. After about 1920, cheap stamped metal (and ultimately plastic) machines began to replace the superior cast models of prior decades.

Several companies made more than one type of toy sewing machine. A brief description of these companies follows, along with a selection of typical models manufactured by each. In many cases, the model name given is but one of a host of nearly identical machines, some of which have been illustrated. In these cases, it is probable that all were made by the same company.

FOLEY & WILLIAMS (see also F & W AUTOMATIC): This company started making sewing machines around 1885 and continued through the mid-1920s. Like several other makers of toy sewing machines, its main business was large machines for both home and industry. Its most popular toy machines were made around 1900 to 1910 (Examples: PONY, MIDGET).

NATIONAL SEWING MACHINE COMPANY: This company was the successor to the ELDREDGE company and was formed in 1890. It produced large quantities of machines for home use under hundreds of different local names and remained in business throughout the first half of the twentieth century. Obviously, its toy business was a rather small portion of its total production. The toy models produced were typically from the period after 1910 (Example: STITCHWELL).

SMITH & EGGE COMPANY: This well-known New England company sold a variety of metal hardware products during the last quarter of the nineteenth century. The Bridgeport, Connecticut, factory produced locks, lock chains, and other related items. This company also manufactured toy sewing machines and produced a rather large selection of different names and models. As with other makers, many of these models were identical except for the name stamped on the machine. Most of the popular toy machines produced by

Smith & Egge were made around the turn of the century (Examples: LITTLE COMFORT, RELIABLE).

SINGER: All toy sewing machines made by the Singer Company displayed the Singer name and came in a variety of slightly different models. Toy manufacture was begun around 1900 and popular cast models were produced into the 1950s.

IMPORTANT NOTE: Since large numbers of German toy sewing machines were imported to America from 1900 on, and as many of these machines might be mistaken for American models, a few have been included.

Figure 3-1. Goodes (R/6). This sewing machine may have been the earliest popular American toy sewing machine, having been patented in 1872 by Ebenezer A. Goodes. The patent papers read, "I...have invented a new and useful Toy Sewing-Machine." See figure C-15.

Figure 3-2. Midget (F/4), showing the box, clamp, and screwdriver.

Figure 3-3. Midget (A/3). This style was made with many different names. A few are illustrated here.

Figure 3-4. Reliable (F/3).

Figure 3-5. Gem (F/3).

Figure 3-6. Liberty (O/4), on its box (F/3 machine alone).

Figure 3-7. Pony over Midget (R/5). Upon close inspection, one can see that the "Pony" text has been placed over a "Midget" machine. Apparently several of these were sold, as others have turned up. See figure 3-8.

Figure 3-8. A thin layer of paint was applied and the machine was renamed. See figures 3-7 and 3-3.

Figure 3-9. Stitchwell (A/2). A variant of this machine was sold on a treadle stand (see figure 3-57). This machine was marketed under several names, including Wood, Little Hustler, Busy Bee, Williamette, Little Lady, Wee, and others.

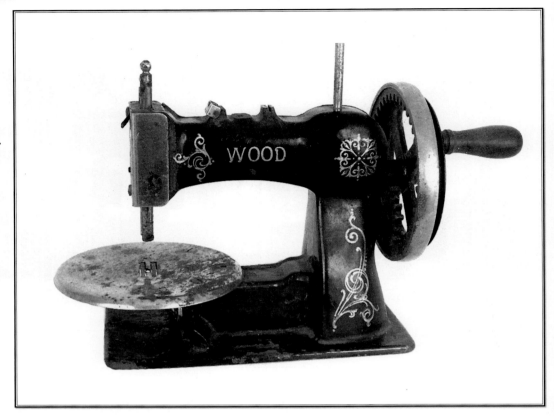

Figure 3-10. Wood (O/3).

Figure 3-11. Little Hustler (F/3).

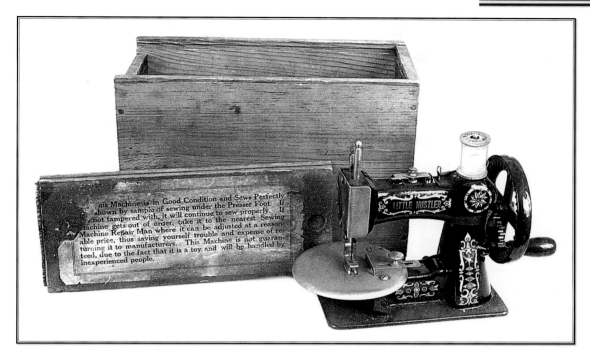

Figure 3-12. Little Hustler (F/4), showing the box and its caption.

Figure 3-13. Little Comfort (O/4), showing the tattered cardboard box (F/3 without box).

Figure 3-14. Little Comfort (F/3). Frequently this model appears with no name on the side and no chain drive. In these cases, it is usually sold merely as a Smith & Egge machine (A/3). There were many different names and slightly differing versions of this machine design.

Early Toy Sewing Machines

Figure 3-15. Perfection (O/3).

Figure 3-16. F. A. O. Schwarz (R/5). This machine is similar to the Little Comfort, except it is brass plated. It was produced for F. A.O. Schwarz, the famous toy retailer.

Figure 3-17. Pony (O/6). Though quite a few are around, this unusual form commands a premium.

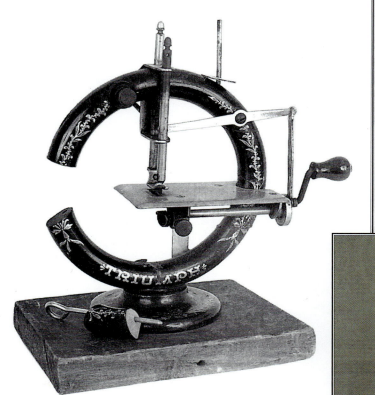

Figure 3-18. Triumph (O/6). Several different names are found on this style of machine, which was probably made by the Foley & Williams Company. The body is wood, and usually some paint or decoration is missing; hence, a higher value should be placed upon any example found in mint condition in its original cardboard box.

Figure 3-19. Yankee (R/6). This particular machine was shipped in a box marked "Triumph."

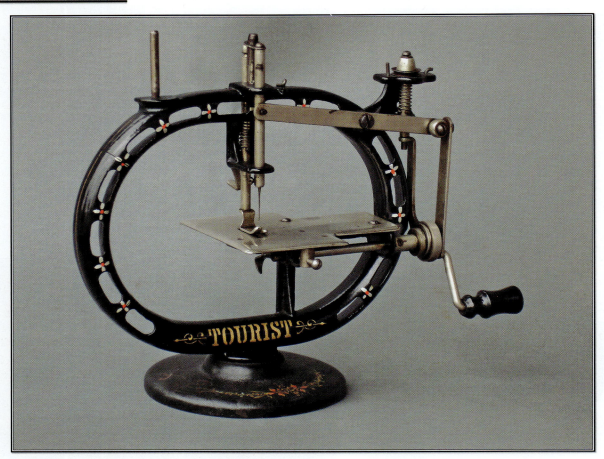

Figure 3-20. Tourist (R/7). This machine has a wooden base and an iron arm.

Figure 3-21. Singer (A/2). Known as the Model 20, this machine was first made around 1900 and continued to be produced with minor variations over the years until after 1940.

Figure 3-22. Singer with electric motor (O/2).

Early Toy Sewing Machines

Figure 3-23. Singer (A/1). This model was produced during the 1950s, in many colors. The most common examples are black and brown; the rarest are red and blue (O/4).

Figure 3-24. Mueller (F/2). This German machine was made in many sizes, ranging from 5" to 12". The company also made lighter toy sewing machines that were stamped rather than cast. Mueller machines date from the turn of the century to after 1930 and were exported to the United States for sale. The 12" model shown was sold in 1911.

Figure 3-25. Mueller (O/5). This elaborate-looking German machine is nickel plated.

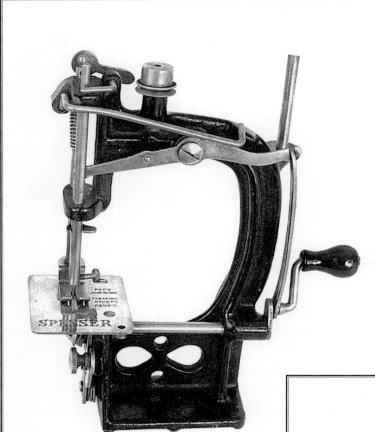

Figure 3-26. Spenser (O/3).

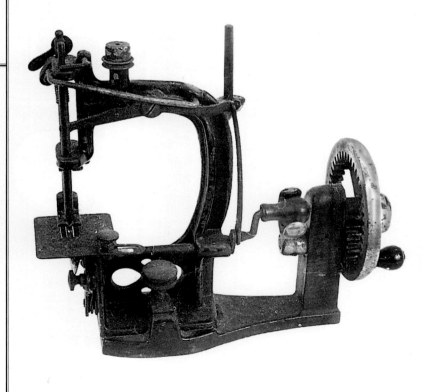

Figure 3-27. Spenser (O/4), mounted on a device that allows faster sewing. One turn of the outer handle causes two turns of the inner handle.

Figure 3-28. Spenser (O/4), showing the box. This model has to be disassembled in order to be placed in its box.

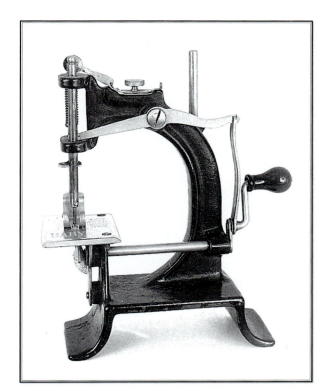

Figure 3-29. Baby (F/3). On the box is the slogan, "Everybody wants a Baby." This machine was advertised as a toy during the 1890s.

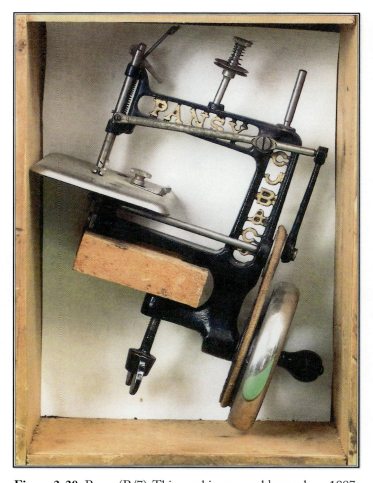

Figure 3-30. Pansy (R/7). This machine was sold as early as 1887.

Figure 3-31. Gem #1 (O/6). This machine and the one in figure 2-32 were made by the American sewing machine company (see p. 21), possibly as promotional items rather than toys — actual examples of the much overused term *salesman's sample*.

Figure 3-32. American Gem (O/6). Both this and the Gem #1 were occasionally equipped with a belt drive mechanism, which was supposed to increase the stitching efficiency of the machine.

Figure 3-33. Tabitha (O/5). The machine is stamped from bright brass. It was made by the Manhattan Brass Company and was sold in the United States and Great Britain.

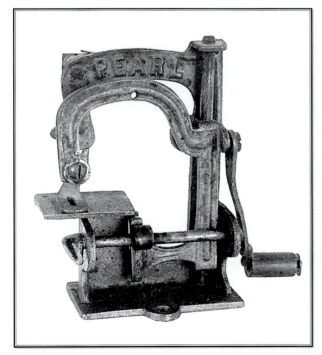

Figure 3-34. Pearl (O/5). This machine is very similar to the Tabitha, but it was cast rather than stamped. It, too, is brass, but the overall rough texture and darker appearance leads one to believe that it was produced earlier. Both machines were made before the turn of the century.

Figure 3-35. Soezy (O/6). Arguably a toy, this machine revives the Hancock mechanism. It was made around the turn of the century and sold as Soezy by Batchelor & Stenson, of New York City, and as Our New No. 10 by the Remedy Co. of New Haven, Connecticut, and probably under other names.

Early Toy Sewing Machines

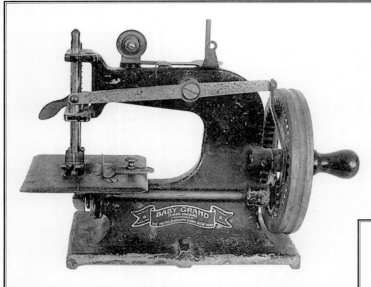

Figure 3-36. Baby Grand (O/3). This machine was made during the 1920s.

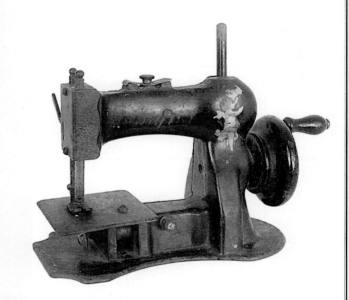

Figure 3-37. Cupid (O/3). This machine was made by the Cupid Manufacturing Co. and can be mounted on a treadle stand (see figure 3-60).

Figure 3-38. German (F/3), circa 1910. The German machines are included in this book because they turn up so frequently in the USA.

Early Toy Sewing Machines

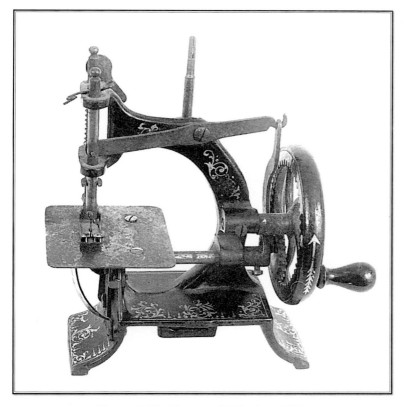

Figure 3-39. German (F/3), circa 1900.

Figure 3-40. German (O/5), circa 1890.

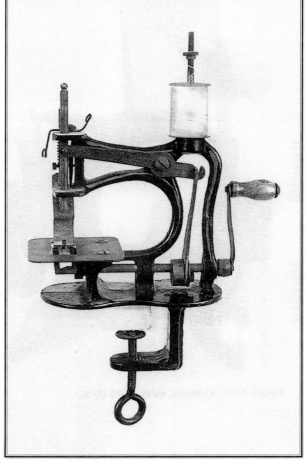

Figure 3-41. German (O/6), circa 1890. The rarity in America of German machines cannot be determined with accuracy, for the numbers imported are unknown, and many examples exist in Europe.

Figure 3-42. Mary (R/7, at least in America). This unusual machine is nickel and feeds the cloth with a walking presser foot, a device featured on the New England varieties of the 1860s.

Figure 3-43. Englewood Junior (O/6). This form was made during the 1920s under several different names.

Early Toy Sewing Machines

Figure 3-44. Linnea (O/5).

Figure 3-45. Yale (R/6). This machine differs somewhat from the machines illustrated in figures 3-43 and 3-44.

Early Toy Sewing Machines

Figure 3-46. Pixie (R/6). This is probably a British machine. It measures only 4" high and features a needle-feed mechanism.

Figure 3-47. This tiny German machine (O/5) is only 2" tall but really sews. It has been found in several different colors and probably dates from the 1930s.

Figure 3-48. German machine (F/1), typical of those manufactured after 1930, made from stamped rather than cast metal. Many different designs were placed on these machines.

Figure 3-49. There were several variations of this unusual German machine (F/2).

Early Toy Sewing Machines

Figure 3-50. Casige (A/1). This machine is stamped "Made in Germany."

Figure 3-51. Casige (A/1). A large variety of stamped metal machines was made from 1930 to 1950. Many are stamped "Made in Germany" or "Made in Germany, British Zone," indicating they were manufactured during the period immediately following World War II. Typically the value is rather low, but since these machines came in many shapes and colors, they make an interesting and colorful display. The model illustrated is a typical example.

Figure 3-52. American Girl (F/1 in the box). This machine was made during the second quarter of the twentieth century.

Early Toy Sewing Machines

Figure 3-53. Betsy Ross (A/1 both with and without box). This sturdy little machine actually sews rather well. It was produced in large numbers during the 1950s and was one of the last made before the present period of plastic.

Figure 3-54. Ideal (O/7). This machine was advertised in *Ladies Home Journal* during the mid-1890s. It seemed only natural that children should have their own treadle sewing machines, and this particular model was one of the more frequently sold types. Though fairly common, these machines are always in demand; hence, they command a relatively high price.

Figure 3-55. Princess (O/7).

Figure 3-56. Gem (R/6). This head is quite similar to the two previous ones. It was made by the J. R. Hebert Company of Brooklyn.

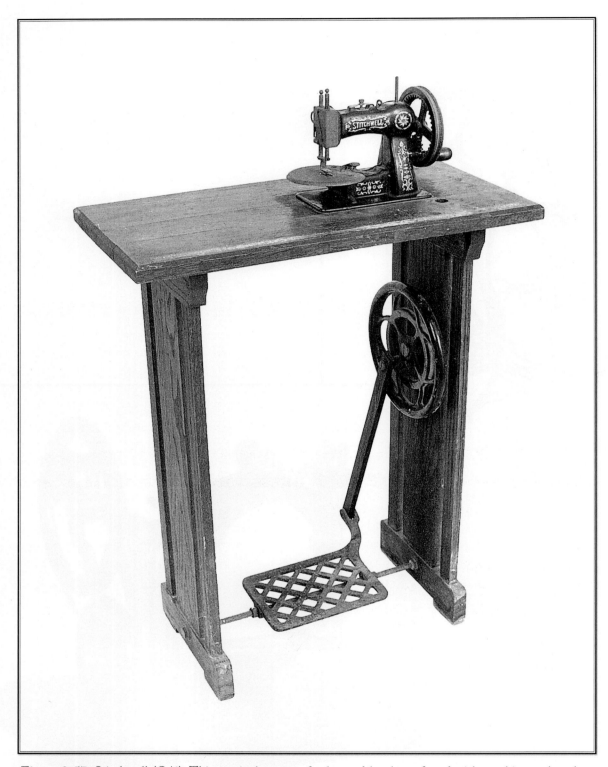

Figure 3-57. Stitchwell (O/6). This particular type of oak stand has been found with machines other than the Stitchwell. Note the difference between the treadle-mounted machine and the strictly hand-operated version in figure 3-9. The flywheel of the treadle model has a groove for the drive belt. Usually the table has two small drawers at either end.

Figure 3-58. Little Daisy (R/8). This is probably the most desirable of the mass-produced child treadle machines. It was made during the 1880s and reflects the Victorian Eastlike style, down to the knob on the drawer, which swings out as illustrated.

Early Toy Sewing Machines

Figure 3-59. Detail of the Little Daisy.

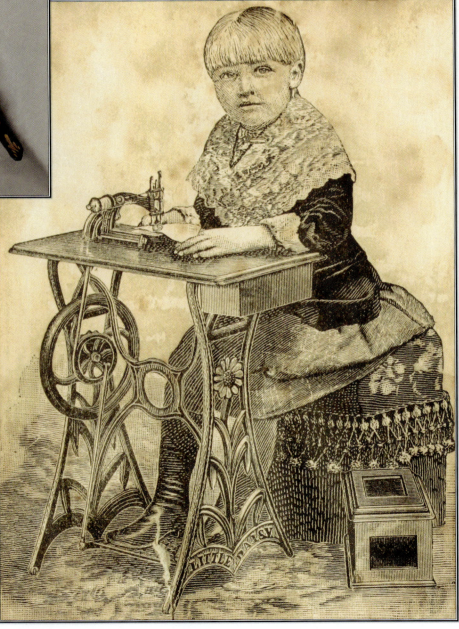

Figure 3-60. This flier was in the drawer of the Little Daisy machine in figure 3-58.

Figure 3-61. Little Tot (R/7). This machine, like the Little Daisy, is smaller than other treadle models for children.

Figure 3-62. Cupid (R/6).

The Restoration of Early Sewing Machines

Metal Restoration

The primary rule of all metal restoration is this: don't add to the damage that time has wrought by repainting any of the designs that once embellished a machine. Repainting designs is very difficult, even for a professional, and an imperfect job will lower the value of your machine. If the urge to paint is more than you can resist, vent your artistic frustrations on a rusted hulk that has been sandblasted clean and needs a completely new paint job.

If the machine is already in excellent condition, little needs to be done except to clean it gently with a non-reactive soap, such as Murphy's Oil Soap, and water. After cleaning, make sure all parts are completely dried, using only a soft cloth, as old paint chips easily. After covering all bare metal parts with a thin coat of lubricating oil, the machine is ready for display.

One phenomenon that occurs with machines that are in otherwise excellent condition is the flaking of brittle paint. If you touch a machine and tiny bits of paint appear on your fingers, you must treat the machine immediately, before significant chips of paint fall off. The problem can usually be remedied by applying, with a soft rag, a mixture of one part linseed oil and one part turpentine (hereafter referred to as linsentine), spreading as thin a coat as you possibly can and trying not to disturb the paint. This application should be made to non-moving parts only, as the linseed oil will gum up and impair the movements of gears and cams. The machine must then be allowed to dry thoroughly, without disturbance, for a week or more. The resulting layer of linseed oil does not yield an impervious finish, but simply acts as a binder and very effectively prevents any more paint from being lost. The turpentine performs the vital function of thinning the linseed oil, thus enabling it to penetrate the smallest of cracks in the paint.

A word of caution should be given: rags, when soaked in the mixture of linseed oil and turpentine, are subject to spontaneous combustion. Although the mixture is perfectly safe once applied to the machine, any rags used to apply it should be disposed of carefully, with plenty of ventilation and a dousing of water. To store any leftover linsentine, use a glass container, as the mixture can chemically react with certain metals and plastics.

If you have a machine or a stand whose surface is a combination of rust (red iron oxide) and paint, first lightly soak some very fine steel wool with linsentine and go over all non-moving parts of the machine gently, but with enough force to eliminate the rust. Interestingly, when the rust has been removed, the exposed layer is a different kind of iron oxide, which, when thinly coated with linsentine, turns almost as dark as the original black paint. After the red rust has been thoroughly cleaned off with linsentine, you should remove any residual traces with an old towel. For a permanent protective coating, you should go over the non-moving surfaces once more with steel wool dipped in linsentine, again wipe off any excess, and allow the machine to thoroughly dry (a week or more).

In the case of a machine that is completely covered with rust on all metal parts and appears to have no original paint, the results of a good cleaning can be quite surprising. Even the thickest layer of rust may be hiding substantial amounts of original paint, which will be uncovered by the linsentine/steel wool treatment. If the metal is completely and totally rusted, with no traces of paint remaining, you need to rub it vigorously with steel wool and turpentine or with a wire-brush attachment to an electric drill. After a thorough cleaning, the metal may be protected with a coat of black spray paint. As was already pointed out, do not attempt to embellish the head or stand with any decorative paint work, for you run the risk of doing more harm than good.

Occasionally, one finds machine stands that have been subjected to someone's redecorating frenzy and have been painted a brighter color than black — lime green and white are perennial favorites. If a machine is discovered in this condition, a solvent such as Kutzit can be used to remove the offending paint, and a protective coat of black paint should be applied.

It can be quite difficult to deal with a head that is completely rusted and frozen. If possible, take the machine apart. Loosen screws with WD-40 or some other loosening agent and disassemble the machine as much as possible, making careful note of where each part and each screw goes. Clean pieces individually with 400 – 600 grit emery paper that has been moistened. If you use emery paper that is coarser than 400, you will end up putting scratch marks in the metal. After all rust has been removed, go over the parts again with a very fine steel wool, and then put the machine back together. Do not try to remove every pit or every spot of black iron oxide — these flaws are reasonable for a venerable, somewhat mistreated machine to exhibit. After a little oiling, the machine should operate. Even the most rusted mess can turn into a respectable antique when the proper steps have been taken.

Another phenomenon should be mentioned. You will occasionally find a machine that appears to be in excellent condition, yet none of the parts will move. This occurs because the oil that was used during the nineteenth century was usually whale oil. After a hundred years of idleness, the oil thickens up like glue. This can be a very difficult problem to correct. You do not want to take the machine apart, because, in the manufacturing process, machines were usually painted after being assembled. If you attempt to disassemble the machine, you will disturb the paint that lies in a solid coat over screws and parts. The only remedy is the continual application of a loosening agent to all moving parts while you attempt to turn the flywheel (if one is present). Great patience is required, but eventually the parts will begin to move very slowly, with great resistance. If the machine is stubborn, as is usually the case, it is best to wait for the agent to soak in and to proceed with another application. It is difficult to give an exact waiting time, for it really depends upon the severity of each individual machine's condition. You should begin by renewing your efforts after a few minutes, then a few hours, days, and even weeks (one of the author's machines required a year's patience, with applications of WD-40 made every three weeks or so). Remember that no machine is hopeless; with much effort, time, and patience, the mechanism will move freely again. At this point, most of the old dried oil will have been liquefied through both friction and the application of your loosening agent. Now clean off any gummy residue and coat the bare metal with a lubricating oil such as Three-in-one.

You will find in the course of collecting that not all machines were decorated with the same materials. Some were painted black with colorful flowers embellishing the head and/or iron stand; some were, in addition, inlaid with mother-of-pearl, and some were silver plated. If the metal on the arm of a machine is unpainted, but shiny dark gray, it might be hiding a bright surprise. Rub a small spot briskly with your thumb — if the spot becomes shiny and your thumb dark, there is most likely a complete layer of silver beneath.

Frequently, you will find a machine that contains tarnished brass parts. The temptation to polish these parts should be resisted, unless they are discolored with green copper oxide. In this case, try rubbing the affected area with a fine cloth that has been dabbed in turpentine. The purpose here is not to polish the brass, but to remove the oxidation and any dirt that may be present. If the brass on a machine is decorative as opposed to functional, and if it has been polished before, it can be polished again by any of the usual methods.

Wood Restoration

If you have experience refinishing wood, feel free to try your own favorite technique. If not, the following method works very well for sewing machines, particularly because there is relatively little surface area to a sewing machine table; thus, more attention can be given.

When the original varnish is still intact, the wood can be simply cleaned off with a mild soap, such as Murphy's Oil Soap. Sanding is required only if the finish has worn off and the wood has turned dark or gray. When the wood part of the stand has, unfortunately, been painted (almost never done during the manufacturing process), the paint can be removed by a solvent such as Kutzit.

If bare wood has been exposed to the elements, the surface will typically have a grayish tone (the usual color for weathered walnut), and the following steps should be taken. Remove the machine head and any other projections that might be attached to the table, and sand with 120 grit sandpaper until the natural, lighter color of the wood shows through. Under no circumstances should you use a belt sander! After your first level of sanding has been completed, advance to a finer 220 grit sandpaper and sand again until the wood surface is satin smooth. A final rubbing with some fine steel wool usually helps also. Once the wood surface has been prepared, apply some fresh white shellac. In years past, shellac has been used as a finish in its own right. However, here we use shellac as an initial sealer so that the final coat of oil will not seep into the wood and alter the natural sheen of the grain. The fresh shellac should thus be rubbed very briskly into the wood with a lint-free cloth. Make sure that you rub the shellac into the wood, and do not leave a layer on the surface. After you have completely sealed the wood in this manner, let the shellac dry about 15 to 30 minutes in a moisture-free environment at room temperature.

The next step is a thorough rubdown with extra-fine steel wool. When the surface is once again smooth, tung oil should be applied (Formby's semi-gloss gives a nice finish). Pour a large dollop or two on the wood and rub briskly with the bare palm of your hand over the entire surface of the table. After a few moments, the oil will begin to thicken (which will be evident when the oil becomes sticky and your hand no longer glides over the surface). Keep rubbing for a few minutes; the heat your hand generates will aid in the drying process. When you can barely slide your hand at all, stop rubbing and allow the surface to dry for 24 hours. The same process can be applied to all drawers and box covers. One or two coats are sufficient to create a beautiful, lustrous surface, but a more protective finish can be achieved with subsequent applications. (Some restorers have been known to apply as many as ten!)

Veneer Replacement

Although most pre-1880 treadle machines utilize stands whose tables are solid walnut, one occasionally finds wood that was veneered, and the veneer is sometimes damaged or partly missing. It is relatively easy to match old walnut veneer by sacrificing a veneered table from a common machine such as an 1880 Willcox & Gibbs. In the case of early Grover and Baker portable machines, which were veneered with rosewood, you can use veneer from the inside of the little door at the right of the machine.

To remove veneer, place a towel that has been moistened with a mixture of 20 parts water to 1 part white vinegar directly in contact with the area to be removed, and cover with some foil or plastic. After a couple of days, and with the help of a putty knife, the veneer should peel up. Actual repair is best left to an expert; however, one can be sure of a better job if the person doing the repair is supplied with veneer that matches closely the existing surface.

Replacing and Repairing Parts

If the treadle stand of a machine is broken, it is usually snapped cleanly in one or two places. If this is the case, go to a good welding shop to have it brazed. Make sure you tell the welder that it is extremely important that the edges are lined up precisely, and that all brazing is to be done only on the side that is least noticeable. You might suggest that he grind a small notch partway into the break right where the join is to be made, so that the final result will be stronger, yet not as noticeable as it would be if he merely placed a bead of brass over the crack. Later, you can paint over any area where the paint has been damaged by the heat of the process.

We have more of a problem if a machine head is missing a part. Of course, it is certainly permissible to substitute a part from an identical model. Unfortunately, the rarest machines, which one is naturally the most interested in restoring, don't come in sufficient numbers to warrant the sacrifice of one machine for another (if you can find two at all). The fastidious restorer thus frequently finds himself making substitute parts. For this undertaking, the Dreml tool is a good ally. Its variety of tiny grinders and sanders are excellent for shaping small pieces of metal. To ensure as much authenticity as possible, the metal should be taken from another antique sewing machine. Ideally, your workshop should include a common nineteenth century machine as a source for old metal — the Singer New Family, because of its many small parts and screws, is a good model to sacrifice.

If a projection of the machine is broken off (for example, a part of the arm), or if the broken part is decorated and the decoration is to be preserved, one cannot resort to the welding torch. The only remedy is to find a machinist who can pin the two parts back together. A hole or two must be drilled in both pieces, and a small, tight-fitting metal dowel is used as a joiner. Unfortunately, there is no glue that makes a good metal repair.

Of course, the object of all restoration is to make a machine look as presentable as possible. If you feel that you cannot repair a machine with a broken or missing part, by all means leave it in its present state. It is better not to make a repair at all than to make a poor one.

Bibliography

Barker, C. B. & Co. *Price List of Genuine Sewing Machine Parts*. New York, NY: 1882.

Bays, Carter. "Collecting Early American Sewing Machines," a series of eight articles appearing in *The Antique Trader Weekly*, March 1981 – 1982.

———. "Collecting Toy Sewing Machines." *The Antique Trader Weekly*, March 30, 1983.

———. "How to Estimate the Number of Machines Manufactured." Unpublished manuscript, 1982.

———. "Sewing Machine Patent Models." *The Antique Trader Weekly*, September 15, 1982.

———. "Toy Sewing Machines Came in Many Shapes." *Antique Week*, May 21, 1984.

Bolton, James. *His Recollections of His Forty Years' Experience with the Singer Manufacturing Company*. Unpublished manuscript.

Bosworth, Charles F. "A Narrative of the Life of Charles Frederick Bosworth." Unpublished manuscript, 1905; copied by his son in 1941 and now kept at the Petersham (MA) County Historical Society.

Brandon, Ruth. *A Capitalist Romance: Singer and the Sewing Machine*. Philadelphia, PA: J. B. Lippincott Co., 1977.

Conservation-Analytical Laboratory. *To Clean Tarnish from and Polish Brass or Bronze*, leaflet 301. Washington, DC: the Smithsonian Institution, 1977.

Conservation-Analytical Laboratory. *Removal of Rust from Sword/Gun/Precious Surface*, leaflet 320. Washington, DC: the Smithsonian Institution.

Cook, Rosamond C. *Sewing Machines*. Peoria, Illinois: The Manual Arts Press, 1922.

Coons, Lorraine. *Women Home Workers in the Parisian Garment Industry, 1860 – 1915*. New York and London: Garland Publishing Inc., 1987.

Cooper, Grace Rogers. *The Sewing Machine: Its Invention and Development*. Washington, DC: the Smithsonian Press, 1976.

Cooper-Hewitt Museum. *American Enterprise: Nineteenth-Century Patent Models*. New York, NY: the Cooper-Hewitt Museum and the Smithsonian Institution, 1984.

Crumbaker, Leslie G. *The Baker Estate; or, Ridge Hill Farms of Needham, Mass*. Needham, MA: Needham Historical Society, 1975.

Davies, Robert Bruce. *Peacefully Working to Conquer the World*. New York, NY: Arno Press, 1976.

Depew, Chauncey M. *One Hundred Years of American Commerce*. New York, NY: D. O. Haynes & Co., 1895.

Farnum, Bret. "What Happened to Those Old Patent Models? Ask the Man Who Owns 30,000!" *Collectors News*, May 1981.

Forsdyke, Graham and Maggie Snell, *ISMACS News*, issues 15 – 37. 1988 – 2000.

Gilbert, K. R. *Sewing Machines*. London: Her Majesty's Stationery Office, 1970.

Henson, William. "Restoration of Modern Machinery." *Museum News*, June 1971.

Jones, Edgar R. *Those Were the Good Old Days*. NY: Simon & Shuster, 1959.

Journal of Domestic Appliances and Sewing Machine Gazette, 6, 1878.

Knight, E.H. *Knight's American Mechanical Dictionary*. Boston, MA: Houghton, Mifflin and Co., 1882.

Lewton, Frederick L. "The Servant in the House." *Annual Report of the Smithsonian Institution*, publication 3056. Washington, DC: the Smithsonian Institution, 1929.

Long, Clarence D. *Wages and Earnings in the United States 1860 – 1870*. Princeton, NJ: Princeton University Press, 1960.

New York Daily Tribune, May 22, 1863.

Organ, R. M. *Cleaning of Wooden and Metallic Parts of a Sewing Machine*, Conservation-Analytical Laboratory leaflet, Washington, DC: the Smithsonian Institution.

Parton, James. "History of the Sewing Machine." *Atlantic Monthly*, May 1867.

Perlongo, Bob. *Early American Advertising*. New York, NY: Art Direction Book Co., 1985.

Peterson, Cliff. A series of eight catalogs offering patent models for sale. Santa Monica, CA: 1980 – 1982.

Peterson, Harold L. *Conservation of Metals*, technical leaflet 10. Nashville, TN: the American Association for State and Local History, 1968.

Presbrey, Frank. *The History and Development of Advertising*. Garden City, New York, NY: Doubleday, Doran & Co., 1929.

Public Auction Sale, 1000 Authentic U.S. Patent Models, a series of 10 auction catalogs. Garrison, New York, NY: O. Rundle Gilbert, 1973 – 1978.

Bibliography

Scientific American, several issues, 1846 – 1868.
Scott, John. *Genius Rewarded; or, the History of the Sewing Machine*. New York, NY: the Singer Manufacturing Co., 1880.
Sewing Machine Advance. "Allen B. Wilson." September 15, 1879.
Sewing Machine Advance, several issues, 1878 – 1882.
Sewing Machine News, several issues, 1879 – 1885.
Stebbins, L. *Eighty Years Progress*. Hartford, CT: L. Stebbins, 1869.

Toschi, Claire. *Toy Stitchers*, issues 1 –18, Millbrae, CA: C. Toschi, 1990 – 1992.
Thomas, Glenda. *Toy and Miniature Sewing Machines, Book II*. Paducah, KY: Collector Books, 1997.
Urquhart, J. W. *Sewing Machinery*. London: Crosby Lockwood and Co., 1881.
Vincent, Margaret. *The Ladies' Word Table*. Allentown, PA: the University Press of New England, 1988.
Wisconsin State Historical Society, *Singer Manufacturing Company Records*, box 168, folder 1.

In addition to the preceding materials, the author also used instruction books or pamphlets for the following sewing machines — Aetna, American, American Hand, Common Sense, Davis, Domestic, Elliptic, Fairy, Family, Family Gem, Folsom, Gold Medal, Grover and Baker, Home, Howe, Lathrop, Little Giant, Madame Demorest, Remington, Singer, Victor, Wardwell, Washington, Weed, Wheeler and Wilson, White, Willcox & Gibbs, Williams & Orvis — as well as advertisements from several sources for the Atwater, Bartlett, Beckwith, Blees, Bosworth, Boudoir, Common Sense, Daisy, Davis, Diamond, Domestic, Dorcas, Elastic Motion, Eldredge, Elliptic, Empire, Erie, Fairy, Family, Finkle & Lyon, Florence, Franklin, Globe, Gold Medal, Goodrich, Grover and Baker, Heberling, Home, Household, Howe, Hunt, Kruse, Ladd & Webster, Leavitt, Little Monitor, Madame Demorest, National, Novelty, Pocket, Remington, Secor, Singer, Universal, Victor, Weed, Wheeler and Wilson, White, Williams & Orvis, and Wilson sewing machines.

Appendix A

Some Data from One Hundred Years of American Commerce

Below is data directly from an 1895 article about the sewing machine industry by Frederick G. Bourne, who was president of the Singer company. This article appears in volume two of Depew's *One Hundred Years of American Commerce*.

A PARTIAL STATEMENT FROM RECORDS OF "THE SEWING-MACHINE COMBINATION," SHOWING NUMBER OF SEWING-MACHINES LICENSED ANNUALLY UNDER THE *ELIAS HOWE* PATENT.

Name of Manufacturer.	1853.	1854.	1855.	1856.	1857.	1858.	1859.	1860.	1861.	1862.	1863.	1864.	1865.	1866.
Wheeler & Wilson Mfg. Co...	799	756	1,171	2,210	4,591	7,978	21,306	25,102	18,556	28,202	29,778	40,062	39,157	50,132
I. M. Singer & Co...........	810	879	883	2,564	3,630	3,594	10,953	13,000 (a)	16,000 (a)	18,396	......	......	......	......
The Singer Manufacturing Co.	...	...	...	...	...	...	...	...	...	...	20,030	23,632	26,340	30,960
Grover & Baker S. M. Co..	657	2,034	1,144	1,952	3,680	5,070	10,280	(b)	(b)	(b)	(b)	(b)	(b)	(b)
A. B. Howe " " ..	...	60	53	47	133	179	921	(b)	(b)	(b)	(b)	(b)	(b)	(b)
Leavitt " " ..	28	217	152	235	195	75	213	(b)	(b)	(b)	(b)	(b)	(b)	(b)
Ladd & Webster " " ..	100	268	73	180	453	490	1,788	(b)	(b)	(b)	(b)	(b)	(b)	(b)
Bartholf " " ..	135	55	31	35	31	203	747	(b)	(b)	(b)	(b)	(b)	(b)	(b)

A PARTIAL STATEMENT SHOWING NUMBER OF SEWING-MACHINES LICENSED ANNUALLY FROM 1867 TO 1876 INCLUSIVE.

Name of Manufacturer.	1867.	1868.	1869.	1870.	1871.	1872.	1873.	1874.	1875.	1876.
The Singer Manufacturing Company...	43,053	59,629	86,781	127,833	181,260	219,758	232,444	241,679	249,852	262,316
Wheeler & Wilson Mfg. Company......	38,055	(b)	78,866	83,208	128,526	174,088	119,190	92,827	103,740	108,997
Grover & Baker Sewing-Machine Co...	32,999	35,000 (a)	35,188	57,402	50,838	52,010	36,179	20,000 (a)	15,000 (a)	....
Weed Sewing-Machine Co.............	3,638	12,000	19,687	35,002	39,655	42,444	21,769	20,495	21,993	14,425
Howe Sewing-Machine Co.............	11,053	35,000 (a)	45,000 (a)	75,156	134,010	145,000 (a)	90,000 (a)	35,000 (a)	25,000 (a)	109,294
A. B. Howe " "	......	......	......	......	20,051	......	......	......	......	......
B. P. Howe " "	......	......	......	......	......	14,907	13,919	......	......	......
Willcox & Gibbs Sewing-Machine Co...	14,152	15,000	17,201	28,890	30,127	33,639	15,881	13,710	14,522	12,758
Wilson (W. G.) " "	......	......	......	......	21,153	22,666	21,247	17,525	9,508	......
American B. H. & S. M. Co...........	......	......	7,792	14,573	20,121	18,930	14,182	13,529	14,406	17,937
Florence S. M. Co...................	10,534	12,000	13,661	17,660	15,947	15,793	8,960	5,517	4,892	2,978
Shaw & Clark Sewing-Machine Co.....	2,692	3,000	......	......	......	......	......	......	......	......
Gold Medal " " "	......	......	......	8,912	13,562	18,897	16,431	15,214	14,262	7,185
Davis " " "	......	......	......	......	11,568	11,376	8,861	......	......	......
Domestic " " "	......	......	......	......	10,397	49,554	40,114	22,700	21,452	23,587
Finkle & Lyon Mfg. Co. and Victor....	2,488	2,000	1,339	2,420	7,639	11,901	7,446	6,292	6,103	5,750
Ætna Sewing-Machine Co............	2,958	3,500	4,548	5,806	4,720	4,262	3,081	1,866	1,447	707
Blees " " "	......	......	......	......	4,557	6,053	3,458	......	......	......
Elliptic " " "	3,185	......	......	......	4,555	......	......	......	......	......
Empire " " "	2,121	5,000	8,700	......	......	......	......	......	......	......
Remington Sewing-Machine Co.......	......	......	......	3,560	2,965	4,982	9,183	17,608	25,110	12,716
Parham " " "	......	......	1,141	1,766	2,056	......	......	......	......	......
Bartram & Fanton Mfg. Co...........	2,958	......	......	......	1,004	1,000	1,000	250	......	......
Bartlett Sewing-Machine Co..........	......	......	......	......	614	1,000	......	......	......	......
J. G. Folsom......................	......	......	......	......	280	......	......	......	......	......
McKay Sewing-Machine Asso........	......	......	......	129	218	......	......	128	161	102
C. F. Thompson....................	......	......	......	......	147	......	......	......	......	......
Union Buttonhole Machine Co.......	......	......	......	......	124	......	......	......	......	......
Leavitt Sewing-Machine Co..........	1,051	1,000	771	......	......	......	......	......	......	......
Goodspeed & Wyman S. M. Co......	2,126	......	......	......	......	......	......	......	......	......
Keystone Sewing-Machine Co........	......	......	......	......	......	2,665	217	37	......	......
Secor " " "	......	......	......	......	......	311	3,430	4,541	1,307	......
Centennial " " "	......	......	......	......	......	......	514	......	......	......

(*a*) Number estimated. (*b*) No data.

Figure A-1. From *One Hundred Years of American Commerce*.

DESCRIPTIVE LIST OF EARLY U. S. PATENTS ON SEWING-MACHINES FROM 1842 TO 1855.

Serial Number.	Date.	Name.	Invention.
			1842.
2,466	Feb. 21	J. J. Greenough	Using short thread. Needle with eye in center, pointed at both ends, pulled through the material with pincers, and making shoemaker's stitch.
			1843.
2,982	March 4	B. W. Bean	Short thread, running stitch, ordinary hand-needle, cloth crimped into ridges for passage over the needle.
3,389		G. H. Corliss	"Sewing Engine." Short thread. Similar to Greenough's.
			1844.
3,672	July 22	J. Rodgers	Running stitch. Similar to Bean's.
			1846.
4,750	Sept. 10	Elias Howe, Jr.	*Eye-pointed needle in combination with shuttle for under thread, continuous thread from spools, lock-stitch, automatic feed the length of baster-plate.*
			1848.
5,942	Nov. 28	J. A. Bradshaw	Lock-stitch, reciprocating shuttle.
			1849.
6,099	Feb. 6	C. Morey & J. B. Johnson	Chain-stitch, *barbed needle.*
6,437	May 8	J. S. Conant	Chain-stitch.
6,439	May 8	J. Bachelder	*Two or more threads, chain-stitch, continuous feeding device, horizontal table, and overhanging arm.*
6,766	Oct. 2	S. C. Blodgett & J. A. Lerow	Lock-stitch, shuttle rotating in a lateral annular race. Continuous feed by endless rotating baster-plate.
			1850.
7,296	April 16	D. M. Smith	Running stitch, short thread.
7,369	May 14	O. L. Reynolds	Chain-stitch.
7,622	Sept. 3	B. Thimonnier, Sr.	Chain-stitch.
7,659	Sept. 24	J. Bachelder	Chain-stitch.
7,776	Nov. 12	A. B. Wilson	*Lock-stitch, vibratory shuttle pointed at both ends, reciprocating feed-bar.*
7,824	Dec. 10	F. R. Robinson	Short thread.
			1851.
7,931	Feb. 11	W. O. Grover & W. E. Baker	*Chain-stitch, two or more threads.*
8,282	Aug. 5	W. H. Akins & J. D. Felthousen	Lock-stitch.
8,294	Aug. 12	I. M. Singer	Lock-stitch, *feed-wheel, thread controller.*
8,296	Aug. 12	A. B. Wilson	Lock-stitch, *rotary hook, for carrying upper thread around bobbin containing under thread.*
			1852.
8,876	April 13	I. M. Singer	Lock-stitch, thread controller, and tension device.
9,041	June 15	A. B. Wilson	Lock-stitch, rotary hook. *Four-motion feeding bar.*
9,053	June 22	W. O. Grover & W. E. Baker	Chain-stitch, two threads.
9,139	July 20	C. Miller	Back-stitch, vibratory shuttle.
9,338	Oct. 19	O. Avery	Chain-stitch, two needles, two threads.
9,365	Nov. 2	C. Hodgkins	Chain-stitch, two needles, two threads.
9,380	Nov. 2	J. G. Bradeen	Short thread, running stitch.

Figure A-2. From *One Hundred Years of American Commerce.*

1853.

9,556	Jan. 25	F. Palmer	Feeding device.
9,592	Feb. 22	W. H. Johnson	Chain-stitch, two needles, two threads.
9,641	March 29	T. C. Thompson	Lock-stitch, magnetic shuttle and race for keeping shuttle in contact with race.
9,665	April 12	W. H. Johnson	Cloth holder and feeding device.
9,679	April 19	W. Wickersham	Sewing leather, barbed needle, two threads.
10,344	Dec. 20	H. L. Sweet	*Binder*, for binding hats, etc.
10,354	Dec. 20	S. C. Blodgett	Chain-stitch, two needles, two threads.

1854.

10,386	Jan. 3	S. C. Blodgett	*Hemmer*, for sewing umbrellas.
10,597	March 7	W. H. Johnson	Chain-stitch, one thread, *needle feed*.
10,609	March 7	C. Miller	*Buttonhole*, two threads.
10,615	March 7	W. Wickersham	Sewing leather, chain-stitch, *two needles, two parallel rows of stitching*.
10,622	March 7	C. Hodgkins	Chain-stitch, two threads.
10,728	April 4	W. H. Akins	*Cop for shuttle*.
10,757	April 11	S. J. Parker	Lock-stitch, *transverse reciprocating shuttle*.
10,763	April 11	J. Harrison, Jr.	Lock-stitch, reciprocating shuttle. Upper and under thread controller.
10,842	May 2	I. M. Singer	Chain-stitch, two threads; *embroidery attachment carrying third thread*.
10,875	May 9	S. Coon	Lock-stitch; reciprocating shuttle, thread controller.
10,878	May 9	H. Crosby, Jr.	Lock-stitch; revolving hook, thread controller.
10,879	May 9	C. Hodgkins	Feed-wheel movement.
10,880	May 9	O. Avery	Chain-stitch, two needles, and two threads.
10,974	May 30	I. M. Singer	Chain-stitch, one thread; latch underneedle, *lifting presser foot*.
10,975	May 31	I. M. Singer	Lock-stitch, shuttle-thread controller and tension.
10,994	May 31	M. W. Stevens & E. G. Kinsley	Lock-stitch, *reciprocating shuttle in cylinder bed, with feed-wheel*.
11,161	June 27	Walter Hunt	Lock-stitch, reciprocating shuttle. Needle feed.
11,240	July 4	W. Butterfield	Chain-stitch, waxed thread for leather. Barbed needle, wheel feed.
11,284	July 11	G. A. Leighton	Chain-stitch, two threads.
11,507	Aug. 8	A. Swingle	Sewing leather, chain-stitch, one thread.
11,531	Aug. 15	S. H. Roper	Short thread, backstitch.
11,571	Aug. 22	E. Shaw	Sewing leather.
11,581	Aug. 22	M. Shaw	Sewing leather. Clamp-guides.
11,588	Aug. 22	S. S. Turner	Sewing leather. Single thread, chain-stitch.
11,615	Aug. 29	J. B. Nichols	Binder and folder.
11,631	Aug. 29	S. S. Turner	Sewing leather, wheel-feeding device.
11,680	Sept. 12	P. Shaw	Wheel-feeding device.
11,884	Nov. 7	D. C. Ambler	Lock-stitch, two needles, *overseaming for felling lap-seams*.
11,934	Nov. 14	D. Harris	Lock-stitch, upper-thread controller.
11,971	Nov. 21	C. Parham	Lock-stitch, *shuttle carrier*.
12,011	Nov. 28	T. E. Weed	Thread controller.
12,014	Nov. 28	O. G. Boynton	Binder.
12,015	Nov. 28	T. J. W. Robertson	Lock-stitch, stationary shuttle.
12,066	Dec. 12	W. Lyon	Feeding device.
12,074	Dec. 12	G. W. Stedman	Chain-stitch.
12,116	Dec. 19	A. B. Wilson	Feeding device.

Figure A-2, continued.

Appendix B

Dating Machines by Serial Numbers

The table below was compiled from the data presented in Cooper. To use the table, find the row entry that corresponds to your machine. Then look up the highest serial number that is less than or equal to the serial number on your machine. The date of manufacture is given for that column. If the number on your machine is larger than any serial number for that machine, then your machine was made later than, or during, the last year given. For example, a Singer with the serial number 14072 was, according to the table, made in 1859. A Wheeler and Wilson with the serial number 16201 would have been made in 1858. A Willcox and Gibbs with a serial number of 452101 was made after 1876, etc.

A word of caution is in order. When the table is used to find the dates of manufacture for the Grover & Baker machines of figure 2-105, it indicates that the #362 machine was made in 1851 and the #946 machine in 1852. But the vertical needle bar for both machines contains patent dates from 1853. Similarly, a Wheeler & Wilson machine identical to that of figure 2-316 has been found with a cloth plate stamped with serial "No. 24," indicating a manufacture date of 1851. But elsewhere on the plate we have "Wheeler & Wilson/Bridgeport, Conn." Supposedly, the company didn't move to Bridgeport until 1856.

Hence, the accuracy of the table is in question, and one should not conclude with absolute certainty that some given machine was made in a particular year. However, it is probably safe to assume that the table is accurate to within a couple of years.

SERIAL NUMBERS VS. DATE OF MANUFACTURE

	1850	1851	1852	1853	1854	1855	1856	1857	1858	1859	1860	1861	1862	1863
BARTHOLF		1	21	51	101	236	291	322	357	388	591	1338		
FINKLE (THRU VICTOR)								1		201	451	701	951	1501	3001
FLORENCE												1	501	2001	8001
GROVER AND BAKER			1	501	1001	1659	3894	5039	7001	10682	15753	26034	44870	63706	82642
A. B. HOWE						1	61	114	167	300	479	1400		
(HUNT) LADD, WEBSTER					1	101	369	443	623	1076	1566	3354		
LEAVITT				1	29	246	398	633	828	903	1116	1437	1758	2078
SINGER	1	101	901	1712	2522	3400	4284	6848	10478	14072	25025	43001	61001	79397
WHEELER AND WILSON		1	201	651	1450	2206	3377	5587	10178	18156	39462	64564	83120	111322
WILLCOX AND GIBBS									1	10001	20001	30001	40001	50001	60001

	1864	1865	1866	1867	1868	1869	1870	1871	1872	1873	1874	1875	1876
BARTLETT			1	1001	3127								
BARTRAM & FANTON				1	2959	3959	4959	5959	6963	7962	8962	9212	
BECKWITH								1	3501	7501	12501	18001	23001
FINKLE (VICTOR)	7001	9001	11001	13001	15491	17491	18831	21251	28891	49791	48241	53531	59636
FLORENCE	20001	35001	50001	60001	70535	82535	96196	113856	129803	145593	154556	160073	164965
GROVER & BAKER	101478	120314	139149	157887	190887	225887	261005	338408	389247	441258	477438	497439	512440
A. B. HOWE					(figures not available but in 1871 more than 20,000 were made.)								
HOWE MACHINE CO.				1	11000	46001	91844	167001	301011	446011	536011	571011	596011
LEAVITT	2401	2901	3901	4901	5952	6952	7723						
SINGER	99427	123059	149400	180361	223415	283045	369827	497661	678922	898681	1121126	1362806	1612659
WHEELER & WILSON	141100	181161	220319	270451	308506	357857	436723	519931	648457	822546	941736	1034564	1138304
WILLCOX & GIBBS	70001	80001	90001	100001	115001	130001	145001	160001	190128	223767	239648	253358	267880

NOTES: WHEELER AND WILSON NUMBERS APPLY ONLY TO MODELS MADE BEFORE 1876.
FOR SINGER MACHINES, BE SURE TO USE THE HIGHEST SERIAL NUMBER.

Figure B-1. Table compiled from Cooper, showing the dates of manufacture as determined by serial number.

Appendix C

Patent Models and Unidentified Machines

The Patent Model Story

Until 1880, inventors were required to submit working models of their inventions along with their patent applications. This requirement was in force for nearly half a century; as a result, by 1875 the government storage facility for the models was filled beyond capacity — models were being placed on window sills, bookshelves, etc. In fact more than 175,000 models were in existence at this time, and, although a fire in 1877 helped by eliminating some 76,000, something simply had to be done to alleviate the storage problem. Hence, in 1908, the doors of the Union Building (the models had been moved there in 1893) were opened to the Smithsonian, which used the opportunity to pick out certain important inventions by Edison, Singer, Howe, and others. Unfortunately, only about 1,000 models were disposed of in this manner, and the storage problem remained. Thus, in 1925 and 1926, the Coolidge administration, seeking ways of saving money, decided to get rid of the entire collection. Heirs and descendants were allowed to acquire models, and the Smithsonian was again given the opportunity to select whatever it wanted.

Now, it so happened that the curator of textiles at the time, Dr. Frederick Lewton, was extremely interested in sewing machines. When the Smithsonian was offered its pick of patent models, it was no surprise that Dr. Lewton tried to obtain as many sewing machine patent models as conditions would allow, thereby adding more than 700 to the collection. As a result, the Smithsonian has, without question, the world's best collection of sewing machine patent models.

However, several hundred were not retrieved, perhaps because they were not considered significant by Dr. Lewton at the time. Possibly he did not see them, for the models were all packed in large crates, usually uncategorized, and covered with straw; hence it was impossible, without unpacking an entire crate, to see just what was contained inside, and there were more than 600 crates.

Thus several hundred sewing machine patents remained buried among the 75,000 or so non-related models that were ultimately sold, starting in 1926, to a succession of private individuals. The most recent two owners of the remaining patent models have been O. Rundle Gilbert, who bought them in 1942, and Cliff Petersen, who purchased them from Mr. Gilbert in 1979. During these years, many of the 75,000 models were sold, both by Mr. Gilbert and by Mr. Petersen. As a result, patent models frequently show up in the hands of private individuals and antique dealers. After accounting for loss over the years due to breakage and fire, this number probably amounts to a few hundred. (Mr. Gilbert reportedly lost 20,000 models due to a fire in 1945.)

How to Identify a Patent Model

All patent models were stored at the patent office with identification tags, which were usually secured to the model with red cloth tape (see figure C-2), although sometimes they were tacked directly onto a wood surface (figure C-9). These tags give the patentee, date, and patent number; hence, when a machine is found with a tag, one can simply order the papers and drawings from the patent office to verify that the tag is on the proper model.

Unfortunately, the tag is frequently missing. In this situation, we might never be certain that we have found a patent model. If the untagged model came from one of the Gilbert or Petersen auctions, then we know for certain that it is a patent model; we just do not know who received the patent or when. A thorough study of the patent books can occasionally turn up the patentee, if we are lucky enough to have a model whose descriptive drawings resemble the mechanism at hand. In the case of a questionable model with no tag, purchased from a dealer, we will not be so lucky. Furthermore, in the case of sewing machines, an occasional mechanism was built totally by an individual just for its own sake, with no patent in mind. On the other hand, many patent models consisted of a suitably modified existing machine. Thus, we might find a Singer #1 machine that was altered to exhibit some new tension device; this machine then became the patent model for the new tension. Sometimes the patent was applied for after the machine included the patent in its design. In this case, the submitted model was merely an example of the machine directly from the factory.

It is for these reasons that some of the unidentified machines illustrated here may or may not be patent models. Several such machines have been illustrated, along with some bona fide patent models, whose authenticity is well-known because they came from either Mr. Gilbert or Mr. Petersen and they have their tags (which have been removed or hidden for most of these photographs). Some of the illustrated machines are undoubtedly commercially produced versions, while others were hand made as patent models, or hand made just to be used.

Appendix C

Figure C-1. Patent model, 1854, S. Parker. He was one of the originators of the AMERICAN MAGNETIC (see figure 2-12).

Figure C-2. Patent model, 1856, I. M. Singer. Most Singer patents were submitted on commercially manufactured machines. This patent model (for an improvement in hat stitching) was constructed from wood and brass. Notice the tag, placed on the model by the patent office. Tags for some other figures of patent models were removed or hidden for these photographs.

Appendix C

Figure C-3. Patent model, 1857, John W. Marsh. This machine featured a sliding cloth feed mechanism.

Figure C-4. Patent model, 1859, R. Eickemeyer. This model introduced an overseaming stitch, which was used in hat manufacture.

Appendix C

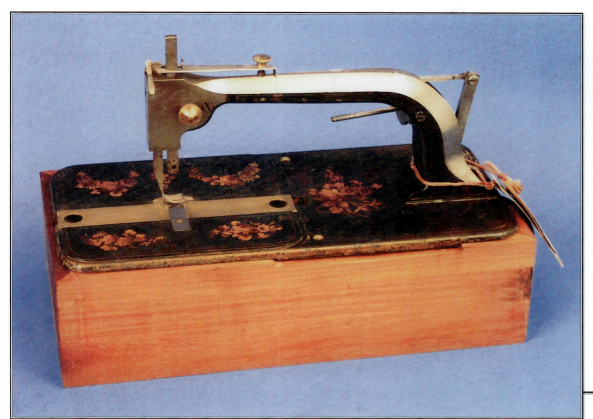

Figure C-5. Patent model, 1859, Wm. Hicks. This example may have been a commercially produced machine.

Figure C-6. Patent model, 1860, J. Steiner. This patent produced a buttonhole seam. Much of this model was made from parts that had been gleaned from old machines.

Appendix C

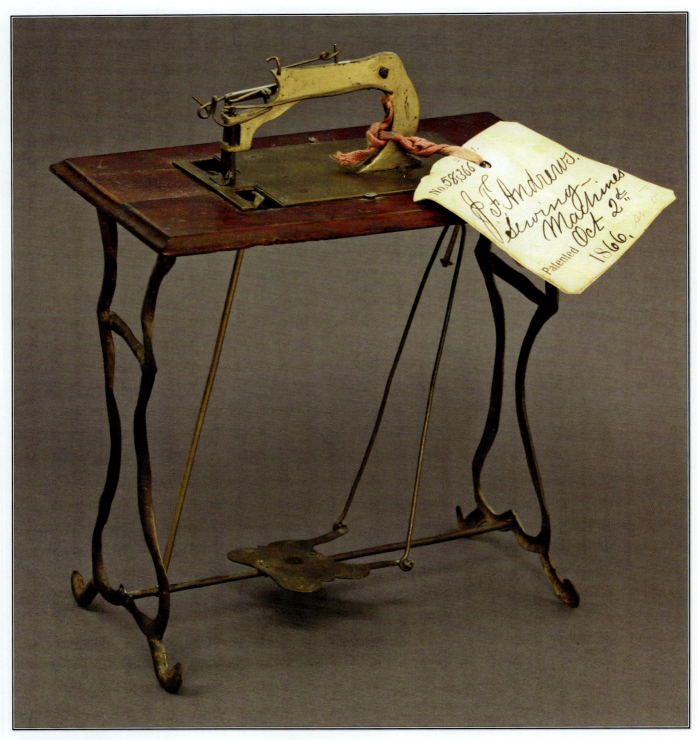

Figure C-7. Patent model, 1866, J. F. Andrews. Although only 4" across, this small brass machine is detailed in every way. The shuttle race holds a shuttle (not part of the model) that is less than ½" long.

Figure C-8. Patent model, 1868, T. W. Pepper. This machine featured a lever (the vertical handle at the right) that allowed one to change stitch direction (the choice was "N," "S," "E," or "W").

Appendix C

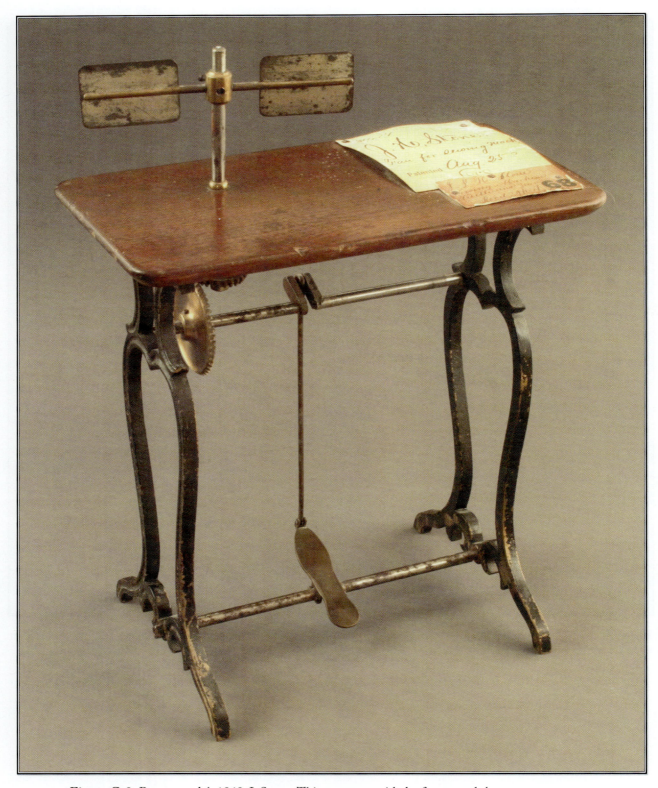

Figure C-9. Patent model, 1868, J. Stone. This patent provided a fan to cool the weary seamstress.

Figure C-10. Patent model, 1868, J. Vandizer. This model was constructed entirely from oak and lead, with the exception of one spring and several small screws.

Appendix C

Figure C-11. Patent model, 1868, D. A. Porter. The entire fancy machine was submitted for a patent that involved only a tension device.

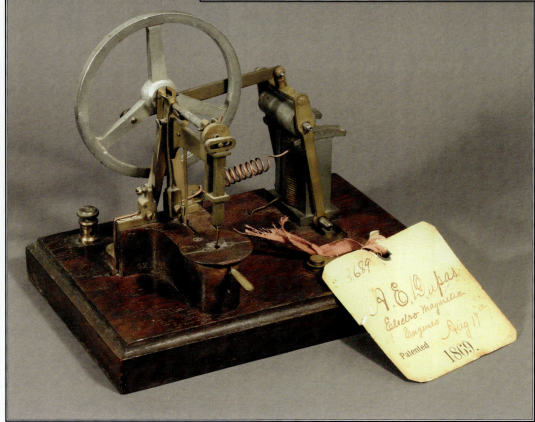

Figure C-12. Patent model, 1869, A. E. Dupas. This may have been the earliest American patent for an electric sewing machine. It is doubtful that any Dupas-type motors were produced.

Appendix C

Figure C-13. Patent model, 1869, M. M. Barnes. Like many other patents, this one was applied to a machine already in production. The machine appears to be related to the Weed Family Favorite machine.

Figure C-14. Patent model, 1871, W. Higgins. The iron base of this model is from a Grover and Baker casting.

Appendix C

Figure C-15. Patent model, 1872. E. A. Goodes. This is the patent for the machine illustrated in figure 3-1. The patent was for a special box. Inside the box, the machine would be firmly anchored upside down to the underside of the top. To use the machine, one would unhook the lid, open the door, rotate the top, machine and all, close the door and refasten the hook.

Figure C-16. Patent model, William Fay, 1874. The patent is for a motor, but the "motor" provided by this model was just a brass box. Some patent models do not actually demonstrate working mechanisms for the devices they are patenting.

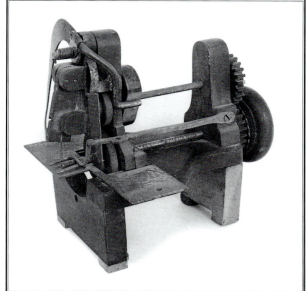

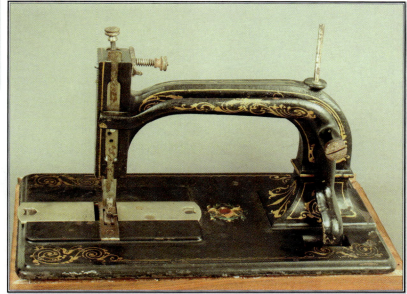

Figure C-17. Patent model, 1875, C. Palmer. This model was constructed mostly from wood.

Figure C-18. Wagner, 1876, obtained from the O. Rundle Gilbert collection.

Figure C-19. Patent model, 1876. Another Wagner patent.

Appendix C

Figure C-20. From the Gilbert collection. Although missing its tag, this is probably the patent for the Independent sewing machine.

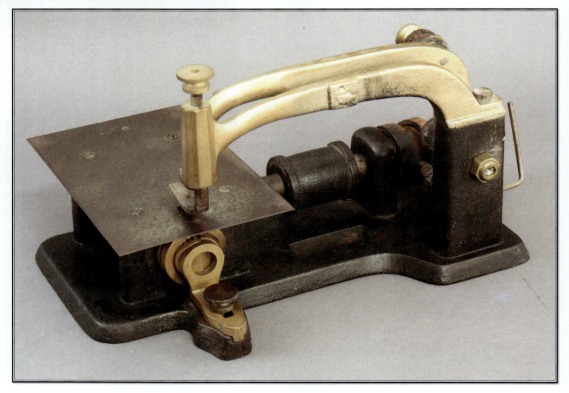

Figure C-21. This patent model also came from the Gilbert collection. The machine is an early patent for an oscillating hook, an important mechanism that is used in most lockstitch machines today. Unfortunately, the machine is missing its tag.

Appendix C

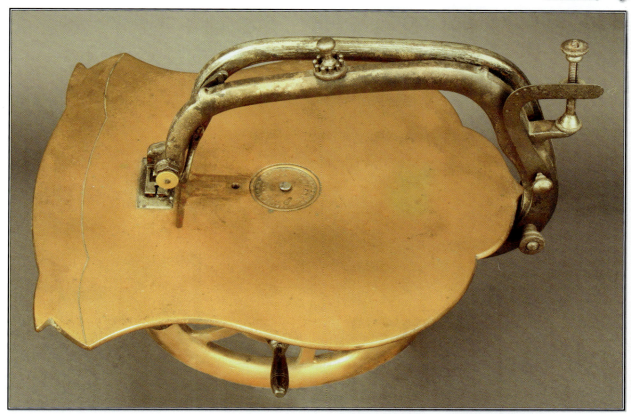

Figure C-22. This solid brass machine may be the patent model for Woodruff's American Eagle sewing machine.

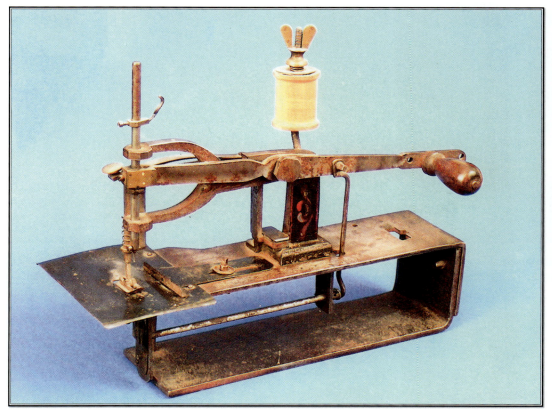

Figure C-23. This handmade machine is probably not a patent model. On the edge of the base, "Singer England" has been stamped. The machine was made around 1860.

Appendix C

Figure C-24. This handmade machine was probably made before 1865. Since it was found without a tag, considerable research will be necessary in order to determine whether it is a patent model.

Appendix C

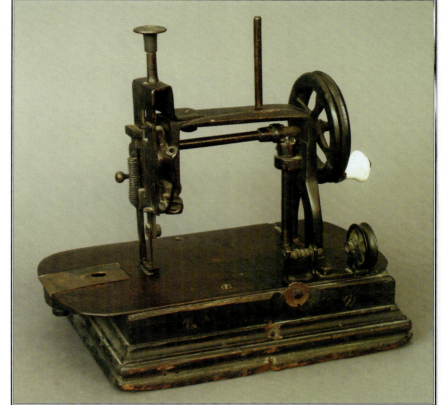

Figure C-25. This machine was made by an individual from spare parts, most of which originally had nothing to do with sewing. For example, the notched brass knob in the front toward the right is an Indian-head penny.

Figure C-26. This machine was possibly made by an individual, possibly mass produced. Unlike the machine in figure C-25, the mechanism is very professional looking. The riddle will be answered if another like it turns up.

Appendix C

Figure C-27. This commercially produced machine was probably made during the late 1860s or early 1870s. Unfortunately, the name that was printed on the machine has worn off. This problem occurs with many early sewing machines.

Figure C-28. The name of this hand-operated machine is unknown. It was probably made around 1865.

Appendix C

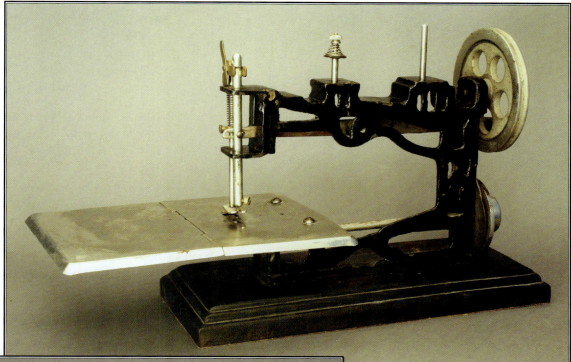

Figure C-29. This machine has a rather unusual casting, but unfortunately, its maker remains unknown.

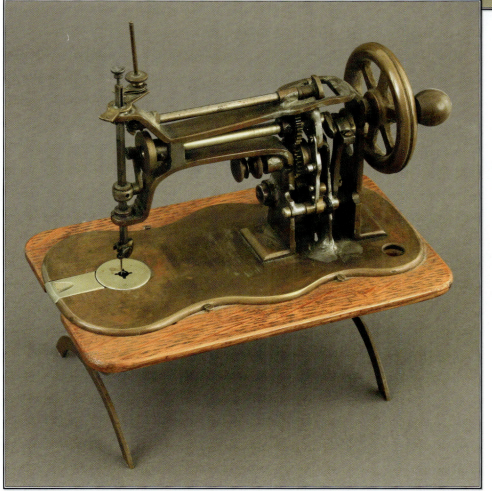

Figure C-30. Here, unbelievably, we have a true salesman's sample. The machine is only 6" across, but extreme attention has been paid to the detail of a very complicated mechanism. The machine sews a concentrated stitch, rotating through 360 degrees to form a button tuft on upholstery. Complete with ¼" bobbin, it very likely actually sews.

Appendix C

Figure C-31. An unknown machine, circa 1885, which superficially resembles the New England type — albeit an unusual version. It employs a revolving-hook chain stitch mechanism instead of the more typical reciprocating looper (see figure 1-1). This machine and the one illustrated in figure C-29 are possibly of foreign origin.

Figure C-32. Unknown treadle machine, circa 1860.

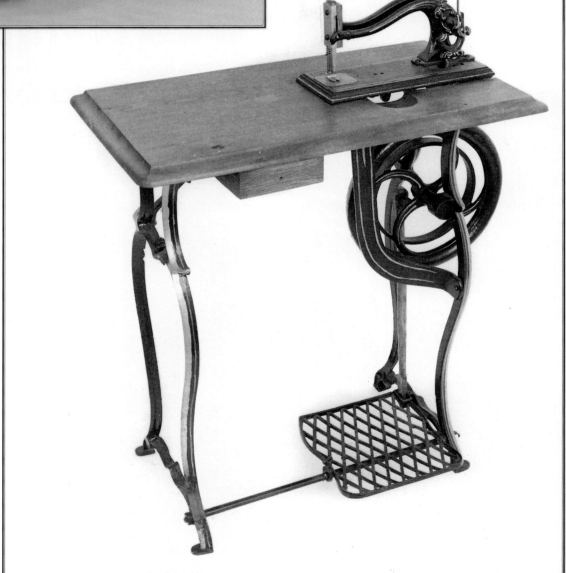

Appendix C

Figure C-33. Unknown treadle machine, circa 1870.

Appendix C

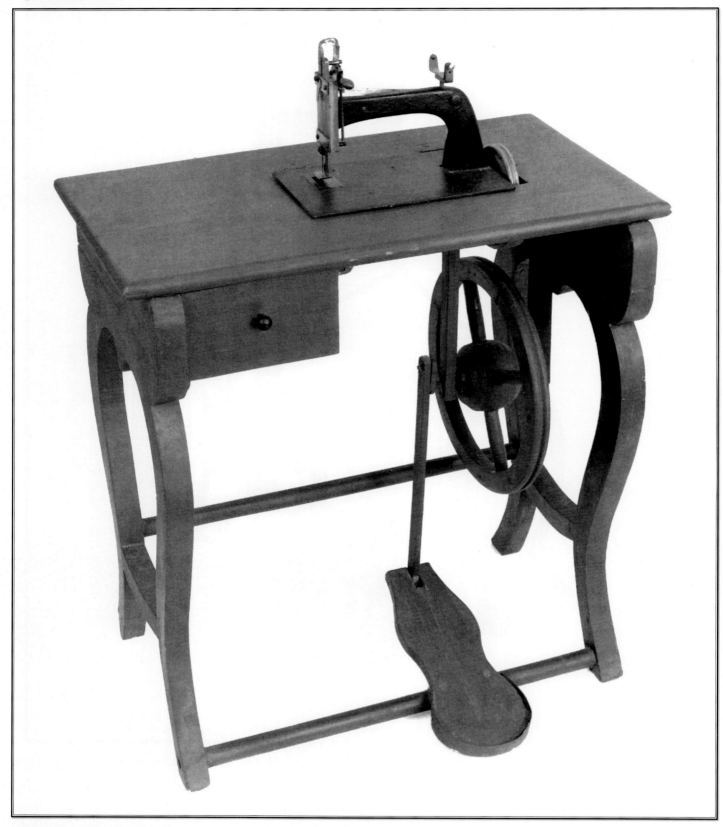

Figure C-34. This machine was made entirely from spare parts, and the stand was built from wood. It was probably constructed around 1865 by somebody who did not wish to pay for a commercially produced machine. Apparently it sews, although not too well.

Appendix D

Evolution of the "Modern" (Vintage) Sewing Machine

Around 1875 to 1880, a transformation in the physical appearance of sewing machines was already underway. The many and varied looks of the different manufacturers were being replaced by the familiar singular design of the early twentieth century. In fact, by 1885, with a few exceptions, almost all sewing machines designed for home use looked pretty much the same.

Here we illustrate this trend, beginning with a few of the earlier models and progressing through the first quarter of the twentieth century. This evolution affects not only the physical appearance, but the mechanism as well (see figure D-62).

For the current collector, this trend implies that a collection of typical sewing machines dating from, say 1900 through 1925, would be rather boring if one were interested in only the outward appearance. This homogeneity of mechanism is contrasted only by an occasional colorful name that appears on a machine, or by an unusual cabinet.

Hence, such a collection of late or vintage machines would find its intrinsic value more in the cabinets or names on the machines than in the machines themselves. Thus, an elaborate oak buffet style would be worth more than a typical domed Bentwood portable cased machine. And a name like Waxahachie Hardware Co. would arouse more interest than a name like Acme. (See appendix G for comprehensive lists of twentieth-century sewing machine names.)

Value of Vintage Machines

The relative value of a sewing machine made in the first quarter of the twentieth century is usually at the low end of the scale. A typical value code would be 1 or 2, but this would increase for elaborate cabinet work or for a machine in excellent condition.

To arrive at a correct dollar figure, one should perhaps consider the value more as a piece of furniture than as a sewing machine. In any case, value speculation for vintage machines is beyond the scope of this book.

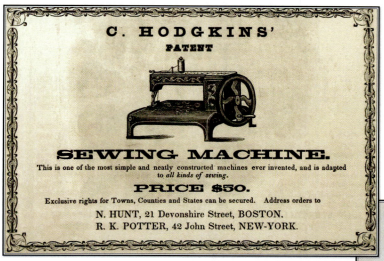

Figure D-1. Hunt machine, circa 1855. This was the predecessor to the Ladd & Webster machine. Its style began to resemble the style that almost all machines ultimately evolved to.

Figure D-2. Lyon, circa 1870. Mr. Lyon had been associated with the Weed Company.

Appendix D

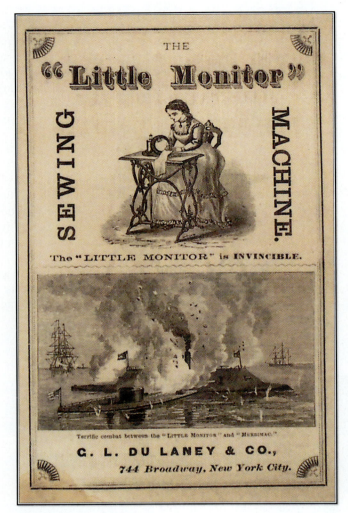

Figure D-3. Little Monitor, 1870. Many makers published small fold-out booklets that illustrated their various models and occasionally included testimonials from happy customers. This particular booklet exhibited three styles. Booklets from larger, more successful makers featured many more.

Figure D-4. Independent, 1873. Another example of a booklet; here we have only two models to choose from.

Appendix D

Figure D-5. Wilson, 1874. Here, the booklet has been unfolded to show a couple of the many different models. The Wilson company produced hundreds of thousands of sewing machines. The No. 12 is an early example of a style that persisted for 40 years.

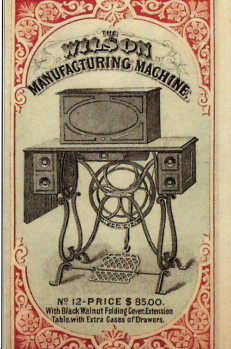
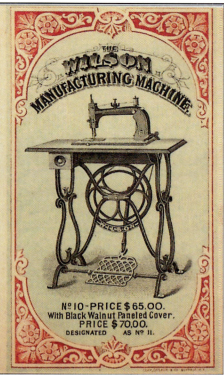

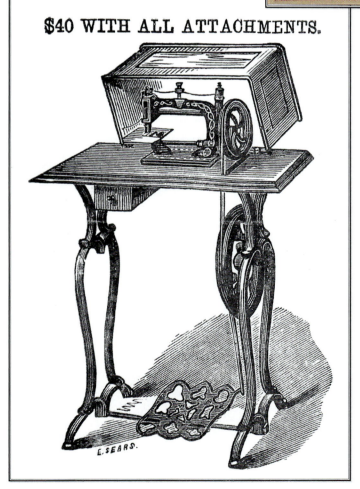

Figure D-6. Bartlett, circa 1875. From a magazine; the paper is so thin you can see the printing on the other side.

Appendix D

Figure D-7. Howe, 1878. We see that even at this early date, electricity was an option. It is unclear from the illustration just how speed was controlled, or how the motor was connected; i.e., note that the flywheel connected to the original treadle (and hence the belt drive) lies inside the iron leg, whereas the belt drive from the motor goes outside the leg. It is possible that this model was never actually produced.

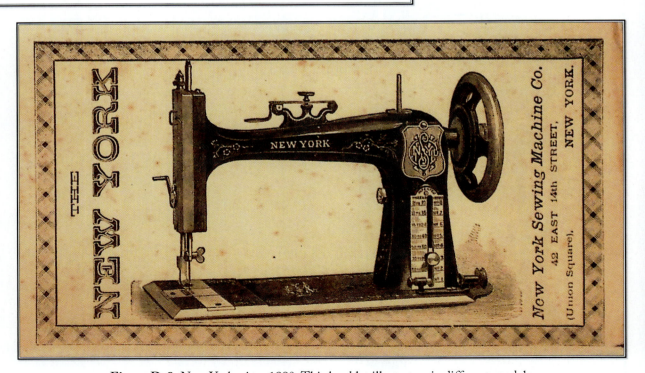

Figure D-8. New York, circa 1880. This booklet illustrates six different models.

Appendix D

Figure D-9. Home Sewing Machine, circa 1878. There are eight models in this booklet.

Figure D-10. A fashion statement. These ladies are not dressed for sewing.

Appendix D

Figure D-11. Colton Water Motor, circa 1880. Electricity had not become commonplace yet, but automated power was occasionally offered.

Figure D-12. Morrison, 1882. The machine is typical enough, but the cabinet is very unusual.

Appendix D

Figure D-13. Helpmate, 1882. This flier is somewhat colorful. Most were not.

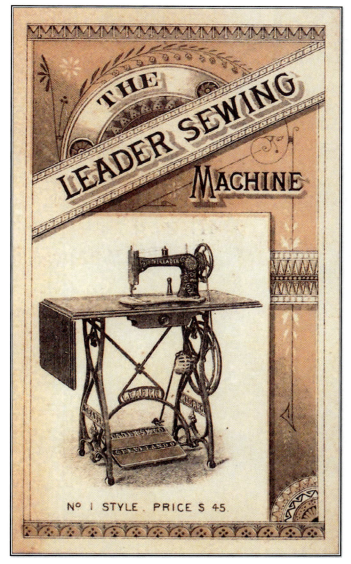

Figure D-14. Leader, 1882. Most fliers posted the retail prices directly under the particular model.

Figure D-15. Jewel, 1885. According to the flier, this machine was manufactured by the Jewel Company in Toledo, Ohio. The name Jewel appeared on later machines made by other companies.

Figure D-16. Howe, circa 1885. Cardboard trade cards were extremely popular from around 1870 to after 1900. Many were whimsical and rather far-fetched.

Figure D-17. Domestic, circa 1885. This company produced a large number of colorful trade cards.

Figure D-18. New Home, circa 1885. Like those of the Domestic Company, the popular New Home sewing machine trade cards are common, varied, and cute.

Appendix D

Figure D-19. New Home, circa 1885.

Figure D-20. White, circa 1885. Some companies produced colorful advertisements in various shapes.

Appendix D

Figure D-21. Domestic, circa 1885.

Figure D-22. New Lovell, circa 1885.

Figure D-23. New Home, 1888. This company, like many others, exported machines to Europe. The style is typical for the period.

Figure D-24. Demorest, 1889.

Appendix D

Figure D-25. New National, 1890.

Figure D-26. Davis, 1892. The styles typically reflected the furniture styles of the period.

Figure D-27. Davis, 1892. This little booklet illustrates several Davis models. Here, the cover (left) and the opposing inside page (right) are shown. It is uncertain just what political statement the artist was trying to make with the rather indelicate cover.

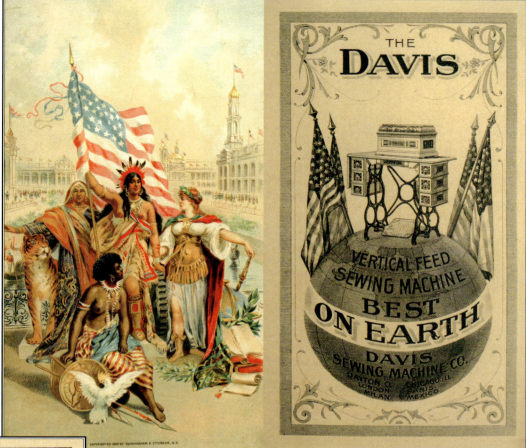

Figure D-28. New Home, circa 1895. This booklet contains seven models that vary in price from $50.00 to $80.00.

Appendix D

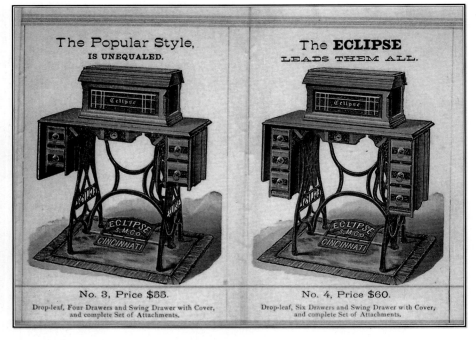

Figure D-29. Eclipse, 1895.

Figure D-30. O'Neill, 1899.

Figure D-31. Defiance, 1900.

Figure D-32. Peerless, 1901.

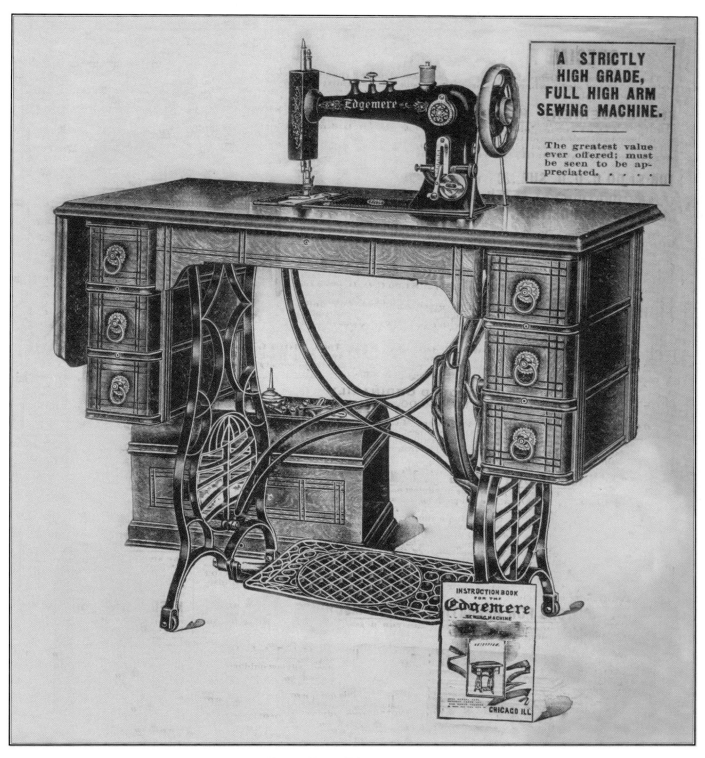

Figure D-33. Edgemere, 1902.

Appendix D

Figure D-34. Singer, 1902. The Bentwood cover for portable machines appeared around 1900 and was popular for more than 20 years.

Figure D-35. Singer, 1902.

Appendix D

Figure D-36. Bonita, 1904.

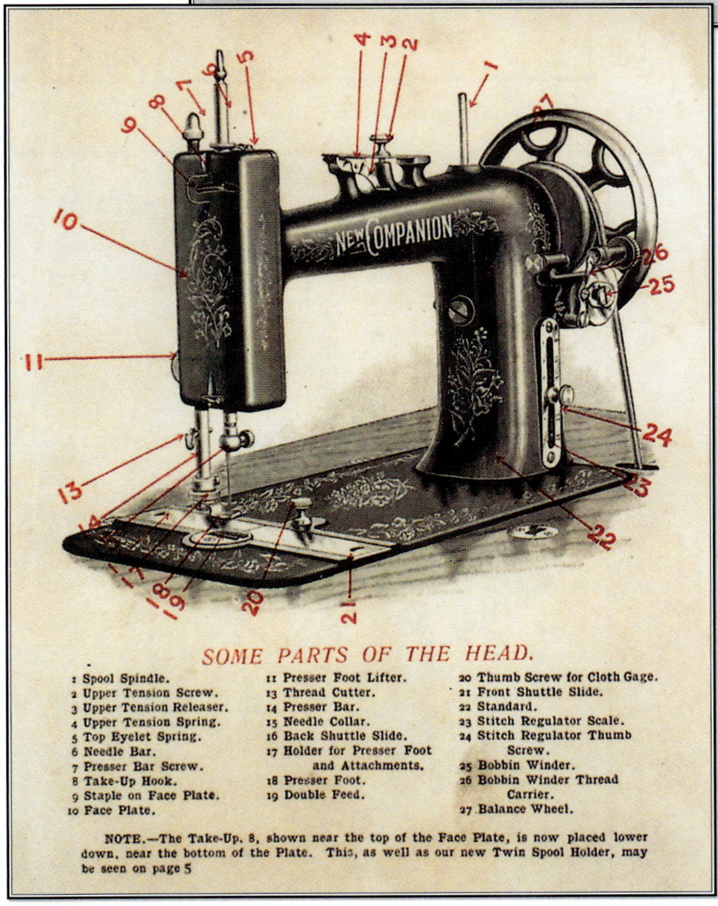

Figure D-37. New Companion, 1904. When companies changed models, they frequently put "New" in front of the name. Some companies became better known with the *New* appendage (example: New Home).

Appendix D

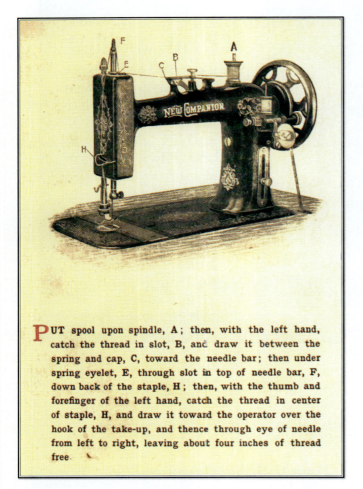

Figure D-38. New Companion threading instructions. Most vintage sewing machines utilized similar principles, which are usually easy to figure out, to thread their machines. A typical reason for machine failure was that the little and varied thread guides frequently wore down, with narrow slots forming where the thread continuously rubbed. This caused irregularities in the stitch. At this point, a new machine was usually purchased. These worn slots can give clues as to how the machine is properly threaded.

Figure D-39. New Home, circa 1905.

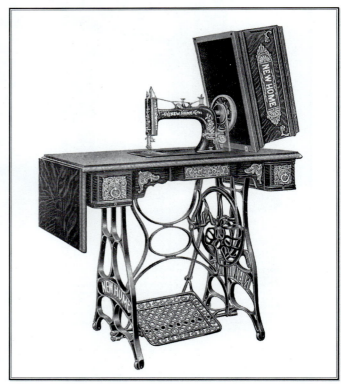

Figure D-40. New Home, circa 1905. During this period, the styles of figures D-23 and D-50 were both common.

Appendix D

Figure D-41. New Home, circa 1905.

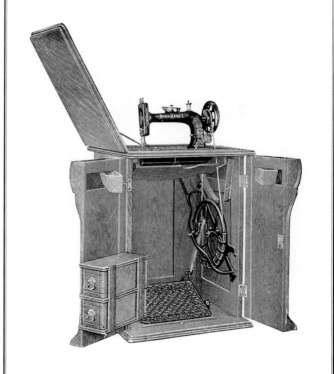

Figure D-42. New Home, circa 1905.

Figure D-43. New Home, circa 1905.

Appendix D

Figure D-44. New Home, circa 1905.

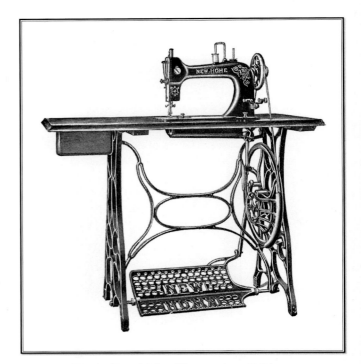

Figure D-45. New Home, circa 1905.

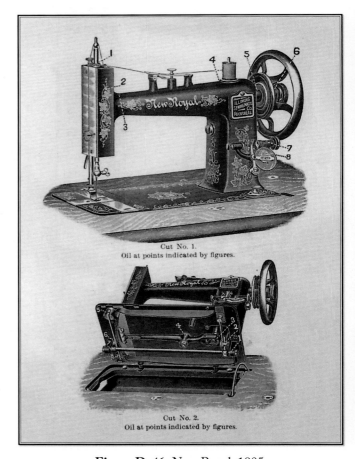

Figure D-46. New Royal, 1905.

Appendix D

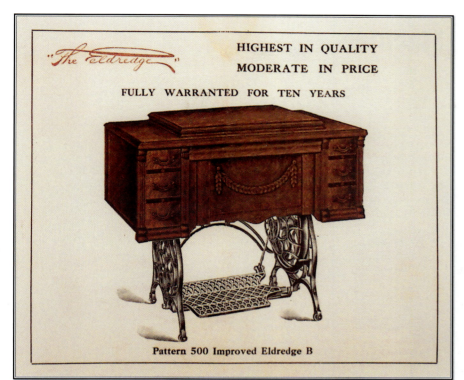

Figure D-47. Eldredge, 1905. Color was increasingly introduced into advertisements.

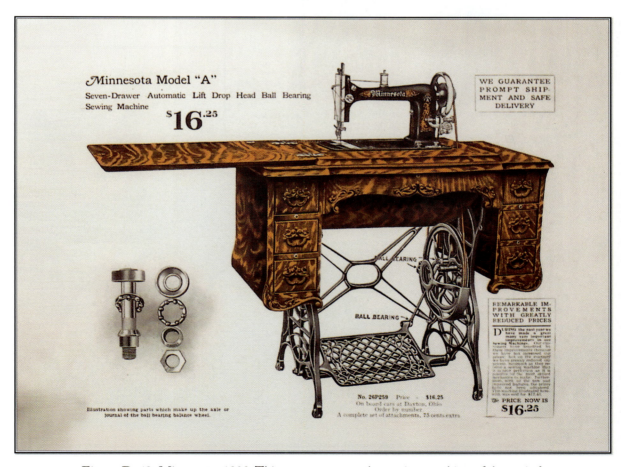

Figure D-48. Minnesota, 1908. This was a very popular sewing machine of the period.

Appendix D

Figure D-49. Norwood, circa 1910.

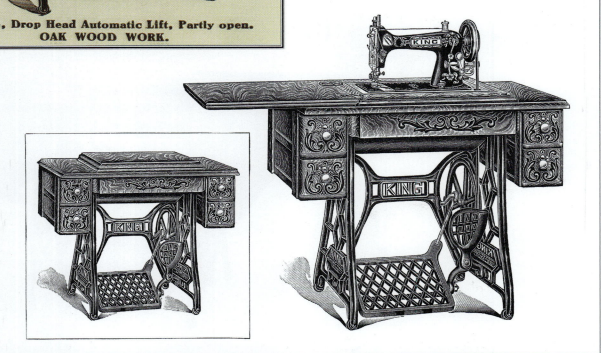

Figure D-50. King, 1910. This style is typical for machines made after 1910 in that the head could be lowered into the cabinet.

Appendix D

Figure D-51. New Home, circa 1910. The little-boy-having-his-pants-sewn theme was used by several different manufacturers (see figure I-23).

Figure D-52. Franklin, 1910. This popular brand was marketed by Sears, but it was actually manufactured by another company, the National Sewing Machine Company, which was located not far from Chicago, the home base of Sears.

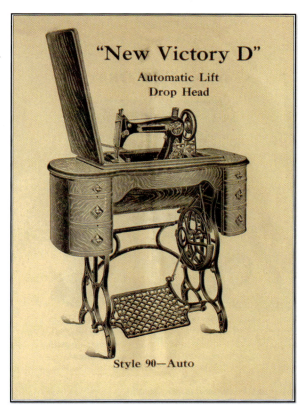

Figure D-53. New Victory D, circa 1910.

Appendix D

Figure D-54. Davis, circa 1910. During this period, many companies produced portable machines that were typically housed in oak boxes with dome-shaped covers.

Figure D-55. Franklin, circa 1915.

Figure D-56. Fountain, circa 1915.

Appendix D

Figure D-57. Sears, 1920. In addition to promoting the Franklin name, Sears produced its own machine. (Naturally, it did not actually manufacture its own machines, which were made by the National Sewing Machine Company of Belvidere, Illinois.)

Figure D-58. New Goodrich, 1920.

Appendix D

Figure D-59. Rockford, circa 1925. Finally, electricity was beginning to replace foot power.

Figure D-60. Priscilla, 1925. Naturally, most companies continued to offer foot-powered machines.

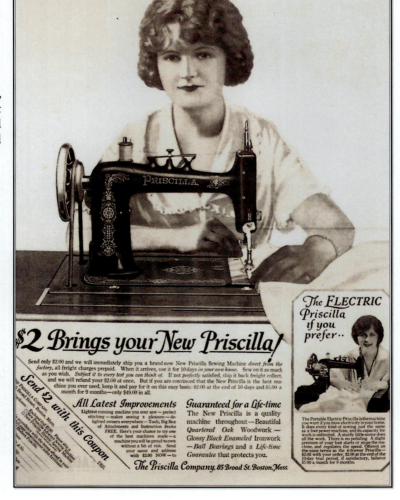

Figure D-61. Damascus Grand, 1928. Although electricity was finally being utilized, the foot powered machine continued to be made. Note that brass drawer handles were not used on this. Wooden ones were less expensive.

Appendix D

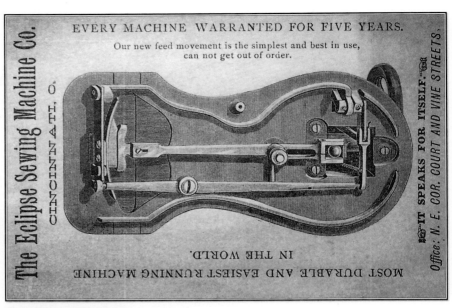

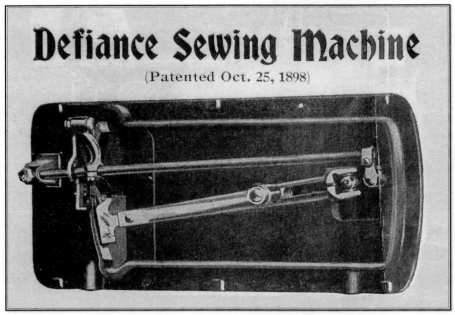

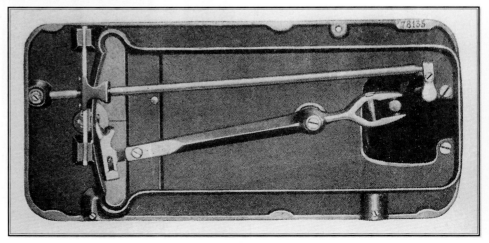

Figure D-62. Typical mechanisms, from top to bottom: 1885, 1898, 1920. It is important to note that for a long time, almost all machines featured very similar mechanisms and pretty much had the same outward appearance.

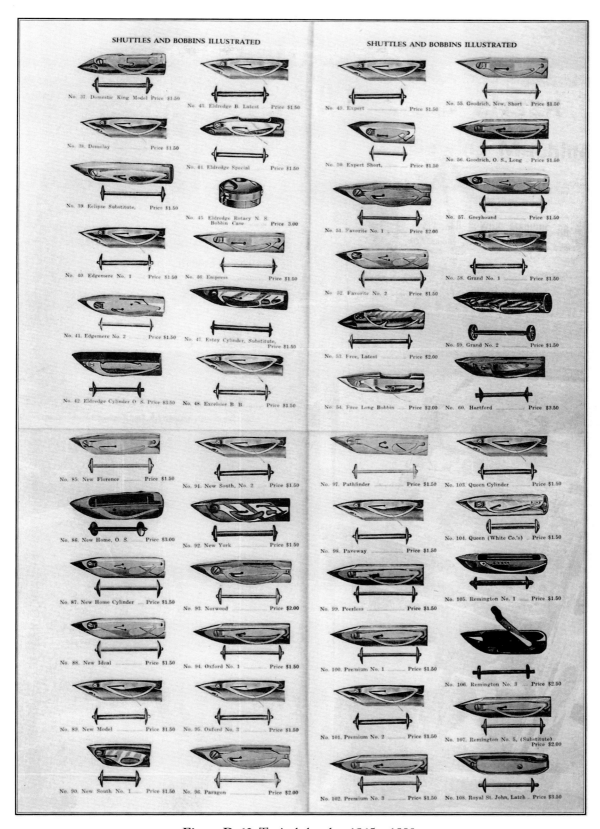

Figure D-63. Typical shuttles, 1865 – 1890.

Appendix D

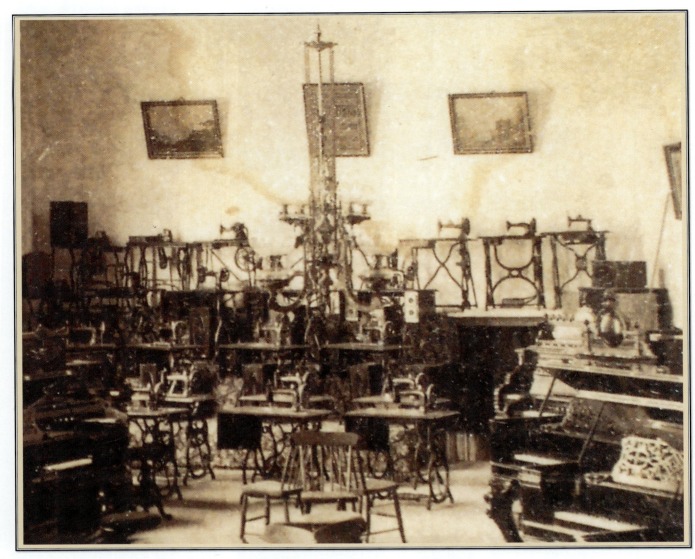

Figure D-64. There was a market for used sewing machines as early as 1875. This is a view of a store that sold used pianos and sewing machines. Back then, phrases like "previously owned" did not clutter the language.

Figure D-65. Singer machines and the countries they were sold in, circa 1900. This popular and colorful set of cards was produced in large quantities. It would be interesting to know how many people actually wore such fashionable attire while sewing.

Appendix E

Singer Manufacturing Machines (1900 – 1910)

Most major sewing machine companies produced, in addition to machines for the home, machines designed for specific manufacturing purposes. The models illustrated here represent but a small portion of those made by the Singer company around the turn of the century. Many of these models were sold, with minor changes, for over 50 years.

Note that although Singer purchased the Wheeler & Wilson company around 1905, it continued to use the Wheeler & Wilson name for a few years. Machines produced at the Wheeler & Wilson factory in Bridgeport, Connecticut, were sold with Singer model numbers that contained a *w*.

Figure E-1. This 1905 Singer (No. 46K27, O/2) was used for manufacturing gloves and furs. It is frequently mistaken for a much earlier machine.

Figure E-2. The 46K14 was a 1905 machine designed for manufacturing gloves.

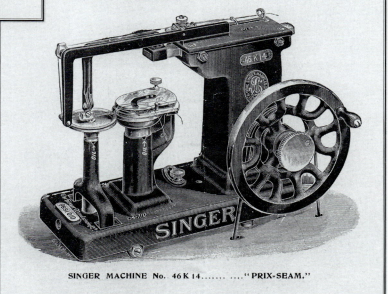

Appendix E

Figure E-3. The 46K1 was used to sew the finger ends of gloves. Though made in 1905, this machine has the look of the Letter "A" machine of the early 1860s.

Figure E-4. This 1910 machine sews 12 parallel rows of lockstitching. Its model number was 41-12. There were also 41-3 and 41-5 models.

Appendix E

Figure E-5. The 76-1, though made in 1905, appears identical to the 1880s Heberling running stitch machine.

Figure E-6. Produced in Bridgeport at the Wheeler & Wilson factory, this 1907 Singer machine retained the Wheeler & Wilson name and was sold as Singer model 45-w. It could sew 2,000 stitches per minute in leather.

Appendix E

Figure E-7. By 1912, the Wheeler & Wilson name had been phased out, but the machine of figure E-6 continued to be made at Bridgeport.

Figure E-8. The 103w1 could be fitted for "stiff hat work" or "soft hat work." It was made in 1909.

Figure E-9. This is what the 1850s Singer #1 had evolved into by 1900. The flywheel for this machine is 13" in diameter. This machine, the 3-1, was used for making harnesses.

377

Appendix E

Figure E-10. The 1908 model 18-2 was used for stitching shoes.

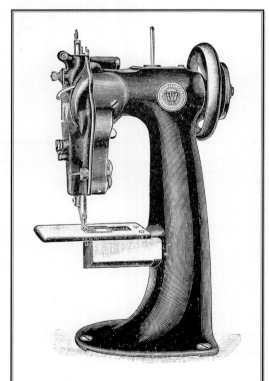

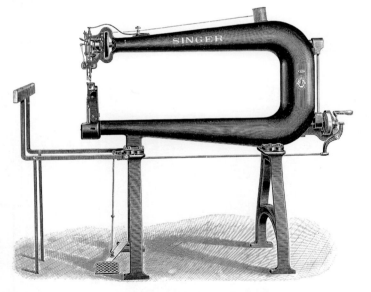

Figure E-11. This 1907 Class 67 model has an arm that is more than four feet across. It was used for sewing carriage dashes, fenders, and "motor-car mudguards."

Figure E-12. The 123w1 was used to sew leather over the handles of handbags and pocketbooks.

Appendix F

"The Great Factory"

These woodcuts from Scott depict the Singer factory as it was operating around 1880 (it had been built about 10 years earlier).

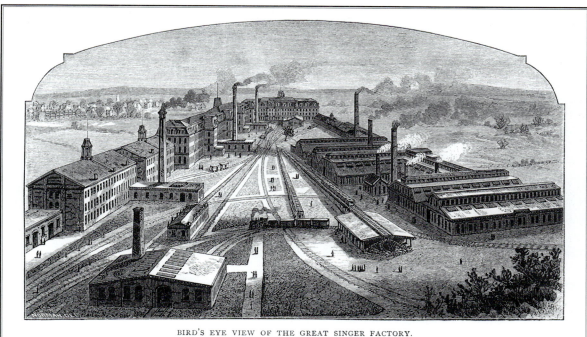

BIRD'S EYE VIEW OF THE GREAT SINGER FACTORY.

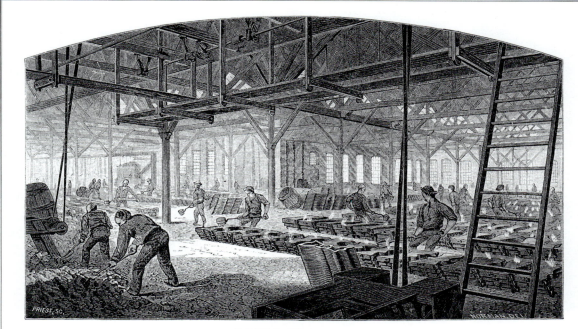

CASTING IN THE FOUNDRY.

Appendix F

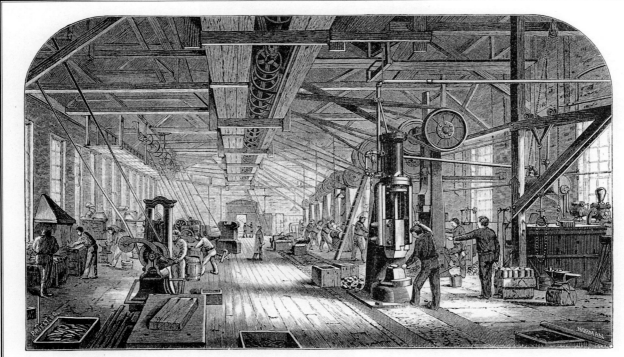

FORGING SHOP.

SCREW DEPARTMENT.

Appendix F

ASSEMBLING ROOM.

POLISHING ROOM.

Appendix F

"SETTING-UP" THE MACHINES.

TESTING THE MACHINES.

Appendix F

JAPANNING FURNACES.

THE SINGER COMPANY'S STEAMER, "EDWARD CLARK."

Appendix G

A Comprehensive List of Vintage Sewing Machines (circa 1900 – 1925)

Herein are given almost every name of any vintage sewing machine that one may encounter. As mentioned in appendix D, there are thousands! However, all these names were associated with machines that were actually manufactured by only a handful of companies, whose histories are given here.

Almost all machines in this list have the same general appearance and similar mechanisms (see figure D-62), although the shuttle was being slowly phased out and replaced by the stationary bobbin, wherein the stitch was formed by either a revolving hook (see figure 2-1) or by an oscillating hook, the current modern lockstitching mechanism.

The brief histories below of twentieth-century sewing machine companies and the long list of machine names that follows were taken from pages 160 – 205 of Grace Cooper's fine work and are reprinted with the kind permission of the Smithsonian Institution's National Museum of American History. The second list comes directly from a 1932 Torrington catalog.

Sewing-Machine Companies

Fanciful names for home sewing machines began to be used in greater numbers in the late nineteenth century, as noted by such appellations as Minnehaha, Splendid, Queen City, and others. For the most part, each new name represented a new company with a different machine, although the question of "difference" could be debated as many of the machines after 1877 looked alike. The smaller companies, especially the new ones, copied the style of the well-known, established machines. The idea of colorful names was not new in the twentieth century, but increasingly became the rule rather than the exception. It was in the last decade of the nineteenth century that companies — like the newly formed National Sewing Machine Company — began selling their machines in increasing numbers to department stores, catalog houses, and other retail outlets, furnishing them with any name selected by the retailer. Sewing machines were even offered as premiums with newspaper subscriptions, and the name of the newspaper would be applied to the machine. Disappearing was the tradition that the machine must bear the inventor's or manufacturer's name. By the early twentieth century, literally thousands of different-named machines were manufactured by fewer than a dozen sewing-machine companies in business at the time. Two companies did not follow this fashion, Singer and Willcox and Gibbs. The Willcox and Gibbs family machine continued to be the simple chainstitch. The "Singer" name reigned supreme, and it was the only one under which that company's machines were sold. But the style of the Singer machine and the design of the trademark were widely copied by many companies both at home and abroad. Other companies sold under their own names, but also added to the vast array of new names. Although sewing machines were not as decorative as they had been in the earlier period, verbally they were more colorful.

A brief history of each of the companies producing the sewing machines that were involved in this commercial name-calling will be given to help establish the dates of these machines. Company records were not kept as to which names were furnished to whom. Some helpful records exist, since sewing machines were built to last for years, and "parts suppliers" for these machines grew to be a respectable business in itself. To offer the correct parts, the parts companies had to inform the potential customer, and themselves, with the name of the manufacturer of the machine; the name stenciled on the machine was not sufficient for a part replacement. Two of the most prominent of these parts companies printed catalogs that have been very helpful. One is the Sewing Machine Supplies and Parts, catalog of the A. G. Brewer Sewing Machine & Supply Company, Chicago, Illinois, whose first edition was published in 1926. In the introduction, the manager of the company writes: "In getting this book out we endeavored to list the items now in demand by the Sewing Machine dealer, both old as well as the latest." The second is Bryson's Verified Complete List of All Interchangeable Parts and Needles, catalog of the C. M. Bryson Company of Cleveland, Ohio, which was copyrighted in 1933. The C. M. Bryson Company had been a sewing-machine sales agency in the late nineteenth century and became a parts supplier in the twentieth century. The company slogan was, "If Bryson does not keep it, you can't get it."

Brief Company Histories

Davis Sewing Machine Company. First established in Watertown, New York, this company moved to Dayton, Ohio, in 1889 – 1890. The reasons given for the move were "first, the pressing necessity of increasing the manufacturing facilities of the company to meet the growing demand for their machines, and next, the great advantage offered for manufacturing in the West. . ." Large factory buildings were constructed in Dayton and business flourished for more than 30 years. Although the name Davis Sewing Machine Company was retained, the actual manufacture of machines was taken over, at some time before 1924, by the H. M. Huffman Mfg. Co. On December 24, 1924, the Dayton operation ceased as the "National Sewing Machine Co., Belvidere, Ill. purchased good will, trade names and right to manufacture sewing machines under name Davis and all other names previously owned by Davis S. M. Co."

Domestic Sewing Machine Company. The Domestic machines were first manufactured in Norwalk, Ohio. The manufacturing rights were sold to a company in Newark, New Jersey, about 1871; the company was under contract to sell all the machines that they produced to the Domestic Sewing Machine Company in Ohio. In 1896 the two companies in New Jersey and Ohio were consolidated, although the factories continued to be located in New Jersey until about 1906. Between that date and 1914, Domestic machines were built in Buffalo, New York. In 1922 a New York City office for the Domestic Sewing Machine Company was opened. In 1924 the Domestic company became a wholly owned subsidiary of the White Sewing Machine Company and was located in Cleveland, Ohio. Domestic electric machines for home use were still being manufactured in the Cleveland factory in 1974.

A. G. Mason Manufacturing Company. A. G. Mason had been a general agent in Cleveland for the Davis Sewing Machine company until 1903 when he began to manufacture sewing machines under his own name. He concentrated on building up sewing-machine departments in large retail stores. He gave particular attention in his manufacture of sewing machines to producing medium-priced, high-quality machines sold under special names chosen by the retail dealer. A. G. Mason died in 1916, and the company became a subsidiary of the Domestic Sewing Machine Company.

Household Sewing Machine Company. Beginning as the Providence Tool Company manufacturing household sewing machines, the company name was changed to Household Sewing Machine Company in 1890 and manufacture continued in Providence, Rhode Island, until 1906. Several other machine names were used for their products in addition to "Household."

Foley & Williams Manufacturing Company. This company developed about 1885 from the earlier H. B. Goodrich Company of Chicago, Illinois. The Foley and Williams company remained in business through 1924, but in the 1926 Brewer catalog they are listed as "out-of-business." Shortly after this, the company was reorganized as the Goodrich Sewing Machine Company and continued in active business through the mid-1930s.

New Leader Sewing Machine Company. It is not known whether this company was related to the earlier Leader company of Springfield, Massachusetts, which moved to Cleveland before it went out of business in 1884. The earliest record of the New Leader is from 1926, and the company was listed as being in operation as late as 1933. The names given its sewing machines are related to the company name, e.g., New Century Leader.

Standard Sewing Machine Company. Frank Mack and William A. Mack, with years of experience in the sewing-machine business, began their own manufacturing as the Standard Sewing Machine Company, Cleveland, Ohio, in 1884. They both continued with the company until 1893. The Standard company continued to manufacture sewing machines in Cleveland through the early decades of the 20th century. Both electric and treadle machines were advertised in the early 1920s. The Standard Sewing Machine Company was sold to the OSAAN Fur Machine Company which was acquired by the Singer company in 1931.

Free Sewing Machine Company. This company, located in Rockford, Illinois, was an outgrowth of the Royal Sewing Machine Company that built a new factory in Rockford in 1890. By the end of December 1894, the Royal company had sold out to Gilbert Woodruff. In 1895 the Illinois Sewing Machine Company was founded using the remaining assets of the

Appendix G

earlier company. Will C. Free joined the company in 1898 and became the president in 1910. He retained the Illinois Sewing Machine Company as a subsidiary, but organized a parent company — the Free Sewing Machine Company. In 1917, working with Westinghouse, an electric-model sewing machine was introduced under the name "Free-Westinghouse." The company continued in business in Rockford until 1958 when it moved to Los Angeles, California. Manufacture of sewing machines was discontinued in 1969.

National Sewing Machine Company. This company was formed in 1890 as the result of a consolidation of two older companies, the June Manufacturing Company and the Eldredge Sewing Machine Company both of which had been organized in 1879 after the expiration of the Sewing Machine Combination. Both companies had moved their factories from Chicago to Belvidere, Illinois, in 1886. The National Sewing Machine Company sold most of their machines through department stores and mail-order houses; Marshall Field's department store in Chicago began to sell National (Eldredge-built) machines in 1888, John Wanamaker's of Philadelphia purchased its first machine in 1892, and R. H. Macy's in New York in 1897. Eldredge-built machines were first sold to the Montgomery Ward company in 1889 and National continued to furnish them sewing machines. National produced its first electrical machines in 1917, which were sold through the Western Electric Company; their first so-called "period style" consoles were also introduced in 1917. On September 1, 1953, the National Sewing Machine Company was merged with the Free Sewing Machine Company as a wholly owned subsidiary.

New Home Sewing Machine Company. In 1862 Andrew Clark and William P. Barker, under the name of Clark and Barker, began manufacturing New England single-thread hand-turned sewing machines in Orange, Massachusetts. In 1865 Clark bought out Barker and continued in business for several years. A new firm was organized by Clark in 1867 and named the A. F. Johnson and Company. Valuable patents were purchased from Mr. Johnson and incorporated into the machines. The factories were enlarged and manufacture of the Gold Medal and Home Shuttle sewing machines were added to the New England machines. In 1869 the company was again reorganized, this time called the Gold Medal Sewing Machine Company. The manufacture of the Home sewing machine began in 1870; in 1877 when all the major patents — held by the Sewing-Machine Combination — expired, the New Home machine was developed by W. L. Grout, who was the company superintendent and general manager. The new machine was popular, and in 1882 the company name was changed to the New Home Sewing Machine Company. This company continued to manufacture sewing machines in Orange, Massachusetts, selling them under a wide variety of names. In 1930 they became affiliated with the Free Sewing Machine Company and moved to Rockford, Illinois. The company moved, with the Free company, to Los Angeles in 1958. In 1960 the New Home business was purchased by the Janome Sewing Machine Company, Ltd., of Tokyo, Japan, with offices in Santa Monica, California. To date, new Home sewing machines of Japanese manufacture continue to be built.

White Sewing Machine Company. Thomas H. White manufactured sewing machines in Templeton, Massachusetts, and in Orange, Massachusetts, for several years before he moved to Cleveland, Ohio, in 1866. At that time, he organized the White Manufacturing Company and built sewing machines for sales organizations bearing their trade names. In 1876 the company was organized into the White Sewing Machine Company and, for the first time, sewing machines were sold under the name "White." By 1919, 7 percent of the annual production was in the newly introduced electric machines. In 1924 the company acquired the Domestic Sewing Machine Company and the King Sewing Machine Company of Buffalo. The King company had been a subsidiary of Sears, Roebuck and Company and furnished machines to them. In 1925 the companies were consolidated to form the White Sewing Machine Corporation. With this came a ten-year contract with Sears, Roebuck and Company to furnish their machines for a ten-year period. The White company continued to manufacture sewing machines in America through the 1960s. By 1974 the company had become White Consolidated Industries with the White Sewing Machine Company, a distributor for White machines manufactured in Japan. The Domestic Sewing Machine Company remained a subsidiary and continued to manufacture electric machines for home use in Cleveland, Ohio.

Willcox and Gibbs Sewing Machine Company. The Willcox and Gibbs company of New York City was one of the few from the 1850s — the first decade of sewing-machine manufacture — to survive the twentieth century. The family chainstitch machine that had been the company's strong seller was phased out of the active selling program in 1926 – 1927; however, production of this machine, which had changed very little in style from that of the 1860s and 1870s, was continued intermittently with the last lot being produced in 1946. The machines were always sold under the company name, although this style machine was copied by several other companies and sold under their names. Beginning in 1875, the Willcox and Gibbs company began to include manufacturing machines in their lines of production. The first one was the Chainstitch Visible Stitch Straw Hat Sewing Machine. It is believed to have been the first machine for stitching straw braids for the making of hats. For at least sixty years after its introduction, thousands of these machines were sold to the straw-hat industry throughout the world. This one was just the first of a long line of manufacturing machines which they continued to make. These machines included lockstitch ruffling machines, lockstitch long-arm tucking machines, zigzag machines, overlock machines, hosiery welting and trimming machines, feldlock machines, and the American version of the Cornely embroidery machines that were based on the Bonnaz patent. Embroidery sewing machines were their forte and one of their more unusual machines was the Uniart embroidery machine, which could make a stitch as long as ¾" and duplicate the diagonal stitching found only in hand embroidery. Shell scalloping machines and bag machines were also among their long list of specialized sewing machines. The Willcox and Gibbs company discontinued manufacture in 1973.

Singer Manufacturing Company. The Singer company had been one of the three successful ones from the early 1850s. By the late 1860s, it finally surpassed the Wheeler and Wilson company in production and sales; in 1905 – 1907 Singer bought out the company. With this acquisition, they added the manufacture of a rotary-bobbin machine to their vibrating shuttle machines. Singer chainstitch machines had been introduced in the last quarter of the nineteenth century and continued to be popular into the second and third decade of the 20th century. From the beginning, Singer produced heavy-duty manufacturing machines, and family machines were introduced after a few years. Both types of machines continued to be produced, the Singer name proudly displayed on each and every one. By the end of the nineteenth century, the Singer name was known around the world. A Singer manufacturing plant was located in Scotland, but agents were everywhere. Updated cabinets changed with the style and attempts to introduce an electric machine as early as 1889 are credited to the Singer company, but until electricity was commonly found in the household there was no great demand for the machine. The manufacturing machines were designed with special driving attachments so that they could be belted to the main source of power, whatever that might be. The wide variety of manufacturing machines included machines for harness and leather work, machines with two needles and two shuttles for canvas belting, bag machines, hat machines, overedge machines, buttonhole machines, and automatic button sewers. There were machines to stitch tents and wagon covers, to sew elastic banding, glove machines, special machines for darning and patching laundry nets, book and pamphlet machines, hemstitch machines, and long-arm and short-arm machines. The variety is endless. The major factories in the early decades of the 20th century were in Elizabeth, New Jersey, and Bridgeport, Connecticut, which was the old Wheeler and Wilson factory. The "Class 1w" machine produced in Bridgeport as late as 1925 was the same style as the Wheeler and Wilson sewing machine manufactured as early as the 1860s. It was still recommended for "fine lock stitching in the manufacture of shirts, collars, cuffs. . . ." The Singer company remains a very active one. Although many of their current machines are manufactured in foreign plants, some are still produced in the United States.

Appendix G

Sewing-Machine Name	Sewing-Machine Company
Abbott	National
A.B.C.	A.B.C. Machine Co. (1906—)
Abelone Furniture Co.	A. G. Mason Mfg. Co.
Abendale	National
Abenschule	National
Aberdeen	Davis
Abilene	White
Abney Machine Co.	A. G. Mason Mfg. Co.
Abrams Special	White
Absequis de la Colonia	Goodrich
Abstbuck Special	New Home
A. B. and W.	Davis
Acadia	Standard
Acme	Davis
Acme	National
Acme	Standard
Acme Rotary	National
Acrumann	A. G. Mason Mfg. Co.
Acworth	National
Adams	Davis
Adams	White
Adarondack	A. G. Mason Mfg. Co.
Adelaide	Davis
Adkins	A. G. Mason Mfg. Co.
Adla	Goodrich
Adlake	Goodrich
Admiral	Davis
Adrian Hardware Co.	A. G. Mason Mfg. Co.
Advance	Davis
Aero	Standard
Aetna New	National
Agriculturist	Standard
A Happy Home Maker	A. G. Mason Mfg. Co.
Aimsee	Davis
Ajax	Davis
Akron	Free
Alagame	Davis
Alamo City	National
Alaska	National
Albaugh Dover	National
Albenmarle	National
Alberta Peterson	Standard
Alberta Special	A. G. Mason Mfg. Co.
Albion	National
Alde	Standard
Alden	Standard
Alexander	A. G. Mason Mfg. Co.
Alexandria	Davis
Alfords	Davis
Alladin	National
Allday	A. G. Mason Mfg. Co.
Allens Queen	A. G. Mason Mfg. Co.
Alleys Special	Free
Alliance	Davis
Alliance	National
Allison	White
Allison Special	Free
Alma	National
Almacen San Miguel	National
Aloha	Davis
Alosh	Goodrich
Alpha	White
Al Ponetics de Liverpool	National
Alston	Standard
Alta	National
Alto	National
Alva	National
Always-Good	Davis
Always Ready	National
Alzira	White
Amazon	National
Amena	Standard
America	Standard
America	White
American	Davis
American	National
American Beauty	Davis
American Empire	National
American Junior	Standard
American Lady	National
American National	National
American, New	National
American Queen	Goodrich
American Rotary	National
American Standard	Standard
American Union	New Home
American Wonder	National
Americana	Standard
Americo	National
Amerikan	New Home
Amherest	Davis
Ami	Standard
Amidon Bros.	A. G. Mason Mfg. Co.
Amory How and Company	White
Amsler	White
Anchor	A. G. Mason Mfg. Co.
Anchor	White
Anderson	Davis
Anderson	Goodwich
Anderson (A, B, C)	Davis
Andrews	A. G. Mason Mfg. Co.
Andrus Rotary	White
Angelus	Davis
Anita	National
Annabelle	National
Anthracite	Standard
Antharcits	White
Antic	Goodrich
Antitrust	National
Antonio Castillero	Standard
Apartment	Free
Apax	Davis
Apeth	National
Apex	National
Appleton	New Home
Appolo	Free
Appolo	Standard
Apostulu Baptist	Standard
Arbest	New Home
Arbutus	A. G. Mason Mfg. Co.
Arcade	National
Arcade	Standard
Arcadia	A. G. Mason Mfg. Co.
Arey	A. G. Mason Mfg. Co.
Arganaut	Davis
Argote Lopez Co.	A. G. Mason Mfg. Co.
Argyle	Davis
Arkadelphia	A. G. Mason Mfg. Co.
Arlington	Davis
Arlington Anderson	Davis
Arlington Cash	Davis
Arlington Gem	National
Arlington Gem	Standard
Arlington Jewell	Davis
Arlington Queen	National
Armbrust	A. G. Mason Mfg. Co.
Armistead	White
Armour D	Standard
Arms	A. G. Mason Mfg. Co.
Armstrong	A. G. Mason Mfg. Co.
Arnold	A. G. Mason Mfg. Co.
Arnold Arrington	White
Arnold Overseam Sewing Machine	Standard
Arrow	National
Arrow	Standard
Art Superb	National
Artison	Standard
Ashland	National
Asia	White
Aston Special	A. G. Mason Mfg. Co.
Astor, The	Standard
Atchison	National
Athens	A. G. Mason Mfg. Co.
Atkins, The	A. G. Mason Mfg. Co.
Atlanta	National
Atlantic	Davis
Atlantic	Standard
Atlantis	New Home
Atlas	National
At-Will	Davis
Aubrey	White
Auburn	Free
Auburndale	Standard
Auerbach	National
August Junior	National
Aurora	Free
Austin Special	National
Austral	Standard
Austral, New	A. G. Mason Mfg. Co.
Austral Special	National
Auto, The	Free
Autocrat	National
Automatic Rotary	National
Automatic, The	Standard
Autostitch	National
Auto Trust	National
Avena	A. G. Mason Mfg. Co.
Avenue	White
Avery	Free
Avia	A. G. Mason Mfg. Co.
Aviator	Free
Avon	National
Avona	New Home
Baby Grand	Standard
Baca and Bohac	Standard
Bacha	Standard
Backer	Free
Bacon	A. G. Mason Mfg. Co.
Baddley	White
Badger	Badger, Fond du Lac, Wisconsin (1907)
Badt	National
Bailey	Goodrich
Baileys	White
Bain	Standard
Bain	White
Baker	Goodrich
Baldwin	Goodrich
Baldwin	Davis
Baldwin, New	Davis
Bale, N. Y.	A. G. Mason Mfg. Co.
Ball	White
Ball Bearing	White
Ballenger	Goodrich
Ballentinees	Standard
Balliet	National
Balinoral	National
Baltimore	National
Baltimore Special	Davis
Bamberger	Davis
Bamberger	White
Bancon	A. G. Mason Mfg. Co.
Banfield	Goodrich
Banks	White
Banner	Davis
Banner	National
Bannerman	National
Banques	Goodrich
Banta	National
Baptiste	Goodrich
Barbosa Coraceivich	National
Bardwell	White
Barfield	White
Barlow	A. G. Mason Mfg. Co.
Barnards	White
Barnes	A. G. Mason Mfg. Co.
Barnett	Davis
Barnett	White
Barringer	White
Barron	White
Barthalomew	White
Barthalomew	A. G. Mason Mfg. Co.
Bartigo Farmer	National
Bartlett	Davis
Bartlett	White
Bartlett Rotary	National
Bass	Free
Bastedor O Damode	National
Baston, D.Y., Cia	National
Bates	A. G. Mason Mfg. Co.
Batesville	National

Appendix G

Sewing-Machine Name	Sewing-Machine Company
Batron	White
Batrow	White
Batte Furniture Co.	A. G. Mason Mfg. Co.
Battermans	Free
Battermans Special	Free
Batiste Toledo	A. G. Mason Mfg. Co.
Baucan, C.	White
Bauerman	Davis
Bauermeister	Davis
Baumgarten	White
Baumgartner	White
Bauman	A. G. Mason Mfg. Co.
Baumert	White
Bauzon, Chas.	A. G. Mason Mfg. Co.
Baxendale	National
Baxter	Standard
Bayless	White
Bayounes	A. G. Mason Mfg. Co.
Bay State	Davis
Bazar	National
Beach	Davis
Beach	White
Beacon	National
Beacon Imperial	A. G. Mason Mfg. Co.
Beacor D	Davis
Beade, The	Standard
Beagle Hole	Standard
Beahm, Geo.	Standard
Bean	Standard
Bean Special	Free
Beance	National
Bear	Davis
Beardsley	White
Beasley Special	A. G. Mason Mfg. Co.
Beathe	Standard
Beattie Special	A. G. Mason Mfg. Co.
Beaumont	White
Beauty	Free
Beaver	National
Bebauer	Standard
Beck McK. Co.	White
Bedford	National
Beegle	Davis
Bee Hive	A. G. Mason Mfg. Co.
Bee Hive	Standard
Beesons	White
Beham	Standard
B. E. Harmon's Rotary	White
Behlmers	Standard
Behrenden	National
Behrens	A. G. Mason Mfg. Co.
Beigle	Davis
Beirne	Goodrich
Belair	National
Belanger	A. G. Mason Mfg. Co.
Belanger Special	Standard
Bel Isle	National
Bell	Goodrich
Bell Bergum	White
Bell Queen	National
Belle	National
Bellvge	Davis
Belmars	Standard
Belmead	National
Belmont	National
Belmont Special	Free
Belvidere	National
Belview	Goodrich
Ben Hur	Davis
Benjamin	Standard
Benjamin	National
Bennets Best	A. G. Mason Mfg. Co.
Bennita	National
Bentons Favorite	A. G. Mason Mfg. Co.
Benty	National
Benway Special	Free
Berkle	National
Berkley	National
Bershire Rotary	National
Berstrands	White
Berta	National
Bertha	Standard
Bertig Bros.	National
Berwick	Free
Bessie	Standard
Bessies	A. G. Mason Mfg. Co.
Bessies Best	National
Bession	A. G. Mason Mfg. Co.
Best, The	A. G. Mason Mfg. Co.
Bestor	Standard
Bethds	White
Betsy Ross	National
Betz	National
Beuleys	White
Beulah, The	National
Beverly	White
Biddle	Davis
Biddy	A. G. Mason Mfg. Co.
Bierchwals	A. G. Mason Mfg. Co.
Bierchwale	White
Biffor	Goodrich
Big Four	White
Big Sandy	A. G. Mason Mfg. Co.
Big Store	A. G. Mason Mfg. Co.
Biggs	A. G. Mason Mfg. Co.
Biggs and Hanslip	Standard
Billeand	A. G. Mason Mfg. Co.
Billedud	White
Bill Morris Co.	Standard
Bingham	Davis
Binghampton	Standard
Bishop Rotary	White
Bishop	A. G. Mason Mfg. Co.
Bishops Favorite	Standard
Bitkers	Free
Bitkers Favorite	Free
Bivens and Co.	A. G. Mason Mfg. Co.
Bixby and Cox	Standard
Blackburn	Free
Black Diamond	Standard
Blackey	A. G. Mason Mfg. Co.
Blackhawk	National
Blacknell	Standard
Black Leader	New Home
Blacks Reliable	A. G. Mason Mfg. Co.
Blacks Special	New Home
Blade	Davis
Blade	Goodrich
Blade, New	Goodrich
Blahm	White
Blank	A. G. Mason Mfg. Co.
Blanton	White
Blaunt	White
Blocks	National
Blocko	A. G. Mason Mfg. Co.
Blount and E	Standard
Blount Special	Standard
Blossom Hardware Co.	A. G. Mason Mfg. Co.
Blue Bell	Standard
Blue Bird Rotary	Davis
Blue Diamond	Standard
Blue Diamond	Goodrich
Blue Field	Goodrich
Blue Ribbon	Davis
Blue Ridge	National
Bluff City	National
Boans	National
Boanus	National
Boass	National
Bob Laflin	A. G. Mason Mfg. Co.
Bob Stanley	Goodrich
Boehm	A. G. Mason Mfg. Co.
Boetler Special	National
Boettcher	White
Boggs and Buhl	Standard
Bohn	Davis
Bollo Hardware Co.	A. G. Mason Mfg. Co.
Bolton	Goodrich
Bon March	Standard
Bon, The	Davis
Bonanza	A. G. Mason Mfg. Co.
Bonaventure	National
Bond, T., Co.	White
Bond, T., Hardware Co.	New Home
Bond	White
Bonia	New Home
Bon-I-Look	Standard
Bonita	National
Bonley	A. G. Mason Mfg. Co.
Bonner	Standard
Bonota	National
Boody Bros.	A. G. Mason Mfg. Co.
Booker	White
Boones Leader	A. G. Mason Mfg. Co.
Boose and Buhl	Standard
Booster	Goodrich
Booth	White
Booty	A. G. Mason Mfg. Co.
Borden City	National
BorgS	tandard
Borg Special	National
Boss, The	National
Boston	Davis
Boston A	Free
Boston Grand	National
Boston Rotary	Standard
Boston S	White
Boston Store Rotary	Standard
Bouaters	A. G. Mason Mfg. Co.
Bouers	White
Bouquett	Free
Bourland	White
Boutell	National
Bowen	White
Bowerman	A. G. Mason Mfg. Co.
Box Walter	A. G. Mason Mfg. Co.
Boyless	White
Bracht	White
Bracht Bros.	A. G. Mason Mfg. Co.
Bradbury	White
Bradford	Foley & Williams Mfg. Co.
Bradford	Goodrich
Bradley	A. G. Mason Mfg. Co.
Brady Bros.	A. G. Mason Mfg. Co.
Bramer	A. G. Mason Mfg. Co.
Bramlett	A. G. Mason Mfg. Co.
Bramor	National
Brant	Davis
Brasselton	A. G. Mason Mfg. Co.
Bread Winner	National
Breedys Best	National
Breham	Standard
Brenners Rotary	National
Brenton and H	A. G. Mason Mfg. Co.
Brewer A, B, C	Free
Brewer AE-BE-DE	National
Brewer Electric	National
Brewer Electric R	National
Brewer O-Keh	New Home
Brewer Rotary	White
Brewer Rotary E	National
Brickel	White
Bride	National
Briggs	White
Bright Star	National
Brigton	Davis
Brin	A. G. Mason Mfg. Co.
Brisco	National
Bristol	Goodrich
Britian	Davis
Broadway	Standard
Broadway	White
Broatbryay Special	National
Broken Arrow	Standard
Brock	White
Brodbents	White
Broes	White
Brooker	White
Brookly Edison Special	A. G. Mason Mfg. Co.
Brooklyn Queen	A. G. Mason Mfg. Co.

389

Appendix G

Sewing-Machine Name	Sewing-Machine Company
Brooks	White
Brooks Light Running	Standard
Brooks Special	Free
Brookshire	Goodrich
Browholm	White
Brown	A. G. Mason Mfg. Co.
Brown Special	Standard
Brownie	A. G. Mason Mfg. Co.
Browns	Davis
Browns	Standard
Bruce	A. G. Mason Mfg. Co.
Bruce	Free
Bruce	Standard
Bruce Rotary	White
Brumhall	Davis
Brunswick	National
Bry-Special	Davis
Bryan	A. G. Mason Mfg. Co.
Bryant	White
Brys	Goodrich
Brucker	A. G. Mason Mfg. Co.
Bucker	A. G. Mason Mfg. Co.
Buckey	Davis
Buckeye	Davis
Buckeye	Standard
Buckley Bros.	A. G. Mason Mfg. Co.
Budd	White
Buena	Davis
Buetners	National
Buffalo	Free
Buffalo	Goodrich
Buffalo Queen	National
Buffalo Special	Standard
Buhl	National
Bullock	White
Bunch	White
Bungalow	National
Bunker Hill	A. G. Mason Mfg. Co.
Bunnell Special	Goodrich
Bur Oak	National
Burchwale	National
Burdick 1-A	National
Burdick 2-B	Davis
Burdick 3-C	Household
Burdick 4-D	Free
Burg	Davis
Burgess Special	Free
Burgess, The	A. G. Mason Mfg. Co.
Burhart	White
Buris and K.	A. G. Mason Mfg. Co.
Burks	A. G. Mason Mfg. Co.
Burks	White
Burlington	National
Burnett	Goodrich
Burnetts Choice	National
Burns	A. G. Mason Mfg. Co.
Bur Oak	National
Burrleson	White
Burrous Gem	A. G. Mason Mfg. Co.
Burtis Bros.	White
Burton	National
Burton & Co.	White
Busbee	White
Bush	White
Busha Special	A. G. Mason Mfg. Co.
Buster Brown	A. G. Mason Mfg. Co.
Busy Bee	National
Busy Woman	National
Butler	Free
Butler Special	Free
Buttruff	A. G. Mason Mfg. Co.
Byron	Free
Byrson and G.	National
Bywater Special	A. G. Mason Mfg. Co.
Cabinet	National
Cables	New Home
Caborn	Goodrich
Cactus	Goodrich
Cadilac I	National
Cadilac 111	Standard
Caer	Davis
Caines Special	Standard
Calandric	Standard
Caldwell and L	A. G. Mason Mfg. Co.
Calfat	National
California	Goodrich
Callaway	Standard
Calumet	Free
Calyx	Standard
Calyx	White
Calyx Rotary	A. G. Mason Mfg. Co.
Cal-YX Rotary	White
Cambria	Davis
Cambridge	New Home
Cameo	Goodrich
Cameran	Goodrich
Cammilto	Free
Campania	Standard
Campbell	Standard
Campbells Gem	A. G. Mason Mfg. Co.
Cams Special	Standard
Canadian	National
Canadian Empire, The	National
Cannons	A. G. Mason Mfg. Co.
Canton	A. G. Mason Mfg. Co.
Capac Star	A. G. Mason Mfg. Co.
Cape Fear	Free
Capital	National
Capitol	A. G. Mason Mfg. Co.
Capitol	Standard
Capitola	Free
Car	National
Caraflor	White
Caraway	Standard
Cardoza	Davis
Cardozas	Goodrich
Carle	White
Carlin & F	Davis
Carlisle	A. G. Mason Mfg. Co.
Carlock and R	A. G. Mason Mfg. Co.
Carmelita	National
Carmicheal	National
Carnahan	Standard
Carnahan	A. G. Mason Mfg. Co.
Carney, The	A. G. Mason Mfg. Co.
Carnival	Davis
Carola	National
Carolina	National
Carolyn	White
Carpenter	White
Carr Bros.	White
Carr Special	National
Carrara	National
Carren	National
Carroll	Free
Carson Special	A. G. Mason Mfg. Co.
Carswell	Davis
Carter	Goodrich
Carthage Special	A. G. Mason Mfg. Co.
Carthagenian	Standard
Carycon	A. G. Mason Mfg. Co.
Casa Bicalko	A. G. Mason Mfg. Co.
Casa Eperanca	A. G. Mason Mfg. Co.
Casa Florenzeno	A. G. Mason Mfg. Co.
Cascade	Davis
Case, The	National
Cases	National
Cases Leader	National
Cash Department Store	Goodrich
Casino Special	Standard
Casses Number I	National
Cates	White
Cats	White
Causeway	Davis
Cayce Publishing Co.	Free
Cecil	A. G. Mason Mfg. Co.
Celeste	National
Celeste	A. G. Mason Mfg. Co.
Centenial	A. G. Mason Mfg. Co.
Centenial	Standard
Centerfield	Standard
Center and P.	A. G. Mason Mfg. Co.
Central City	Free
Central Methodist	National
Central Model	Goodrich
Centric	Standard
Centura	Davis
Century	Davis
Century Grand	National
Century Mtg. Co.	Free
Century Mfg. Co.	National
Century Rotary	White
Ceres	National
Chachere	Standard
Challenge	National
Challenge	Davis
Chamber, A. K.	A. G. Mason Mfg. Co.
Chamber Bar	National
Chamber Domestic	Goodrich
Chamber, New	Free
Chambert Rotary	White
Champion	National
Champlain	Standard
Chandler D. W.	Standard
Chaney	A. G. Mason Mfg. Co.
Chant and C.	National
Chappel, The	Free
Chapman	National
Charlotte	National
Charm	A. G. Mason Mfg. Co.
Charmer	National
Charmount, La	A. G. Mason Mfg. Co.
Charter Oak	Davis
Charter Oak	National
Chase City	National
Chatham	National
Chattanooga	Davis
Chautauqua	New Home
Cheerful Moment	National
Cheiftain	Davis
Chelsea	Davis
Cheming	Davis
Cherokee	A. G. Mason Mfg. Co.
Cherokee	Free
Chesapeake	National
Chester	White
Chicago	National
Chicago	Goodrich
Chief Wapello	Davis
Childress	A. G. Mason Mfg. Co.
Childs Special	National
Chiles	National
Chillico Hardware Co.	A. G. Mason Mfg. Co.
Chillicothe	White
Chimanco	National
China	National
Chinic	Davis
Chisms Leader	A. G. Mason Mfg. Co.
Chan	White
Christian Courier	National
Christie	National
Christine	A. G. Mason Mfg. Co.
Chronicle, New	National
Chronicle Premium	Goodrich
Chubert	Standard
Chum and B.	A. G. Mason Mfg. Co.
Cisco	Davis
Clarborn	Standard
Clarlender	National
Clark	Davis
Clark, F. S.	A. G. Mason Mfg. Co.
Clark, J. A.	Standard
Clarke Rotary	White
Class	A. G. Mason Mfg. Co.
Classic	National
Clauson and Wilson	A. G. Mason Mfg. Co.
Clays Special	National
Clayton	National
Clemons Bros.	A. G. Mason Mfg. Co.
Cleveland	Davis

Appendix G

Sewing-Machine Name	Sewing-Machine Company
Cleveland, The	Standard
Cleveland Gem	A. G. Mason Mfg. Co.
Cleveland Peerless	A. G. Mason Mfg. Co.
Clifford	National
Cliftoa	National
Cliftoa	Free
Climax	New Home
Clindison Special	National
Clipper	New Home
Clouer	A. G. Mason Mfg. Co.
Clover	Davis
Club, The	Standard
Cobbs	White
Cobbs Special	A. G. Mason Mfg. Co.
Cockran	National
Codgel Special	A. G. Mason Mfg. Co.
Coffee, J. W.	New Home
Coggins, B. F.	A. G. Mason Mfg. Co.
Coin, The	Free
Cohns	National
Cole	Standard
Cole Special	A. G. Mason Mfg. Co.
Coleberg	Free
Co-Lee	A. G. Mason Mfg. Co.
Collers	A. G. Mason Mfg. Co.
Collins	National
Colonial	Davis
Colonial	New Home
Colonial	Standard
Colonial House	National
Colonial Steinway	National
Colorado	Standard
Colquit	A. G. Mason Mfg. Co.
Columbia	Davis
Columbia	New Home
Columbia Record	National
Columbian	National
Columbine	Standard
Columbus	New Home
Columbus	Davis
Columbus, The	A. G. Mason Mfg. Co.
Columbus, R.	White
Columbus Special	National
Comanche	White
Combest	A. G. Mason Mfg. Co.
Comfort	A. G. Mason Mfg. Co.
Commander	Free
Commercial	Davis
Commercial	National
Commercial	Standard
Commercial Electric	New Home
Common Sense	A. G. Mason Mfg. Co.
Common Wealth	Davis
Common Wealth	Free
Companion City	National
Competition	National
Comstock Electric	New Home
Comus	National
Concha	A. G. Mason Mfg. Co.
Concordia	National
Concra	White
Conley	Standard
Conley	White
Conlon	White
Connells Leader	National
Connolly	White
Conover	Davis
Conover, B.	Davis
Conover, The	A. G. Mason Mfg. Co.
Conquest	National
Conquerer	National
Conshatter	Standard
Constitution	Goodrich
Constitution	National
Constitution Atlanta	Goodrich
Continental	National
Continental Rotary	National
Convery	White
Conway & Jordan	A. G. Mason Mfg. Co.
Coogans 20th Century	Standard
Cooks	A. G. Mason Mfg. Co.
Cooley, The	Standard
Coopers	A. G. Mason Mfg. Co.
Co-operative	A. G. Mason Mfg. Co.
Copeland	A. G. Mason Mfg. Co.
Copeland	National
Coquett	Standard
Corasco	Goodrich
Cords	White
Corinth	White
Corley	Goodrich
Corley, The	Standard
Corymer	White
Corn Belt	A. G. Mason Mfg. Co.
Cornelius	A. G. Mason Mfg. Co.
Cornell	Standard
Cornellys Leader	A. G. Mason Mfg. Co.
Corner, The	Standard
Cornerstone	National
Corola	Davis
Coronell	Davis
Coronet	Standard
Corrara	National
Corrolla	A. G. Mason Mfg. Co.
Correct	Free
Cosmo	New Home
Cosper	White
Cosseboom	Standard
Cottage	New Home
Cottage	National
Cottage Queen	New Home
Cotton	Standard
Couilliard	National
Coulson	Davis
Counters	Davis
Countess	A. G. Mason Mfg. Co.
Co-up	White
Courier	National
Courier Journal	National
Couan	A. G. Mason Mfg. Co.
Covington Co.	A. G. Mason Mfg. Co.
Cowell & S.	White
Cox	White
Coyne	Free
Craig	White
Craig Rotary	White
Cramer	White
Cranberry	Free
Crass	White
Craver & E	White
Crawcord	White
Crawford	Davis
Crawford	Standard
Crawford	White
Crawleys	White
Creed	White
Creedmoor	Standard
Cremo	White
Cresent	Davis
Cresent	Free
Cresent	Standard
Cresent	White
Crippin	Household
Criterion	National
Croley	White
Crook-Record	White
Crosby	White
Cross	A. G. Mason Mfg. Co.
Crown	A. G. Mason Mfg. Co.
Crown Jewell	Free
Crown Rotary	White
Crump	White
Crusader, The	Standard
Cruse, E.	A. G. Mason Mfg. Co.
Crutchen, C. M.	Standard
Cuba Libre	Standard
Cubana	Goodrich
Culler, W. C.	A. G. Mason Mfg. Co.
Culliman	Standard
Cullum, L. D.	A. G. Mason Mfg. Co.
Cumberland	Davis
Cumberland Special	Free
Cummings Special	A. G. Mason Mfg. Co.
Currie	A. G. Mason Mfg. Co.
Cutlers	Davis
Cuyahoga	A. G. Mason Mfg. Co.
Cuyahoga	Standard
Czar	Goodrich
D'Amour	National
Daffodil, The	National
Da Horn Sing	Davis
Dahlichs	A. G. Mason Mfg. Co.
Dailey and Co.	National
Dailey, W. S.	Standard
Daisey	Standard
Daisey	Davis
Daisey	Goodrich
Daisey	A. G. Mason Mfg. Co.
Dalay San Sords	White
Dallas, New	A. G. Mason Mfg. Co.
Dallas-W-Co	White
Dallier	White
Damascus	Standard
Damascus	National
Danake	National
Dandremon	Goodrich
Dandy	Goodrich
Dandy	New Home
Dandy, New	Standard
Dan Fords	White
Danforth	A. G. Mason Mfg. Co.
Dania	A. G. Mason Mfg. Co.
Daniels	A. G. Mason Mfg. Co.
Daniels	Standard
Danskeren	Goodrich
Danson	National
Darlington	National
Darner Bros.	White
Darrison	White
Daughtys	White
Duske's Pioneer	National
Dauntless	National
Dauntless	New Home
Dauphine	National
Davenport	National
Davidson	National
Davies	Davis
Davis	Davis
Davis, A. J.	White
Davis, A. J. Son	A. G. Mason Mfg. Co.
Davis, C. M.	White
Davis Rotary C. D. 1. 2.	National
Dawson Special	Free
Dawley 3	Goodrich
Day's Special	National
Dayton	Davis
Daytonia	Davis
Dean Special	A. G. Mason Mfg. Co.
Dean, The	Standard
Dearing	National
De Boren	National
Decatur	National
Decatur, The	Standard
Decora Special	National
Decorah Posten	National
Defender	A. G. Mason Mfg. Co.
Defiance	Davis
Defiance	Standard
Defiance	National
De Kahl	A. G. Mason Mfg. Co.
Delamer Elect	National
Delanorton	Goodrich
Delaplane	White
Delaware	Davis
Delia	Standard
Delight	Davis
Delight	Free
Delight	National
Delmar	National
Delong	White

391

Appendix G

Sewing-Machine Name	Sewing-Machine Company
Delphia	Free
Delta	Free
Deluxe	National
Demerest Dry Co.	White
De Morley	National
Democrat	National
Dempsters	National
Den	National
Den Dansko	National
Denholm	Standard
Dennis	A. G. Mason Mfg. Co.
Dennis Special	Davis
Dennison	National
Dentz	A. G. Mason Mfg. Co.
Denver	Davis
Denver	National
Denver	Standard
Departure	National
Dependable	Standard
De Sola	National
De Sota	National
Despatch	National
Detonia	Davis
Detroit	National
Devereaux	National
Deverlax	White
Devon	National
Dewey	A. G. Mason Mfg. Co.
Dewey, The	Standard
De-Will Co.	White
Dewitt	National
Dey's	White
Diabolo	White
Diamond	National
Diamond D	Standard
Diamond-Models	National
Diamond Royal	Free
Diana	National
Dickson	A. G. Mason Mfg. Co.
Dietzel	A. G. Mason Mfg. Co.
Dispatch	A. G. Mason Mfg. Co.
Dittenger	A. G. Mason Mfg. Co.
Ditzell Imp.	National
Ditzer	National
Dixie	Davis
Dixie	Free
Dixie	National
Dixie	Standard
Dixie Automatic	New Home
Dixie Queen	National
Dixon	White
Dobie Special	New Home
Dobbs	A. G. Mason Mfg. Co.
Dodge Rotary	National
Dodds	A. G. Mason Mfg. Co.
Dodge and Watson	Standard
Dodson and Rice	Standard
Dome Rotary	National
Domestic Buffalo	Domestic
Domestic, New	Goodrich
Domestic, Old	Goodrich
Domestic Rotary	Domestic
Domestic Science	National
Dominion	National
Dominion, The	Free
Donaldson's Rotary	White
Donalds Special	A. G. Mason Mfg. Co.
Donohue, T.	White
Dorcas	National
Dorcas	A. G. Mason Mfg. Co.
Dormer	A. G. Mason Mfg. Co.
Dorothea	A. G. Mason Mfg. Co.
Dorroh-K Co.	White
Dorsey	A. G. Mason Mfg. Co.
Dosenuna	Standard
Dotheron	Standard
Doty	Free
Douglas	National
Douglas	A. G. Mason Mfg. Co.
Downes	Standard
Downes	A. G. Mason Mfg. Co.
Drake	National
Drennen	A. G. Mason Mfg. Co.
Dressmaker	National
Dreus and Crens	Standard
DrisKell	A. G. Mason Mfg. Co.
Droyer	National
Druid	National
Dryden	White
Duchess	National
Duchess	A. G. Mason Mfg. Co.
Duhon	White
Duker	National
Dulitz C	Standard
Du Lux	Goodrich
Dumore	National
Duncan	A. G. Mason Mfg. Co.
Dundee	Standard
Dunham	Davis
Dunklins	A. G. Mason Mfg. Co.
Dunlaps Gem	A. G. Mason Mfg. Co.
Duplex	National
Duplex Rotary	White
Du Quesne	Free
Durant	A. G. Mason Mfg. Co.
Durgan	White
Durham	Household
Durrell	A. G. Mason Mfg. Co.
Durrett	White
Duskell	A. G. Mason Mfg. Co.
Duske's Pioneer	National
Duval	Goodrich
Duyer	Goodrich
Dutchess	National
Dyson	White
Eagle	Standard
Eagle	Standard
Eagle Rotary	White
Eaines	Goodrich
Earl	National
Earlham	National
Easley and D	White
Eastaluchia	Standard
Eastern	National
Easy Rotary	White
Eatonia	National
Eberhart and B.	White
Eberian Flyer	Standard
Eblem	White
Eclipse	Davis
Eclipse	White
Eclipse	New Home
Economist	White
Economy	National
Economy	Domestic
Economy	New Home
Economy Rotary	Domestic
Eddy	White
Edgemere	National
Edgmore	Goodrich
Edgwater	Standard
Edgwood	Standard
Edison A, B, C, D, E, F, G	Goodrich
Edison, The	Standard
Edison Rotary	Standard
Edison Rotary	White
Edwards	Davis
Edwards	White
Edwards, The	Free
Edwards & Bradford	National
Efficient	Davis
Ehlert	White
Elbeco	Davis
Elberta	National
Elbin	Free
El-Carreo	Standard
El-Cente Merco	A. G. Mason Mfg. Co.
El-Center	A. G. Mason Mfg. Co.
Elcock	White
El-Diamante	Goodrich
Eldorado	National
Eldoro	Standard
Eldredge	National
Eldredge Rotary	National
Eldredge 2-spool	National
Eldson	Free
Eldson Imperial	Free
Eld, The	National
Electric	Davis
Electric, The	New Home
Electric City	National
Electric Supply Company	New Home
El-Galto	National
El-Genio	National
Elgin	Davis
Elgin, The	Free
El-Globo	National
El-Hagar	A. G. Mason Mfg. Co.
Elherta	National
Eliasburg	White
Elia	National
Elite	Free
Elite	National
Elite Rotary	White
Elizabeth	A. G. Mason Mfg. Co.
Elkhart	White
Elkins	A. G. Mason Mfg. Co.
Elienhurst	National
Ellens Tar	A. G. Mason Mfg. Co.
Elliot	Standard
Elliot	White
Elliptic	National
Ellis	Standard
Ellis	White
Ellis Store Co.	National
El-Louvre	A. G. Mason Mfg. Co.
Elly	National
Elma	National
Elmira	National
Eimo	Standard
Elmore, New	National
El-Niagra	National
El-Nico	A. G. Mason Mfg. Co.
El-Nouvre	A. G. Mason Mfg. Co.
El-Nueva Coique	Standard
El-Parrae	A. G. Mason Mfg. Co.
Elpico	White
El-Ralampage	Standard
Eiro	National
Elsie	Standard
El-Singer Fatma	Standard
El-Sol Telkart	National
Elva	National
Elwess	National
Ely	Unknown
Emblem	New Home
Emerson	National
Emilia	White
Ernma	National
Emmons	National
Emperor	White
Empire	Davis
Empire	New Home
Empire State	A. G. Mason Mfg. Co.
Emporium	Goodrich
Empress	Davis
Empress	Free
Endora	National
Enfield	A. G. Mason Mfg. Co.
England	National
Englewood	National
English	White
Enterprise	National
Enterprise Rotary	White
Envoy	National
Eopanola	White
Epworth	New Home
Era	National
Era	Goodrich

Appendix G

Sewing-Machine Name	Sewing-Machine Company
Erie	National
Erie Special	Standard
Ermine	National
Erwin	White
Essex	Davis
Essex	A. G. Mason Mfg. Co.
Estell	A. G. Mason Mfg. Co.
Estey, New	National
Euclid	Standard
Euclid	White
Eudora	National
Eunice Hdw.	White
Eureka	Davis
Eureka	New Home
Evangelistern	Goodwich
Evans	National
Everett, The	National
Evergood A, B, C, D, E	National
Everhart	White
Ever Ready	Foley & Williams
Ever Ready	Goodrich
Everybodys	Standard
Everybodys	White
Everyday Life	Free
Excella	White
Excellent	National
Excellent	Standard
Excello	Free
Excells	Free
Excelsior	Davis
Excelsior	National
Excelsior	New Home
Excelsior	Standard
Expert	New Home
Expert	Standard
Fair	Davis
Fairbanks	Davis
Fairbanks	White
Fairlay	Standard
Fair, The	A. G. Mason Mfg. Co.
Fairy	National
Fairview	National
Fait, H.	National
Faithtul Friend	Household
Falcon	New Home
Falcous Gem	National
Fallow	White
Falls City	Free
Falls City	Standard
Fambro	White
Fanieron	Davis
Family Favorite	New Home
Family Friend	National
Family Grand	National
Family Jewel	National
Family, New	A. G. Mason Mfg. Co.
Family Pride	National
Family Queen	Standard
Family Rotary	White
Famous	Davis
Famous	National
Famous	Standard
Famous Bar	White
Farm & Ranch	National
Farmers Alliance	National
Farmers Bride	A. G. Mason Mfg. Co.
Farmers Friend	A. G. Mason Mfg. Co.
Farmer's Guide	National
Farmers Review	Davis
Farmers Rotary	A. G. Mason Mfg. Co.
Farmerson	Davis
The Farmer's Superior Rotary	White
Farmers Supply Co.	A. G. Mason Mfg. Co.
Farmers Union	National
Farmers Voice	Standard
Farro Special	A. G. Mason Mfg. Co.
Fashion	Davis
Fashion	Free
Fashion	Standard
Fashion, New	A. G. Mason Mfg. Co.
Faultless	Free
Faultless	National
Faultless	Standard
Faust	White
Favorite	Davis
Favorite	New Home
Favorite	Standard
Favorite	White
Fawl-Kas	White
Fayette	National
Feather	Household
Ferde Dc Siecle	Goodrich
Fergeson	A. G. Mason Mfg. Co.
Ferrell	White
Ferris	Standard
Fessinger	A. G. Mason Mfg. Co.
Fewells	National
Fidelity	A. G. Mason Mfg. Co.
Fielden	White
Fields	A. G. Mason Mfg. Co.
Fields Rotary	A. G. Mason Mfg. Co.
Fienstein	National
Fife	Goodrich
Fikes	White
Films Favorite	Goodrich
Fingers	White
Finglestein	Free
Finkestein	Unknown
Finkle and Lyon	A. G. Mason Mfg. Co.
Finklesstein	White
Finney	White
Fireside	Davis
Fireside	New Home
Firk Special	A. G. Mason Mfg. Co.
Fischer	New Home
Fischer	Standard
Fischer	White
Fish	White
Fitche Special	Standard
Fitzgerald	Standard
Fitzgerald	A. G. Mason Mfg. Co.
Flag	Standard
Flanigan	Davis
Flanniggin Favorite	A. G. Mason Mfg. Co.
Flaurn	White
Fletwood	A. G. Mason Mfg. Co.
Fletcher	National
Flint	A. G. Mason Mfg. Co.
Florals	National
Flor De Maio	A. G. Mason Mfg. Co.
Flor De Dora	National
Florence	A. G. Mason Mfg. Co.
Florence Rotary	White
Florence Special	A. G. Mason Mfg. Co.
Florence Vib.	New Home
Florida	National
Flyer, The	Standard
F. M. Rotary	White
Foerste	Standard
Footway, The	National
Forbes Best	A. G. Mason Mfg. Co.
Forbes S. G.	Standard
Forbis	White
Ford	National
Forest City	National
Forest City	Standard
Forester	White
Forlows	White
Formon, D. H.	A. G. Mason Mfg. Co.
Forrester R.	White
Forsythes	White
Fort Henry	National
Fort Worth	Davis
Fort Worth Record	National
Forward	A. G. Mason Mfg. Co.
Foster	Goodrich
Fountain	Davis
Four Hundred, The	Standard
Fowles, J. G.	A. G. Mason Mfg. Co.
Foy and Gibson	White
Fram A	National
Francis	A. G. Mason Mfg. Co.
Francis Wallard	National
Franenthal	White
Franklin	National
Franklin	White
Franklin Bros.	White
Franklin Hand A	Davis
Franklin, The	National
Franks	Davis
Free	Free
Free Lock Stitch	Free
Free Press	Standard
Free Silver	Standard
Free Trade	New Home
French, H	National
French and Bassett	Free
Fricke	White
Frictionless	Davis
Friday	National
Friend	White
Frisbis	White
Frontier	Free
Frozen Dog	Goodrich
Fulga Brothers	National
Full Dinner Pail	National
Fuller	National
Fullmer	A. G. Mason Mfg. Co.
Full Wide	A. G. Mason Mfg. Co.
Fulner	White
Fulton	Davis
Fulton	National
Furgeson	White
Furtick	Standard
Furney	A. G. Mason Mfg. Co.
Furs	Standard
Futz	White
Gable	A. G. Mason Mfg. Co.
Gaddis	A. G. Mason Mfg. Co.
Gail	Davis
Gaines	White
Gainsborough	National
Galeusky	White
Galicy Polski	Standard
Galloway	National
Galveston, New	National
Gamoriel	National
Ganda	National
Gannon	National
Garden City	Davis
Garden City	National
Gardener Queen	A. G. Mason Mfg. Co.
Gariey	A. G. Mason Mfg. Co.
Garland	Davis
Garland	New Home
Garland	Standard
Garlicks	Standard
Garlington	White
Garrens	A. G. Mason Mfg. Co.
Garry	White
Garuer	White
Garvin	A. G. Mason Mfg. Co.
Garvis	A. G. Mason Mfg. Co.
Gary	A. G. Mason Mfg. Co.
Gastonia	A. G. Mason Mfg. Co.
Gates	Unknown
Gates City	Free
Gates City Turn Co	Free
Gaucha	National
Gauger	National
Gayiety	National
Gaylor	National
Gayosa	National
Gazell	Goodrich
Geitz Rotary	White
Gellers	Davis
Gem	Davis
Gem	Free
Gem City	National
Genesee	National

393

Appendix G

Sewing-Machine Name	Sewing-Machine Company
Genesee	Standard
Geneva	National
Georgia	Davis
Georgia Hardware Co.	A. G. Mason Mfg. Co.
Gerald	A. G. Mason Mfg. Co.
Gerekes, J. S.	Free
Germeths Favorite	Standard
Germania	National
Germania	Goodrich
Gertrude	Standard
Gholston	A. G. Mason Mfg. Co.
Gibbon	National
Gibson	White
Gignilliant	Standard
Gilbert Queen	A. G. Mason Mfg. Co.
Gillespic and M.	Standard
Gillespic, New	National
Gills	White
Gilmore, H, C, A, B	Free
Gimbel	Davis
Gimbel	A. G. Mason Mfg. Co.
Gimbel Bros.	Standard
Gimbel Rotary	White
Gimbel Special	National
Ginger Loderna	Standard
Ginsburg	Davis
Girard	Free
Gladiator	Davis
Glaciator	A. G. Mason Mfg. Co.
Glasgow	Goodrich
Glass Block	Goodrich
Glasser	National
Gler Miller	Davis
Glern	A. G. Mason Mfg. Co.
Glenn Rotary	White
Glen Oak	National
Glenwood	A. G. Mason Mfg. Co.
Globe	National
Globe	David
Globela	National
Glock Special	Standard
Glod Flash	White
Gloria	Davis
Gloria	White
Gloria Rotary	White
Glorioso	A. G. Mason Mfg. Co.
Goerke	White
Goerke Rotary	White
Goldberg	A. G. Mason Mfg. Co.
Goldberg's Rotary	White
Goldbound	Standard
Gold City	National
Gold Dust	National
Gold Eagle	Goodrich
Gold Hibbard	Davis
Goldmans	White
Gold Medal	National
Gold Medal Rotary	National
Gold Mohr	New Home
Goldsmith	Free
Golden Eagle	National
Golden Giant	A. G. Mason Mfg. Co.
Goldenrod	Goodrich
Golden Rule	Davis
Golden Star	A. G. Mason Mfg. Co.
Golden West	National
Gooch	White
Goodes	Standard
Good Luck	National
Goodness	A. G. Mason Mfg. Co.
Goodman	A. G. Mason Mfg. Co.
Goodnuf	A. G. Mason Mfg. Co.
Goodsich	Goodrich
Goodson	A. G. Mason Mfg. Co.
Goodyear	Goodrich
Gordon Favorite	Standard
Gores Best	A. G. Mason Mfg. Co.
Gorman	A. G. Mason Mfg. Co.
Goshen	National
Gosnells	A. G. Mason Mfg. Co.
Gospel Adv.	National
Gospel News	Standard
Goss and Wake	Standard
Gossett	Standard
Gossett Special	A. G. Mason Mfg. Co.
Gourlay	Standard
Courlay, New	A. G. Mason Mfg. Co.
Gourley	Davis
Govenor	New Home
Gracie	Standard
Graciosa	National
Grafton	National
Gragard	A. G. Mason Mfg. Co.
Graham	Goodrich
Granada Stores	National
Grand	Davis
Grand	Goodrich
Grand	National
Grand Bazaar	A. G. Mason Mfg. Co.
Grand Bulletin	National
Grand Bulletin	Goodrich
Grand Leader	Goodrich
Grand Leader	Standard
Grand Pacific	National
Grand Rotary	National
Grand Rotary	Standard
Grand Union	Davis
Grand Union	National
Grand Union	Standard
Grand Union	A. G. Mason Mfg. Co.
Grange	National
Granger	White
Grange Store	White
Granite State	Standard
Granore	Goodrich
Grant, The	Davis
Grant	Standard
Grant's Gem	A. G. Mason Mfg. Co.
Grass	A. G. Mason Mfg. Co.
Gray	A. G. Mason Mfg. Co.
Grays	White
Grayums	White
Great Northern	Goodrich
Great Western	Free
Greeacre	Standard
Greeg	A. G. Mason Mfg. Co.
Greeman	Unknown
Green	White
Greenbuck	Davis
Greenwood	National
Gregg	White
Grempezuski	A. G. Mason Mfg. Co.
Grenada	A. G. Mason Mfg. Co.
Gretchen	A. G. Mason Mfg. Co.
Gresco-F Co.	White
Greyhound	New Home
Griffin	National
Griffith	National
Gross Special	A. G. Mason Mfg. Co.
Gruene	White
Grander	White
Gualtney-U Co.	White
Guanoco	White
Guarantee	A. G. Mason Mfg. Co.
Guard	Free
Guernsey	Standard
Guggenheimer	A. G. Mason Mfg. Co.
Guide	Free
Guilford	National
Guillett	White
Guiterrez and N.	White
Gulf City	Free
Gulf Queen	Davis
Gunnell	A. G. Mason Mfg. Co.
Gunton	Standard
Guthrie	White
Guthrie	A. G. Mason Mfg. Co.
Guyler	National
Gwaltney, U.	A. G. Mason Mfg. Co.
Gypsy	National
Harvey, The	National
Harvester	White
Harwell	White
Haserot	Standard
Haskett	A. G. Mason Mfg. Co.
Haspador	Davis
Haus	Davis
Haverty Special A, B, C	Free
Hawisha	National
Hawishe	National
Hawkeye	Davis
Hawkeye	Foley & Williams Mfg. Co.
Hawkeye	Goodrich
Hayden	Free
Hazard	A. G. Mason Mfg. Co.
Hazel	National
Hazelhurst	White
Hde. Sol and Co.	National
Hearthstone	National
Heathwood	Standard
Heffner-D	White
Hefron	Free
Hegus, The	Free
Heinz	White
Heinenway	White
Heinrich	Davis
Helaingoford	White
Hellweil	A. G. Mason Mfg. Co.
Helping Hand	National
Helpmuth	A. G. Mason Mfg. Co.
Helsingsfors	A. G. Mason Mfg. Co.
Hemingways	Standard
Henderson	Davis
Henderson	Standard
Henderson, B.	Davis
Henderson certified D	Davis
Heneger	A. G. Mason Mfg. Co.
Henrico	National
Henrietta	Davis
Henwood	Standard
Henry	White
Hepperle	White
Herald	Free
Herbert	White
Herbert, H	Standard
Hercules	National
Herder	A. G. Mason Mfg. Co.
Herman	A. G. Mason Mfg. Co.
Hermitage	National
Herpolscheimer	National
Herrick	A. G. Mason Mfg. Co.
Herrington	A. G. Mason Mfg. Co.
Hesplin	A. G. Mason Mfg. Co.
Heurietta	White
Hewitt	A. G. Mason Mfg. Co.
Heydes Star	A. G. Mason Mfg. Co.
Heydes, The	National
Hgnemans	White
Hiawatha	National
Hibbard	National
Hicks	A. G. Mason Mfg. Co.
Hickory	National
Higginbothan	A. G. Mason Mfg. Co.
Higgins	A. G. Mason Mfg. Co.
High A Family	A. G. Mason Mfg. Co.
High A Victoria	National
Hightburg	National
Hillman	Standard
Hills	Goodrich
Hines	Standard
Hines, The	National
Hinson	A. G. Mason Mfg. Co.
Hinton	A. G. Mason Mfg. Co.
Hitchcock	National
Hjort	White
Hobert	Davis
Hochschild	Standard
Hodde	White
Hoddes	Standard
Hoffman	Standard

Sewing-Machine Name	Sewing-Machine Company
Hackett	National
Harketo Beauty	National
Hadda	A. G. Mason Mfg. Co.
Hagedorn	White
Hager	Davis
Haggard	White
Haines, O. S.	Goodrich
Haines, New	Goodrich
Hairs	White
Halcod	White
Halcomb	White
Haico Rotary	White
Halcyon	Davis
Hales Special	Davis
Hale, The	National
Haleys	White
Hall	A. G. Mason Mfg. Co.
Halley	Standard
Halls Favorite	A. G. Mason Mfg. Co.
Halls Special	Standard
Halls, The	National
Halsey Rotary	White
Hambro-wall	White
Hamilton	Davis
Hamilton	Goodrich
Hamilton	Standard
Hamilton	White
Hammond	A. G. Mason Mfg. Co.
Hampton	Standard
Hampton, C. L.	A. G. Mason Mfg. Co.
Hancock	A. G. Mason Mfg. Co.
Handy	National
Handy	Standard
Handy Sewer	National
Hannie	Standard
Hanson	Standard
Hanson Choice	Free
Hansons	White
Hantic Morn	Standard
Hapgood	Goodrich
HA. Philadelphia	Davis
HA Philadelphia Singer	Standard
Happy Hearts	Goodrich
Happy Hearts	National
Happy Home	New Home
Harbours	White
Harde and G.	White
Hardin	White
Hardine	Standard
Hardis	A. G. Mason Mfg. Co.
Hardison	A. G. Mason Mfg. Co.
Hardy	Standard
Hargets	Standard
Harris	White
Harkeys	A. G. Mason Mfg. Co.
Harlana	Standard
Harley-P.	White
Harmack	Davis
Harman	White
Harold	National
Harper	National
Harris	Davis
Harris	White
Harrison	National
Harrison	Standard
Harry's Special	Free
Hart	A. G. Mason Mfg. Co.
Hartberg	A. G. Mason Mfg. Co.
Hartberger	White
Hartford, New	National
Hartman	National
Hartman	Standard
Hartman	White
Hartmere	Standard
Hartin	National
Harvard	Davis
Harvard	Free
Harvard	A. G. Mason Mfg. Co.
Harvard	White
Harverty A, B, C	Free
Hoffman	White
Hoffman Daisy	Free
Holcomb	A. G. Mason Mfg. Co.
Holcyon	Davis
Holden	A. G. Mason Mfg. Co.
Holds Flyer	Standard
Holland	A. G. Mason Mfg. Co.
Holliday	Free
Holman	National
Holmes	White
Holmes, New	Standard
Homan	Davis
Homan	Standard
Home	Davis
Home	Standard
Home Circle	National
Home Comfort	National
Home Favorite	National
Home Journal	Free
Home Leader	National
Home Pride	National
Home Queen	Unknown
Home and Farm OS	National
Homer	National
Homer Fritz	Standard
Homers	National
Homers Bride	A. G. Mason Mfg. Co.
Homestead	Free
Homestead Rotary	National
Homewood	Goodrich
Honey Cutt	A. G. Mason Mfg. Co.
Honeymoon	Davis
Hong Yuen Co.	Standard
Honor Bright	Goodrich
Hooker	A. G. Mason Mfg. Co.
Hooper	Standard
Hooper	White
Hoosier Standard	Standard
Hoover	A. G. Mason Mfg. Co.
Hope, New	Davis
Hopkins	Free
Hordernia	White
Horner	White
Horn, W. W.	A. G. Mason Mfg. Co.
Horton	White
Ho-se-ma	New Home
Hospodor	National
Hot Kutter	National
Hotpoint Rotary	White
Houghton	Standard
Hourely	White
Housan	Standard
Household	Houshold
Household Leader	Free
Household Pride	Free
Household Queen	National
Household Star	Free
Household Supply Co.	National
Housemaid	National
Houseman	A. G. Mason Mfg. Co.
Housemate	New Home
Housemate Special	Standard
Housemate	Standard
Housewife	National
Houston	Standard
Houston Bros	A. G. Mason Mfg. Co.
Houston Post	Goodrich
Howard	National
Howe	White
Howe, Imp.	Standard
Howe Modern	A. G. Mason Mfg. Co.
Howe Rotary	Standard
Howe Special	Standard
Howell	White
Howland	Davis
Howry	White
Hoye	White
Hudgkins	New Home
Hudson	New Home
Hudson	Standard
Hudson	White
Hueffner	White
Hughes	Standard
Huh Special	Davis
Huletts	White
Hull and Dutton	Standard
Hulse	National
Humberts	White
Humble Pride	White
Humeycutt	White
Hummer	Davis
Hummer	A. G. Mason Mfg. Co.
Humming Bird	Davis
Hunter	White
Huntington	Free
Hues M. Guerro	National
Huos	White
Hurley's Rotary	White
Hurson	Davis
Husband and Patrandry	A. G. Mason Mfg. Co.
Husvennen	National
Hustler	Free
Hyde	White
Hyde Park	Free
Hyman	Standard
Ida	Standard
Idaho	National
Idea	National
Ideal	Davis
Ideal	White
Ideal, New	New Home
Ideal R.	White
Iiola	White
Imperial	Davis
Imperial	New Home
Imperial Beacon	A. G. Mason Mfg. Co.
Imperial Chataqua	Free
Imperial Columbian	National
Imperial Howe	Standard
Improved Howe	Standard
Improved Model	Goodrich
Improved New Leader	New Leader
Improved Royal	Free
Improved Southern	National
Improved Spokand	A. G. Mason Mfg. Co.
Improved Tropp	A. G. Mason Mfg. Co.
Improved Vasar	Free
Impsasttone	Davis
Index	Davis
Index	National
Indiana	Davis
Indiana Farmer	National
Indianapolis Sentinel	Davis
Industrious Hen	A. G. Mason Mfg. Co.
Ingle	A. G. Mason Mfg. Co.
Ingle	White
Ingliss	Standard
Inland Farmer 4	National
Innes, The	Standard
Insurgent	Davis
International	Davis
International	New Home
Inter Ocean	National
Invader	National
Invicible	Standard
Invocation	National
Ioma	National
Iowa I	National
Iowa II	Davis
Iowa IV	Standard
Iowa Queen	National
Iracema	White
Iracena	Standard
Iraquos	Standard
Irian Bros.	White
Ironton	National
Italia	White
Itta-Bena	White
Ivanhoe	Standard
Iver Johnson	A. G. Mason Mfg. Co.

Appendix G

SEWING-MACHINE NAME	SEWING-MACHINE COMPANY
Iverness	Davis
Iver, The	A. G. Mason Co.
I.X.L.	National
Jack e	Goodrich
Jackson	Davis
Jackson	Free
Jackson	Standard
Jackson Special	National
James	Standard
James	White
Jam e	Standard
Jamison	Standard
Jarman	White
Jasper	Standard
Jasnaik	A. G. Mason Mfg. Co.
Jathis	A. G. Mason Mfg. Co.
Jay Grand	White
Jeans	A. G. Mason Mfg. Co.
Jefferson	National
Jeffrenoun	Standard
Jeicel	A. G. Mason Mfg. Co.
Jell co	White
Jennings	New Home
Jerome	National
Jens, O. H.	National
Jetters Gem	A. G. Mason Mfg. Co.
Jettinghoff and B	A. G. Mason Mfg. Co.
Jewell	Davis
Jnusis	A. G. Mason Mfg. Co.
Jewell, The	New Home
Jewell	A. G. Mason Mfg. Co.
Jnusines	National
Joekel	A. G. Mason Mfg. Co.
Johnson	A. G. Mason Mfg. Co.
Johson	Davis
Joli	Standard
Jones	Standard
Jones	A. G. Mason Mfg. Co.
Jonesboro	Free
Jordan Brothers Rotary	White
Josefaal	Standard
Joseph	A. G. Mason Mfg. Co.
Joske	National
Jowick	White
Journal	National
Joy	A. G. Mason Mfg. Co.
Jubilee	White
Judas	Goodrich
Judel	A. G. Mason Mfg. Co.
June, H. A.	Goodrich
Juno	Davis
Juno	Goodrich
Kaczer	A. G. Mason Mfg. Co.
Kaeppel	A. G. Mason Mfg. Co.
Kahn's Pride	Standard
Kalamazoo	Davis
Kalamazoo	White
Kamp	Standard
Kanawha	National
Kane Special	A. G. Mason Mfg. Co.
Kangaroo	Standard
Kangroo	White
Kanokla	Goodrich
Kansas	A. G. Mason Mfg. Co.
Kansas City	Davis
Kansas Farmer	National
Kantank	Free
Kantauk	Free
Karrs Special	A. G. Mason Mfg. Co.
Kasharek	White
Kasparek	Free
Kaufman A, B, C, D	National
Kavanaugh	Free
Kay-Bee	White
Kearl's Special	A. G. Mason Mfg. Co.
Keasler	White
Keech	Free
Keen-Edge	Davis
Keen Klipper	Standard
Keesling	White
Keiser	A. G. Mason Mfg. Co.
Kellers	A. G. Mason Mfg. Co.
Kelly	Davis
Kelly, S. R.	White
Kempisky	Standard
Kendrick	Davis
Kendrick Special	A. G. Mason Mfg. Co.
Kenmore	Standard
Kennedy	Standard
Kennedy	A. G. Mason Mfg. Co.
Ken Quality	New Home
Kensington	National
Kensley	A. G. Mason Mfg. Co.
Kent	Goodrich
Kenton	Davis
Kentucky	National
Kentucky	Standard
Kentucky Beauty	Standard
Kentucky Gem	National
Kentucky Queen	National
Kenwood	National
Kenwood	Standard
Kenyon, M. S.	Standard
Kerris Special	A. G. Mason Mfg. Co.
Kerr Kesterson	White
Keystone	A. G. Mason Mfg. Co.
Kibbers	Goodrich
Kiesee	White
Kilgore	A. G. Mason Mfg. Co.
Kilian B	Standard
Kimble	A. G. Mason Mfg. Co.
Kimbrough	A. G. Mason Mfg. Co.
Kinerys Star	A. G. Mason Mfg. Co.
King	National
King Bee	Free
King Buffalo	New Domestic
King Cotton	Davis
King Ford	National
King land	National
King, New	Davis
King Perfection	National
King Star	A. G. Mason Mfg. Co.
King Sterling	National
King, The	Standard
King Wizard	National
Kingsford	Goodrich
Kingston	National
Kingsville	A. G. Mason Mfg. Co.
Kion San Son	National
Kipp	A. G. Mason Mfg. Co.
Kirby	A. G. Mason Mfg. Co.
Kirk	A. G. Mason Mfg. Co.
Kirkcaldies	Standard
Kirkman	A. G. Mason Mfg. Co.
Kirkpatrick	A. G. Mason Mfg. Co.
Kirk, The	Standard
Kirkwood	Goodrich
Kitchener	White
Kitrell Gem	A. G. Mason Mfg. Co.
Klains Special	A. G. Mason Mfg. Co.
Klein	A. G. Mason Mfg. Co.
Klotes	A. G. Mason Mfg. Co.
Knabe	Davis
Knapps	Goodrich
Kneuaman	A. G. Mason Mfg. Co.
Knickerbocker	Free
Kniffins	A. G. Mason Mfg. Co.
Knight	A. G. Mason Mfg. Co.
Knor II	Standard
Knox	Free
Knox Special	White
Kobacker	National
Koenic	White
Kokoya	Standard
Kolgina	Free
Konitzky	Free
Kooken, J. T.	A. G. Mason Mfg. Co.
Korsmeyer, The	New Home
Kracker Jack	A. G. Mason Mfg. Co.
Krafts Gem	National
Kragens	Goodrich
Kreas	A. G. Mason Mfg. Co.
Krecic	White
Kreigers	National
Kroegers	National
Krogers Special	Free
Krogers	National
Kuehler	A. G. Mason Mfg. Co.
Kuehler Kuenman	White
Kvinden oz Hyemonet	New Home
Kvinden Pride	A. G. Mason Mfg. Co.
Ky Bell	Free
La Argentine	A. G. Mason Mfg. Co.
La Aurora	Standard
La Belle	Free
La Belle	National
La Mexicana	National
La Merocha	Standard
La Moderna	Goodrich
La Nacional	National
La Novedades	National
La Nuevadades	National
La Opera	Standard
La Palma	National
La Panamania	Davis
La Pavoeedora	Davis
La Perfection	Standard
La Boila Cinfuega	National
La Bonita	Goodrich
La Borda	A. G. Mason Mfg. Co.
La Bordadora	A. G. Mason Mfg. Co.
La Borla	A. G. Mason Mfg. Co.
La Canadian	Davis
La Capoise	Standard
La Casa Grandoa	A. G. Mason Mfg. Co.
La Charmont	A. G. Mason Mfg. Co.
La Chricanita	New Home
La Cinfiango	Standard
La Compagngo	Standard
La Compedora	A. G. Mason Mfg. Co.
La Competida	National
La Constancia	Standard
La Costrera	Standard
La Dalescieura	Standard
La Duchesse	Free
La Ecquador	National
La Ecquadorator	National
La Esmeraldo	Goodrich
La Especatz	A. G. Mason Mfg. Co.
La Especial	Standard
La Ertrella	
La Fabricas Universales	New Home
La Facilla	Goodrich
La Famillar	New Home
La Favorite	National
La Favorite	Standard
La Foliscienso	Standard
La Francis	Standard
La Francesca	Standard
La Francia Maritima	New Home
La Frontora	National
La Garalda	National
La Grand	National
La Granda	National
La Homadien	National
La Hondurena	Goodrich
La Ideal	National
La India	National
La International	National
La Jalisciense	Standard
La Joya	A. G. Mason Mfg. Co.
La Joya-del-Hager	New Home
La Librias	New Home
La Ludo	National
La Manabela	National
La Mariposa	New Home
La Marquez	Standard
La Marquise	Free
La Masivilla	National
La Mejor	Standard

Appendix G

Sewing-Machine Name	Sewing-Machine Company
La Meriyana	Standard
La Meriposa	New Home
La Perfection	Standard
La Perfection	A. G. Mason Mfg. Co.
La Perla	A. G. Mason Mfg. Co.
La Perlu-la-Casa	National
La Platta	A. G. Mason Mfg. Co.
La Princess	A. G. Mason Mfg. Co.
La Pueblo	National
La Ramha	A. G. Mason Mfg. Co.
La Regent	Free
La Reina	A. G. Mason Mfg. Co.
La Rosa	A. G. Mason Mfg. Co.
La Rose	Free
La Saporita	National
La Silencosa	New Home
La Simpatica	Standard
La Sin Bomb	National
La Sin Rinal	National
La Soporeso Pueblo	National
La Tarapaco	Standard
La Ultima	Standard
La Valcedora	Standard
La Valex	A. G. Mason Mfg. Co.
La Vercost	National
La Viebriosa	National
Lacey	A. G. Mason Mfg. Co.
Laclede	National
Ladies' Comfort	National
Ladies Favorite	Standard
Ladies Friend	National
Ladies Home Journal	National
Lady Barltimore	Davis
Lady Gay	National
Lafayette	A. G. Mason Mfg. Co.
Laideau	Standard
Lake	A. G. Mason Mfg. Co.
Lakeshore	National
Lakeside	Free
Lakeview	Davis
Lakewood	Goodrich
Lamar	Free
Lamberg	A. G. Mason Mfg. Co.
Lambeck	A. G. Mason Mfg. Co.
Lancaster	Standard
Lancaster	A. G. Mason Mfg. Co.
Landers	A. G. Mason Mfg. Co.
Landrys	A. G. Mason Mfg. Co.
Lanford	A. G. Mason Mfg. Co.
Langs	Goodrich
Lanham	A. G. Mason Mfg. Co.
Lanston	A. G. Mason Mfg. Co.
Lankford	A. G. Mason Mfg. Co.
Lapiers	Goodrich
Lark	Davis
Lark	Free
Lashley	A. G. Mason Mfg. Co.
Laubacks	A. G. Mason Mfg. Co.
Laurance	White
Laurel	Free
Laurence	Free
Laval	Davis
Laverty	A. G. Mason Mfg. Co.
Lavina	Free
Law	A. G. Mason Mfg. Co.
Lawfer	Davis
Laws	White
Lawrence	Free
Lawthers	White
Lazarus Rotary	White
Leader, New	New Leader
Leader, New Century	New Leader
Leader, Our	National
Leader, The	Standard
Leath	White
Leauell	White
Leavell	A. G. Mason Mfg. Co.
Lebecks	Standard
Lechles	Standard
Lees	Davis
Lees	Goodrich
Leeth	A. G. Mason Mfg. Co.
Leggett	Standard
Leigh	National
Leinburg	A. G. Mason Mfg. Co.
Leiss	A. G. Mason Mfg. Co.
Leland	Free
Lemberg	A. G. Mason Mfg. Co.
Lenhart	Goodrich
Lennington	National
Lenora	Davis
Lenox, The	National
Leonard	A. G. Mason Mfg. Co.
Leopold Loeb	A. G. Mason Mfg. Co.
Lerrington	Standard
Leslie, The	National
Lester	White
Leurett	White
Levy Bros	White
Levys	Standard
Levis	Standard
Lewis	White
Lexington	Davis
Lexington	Standard
Lexington	A. G. Mason Mfg. Co.
Liberty	Davis
Liberty	National
Liberty Bell	Free
Liberty Bell	National
Liberty Rotary	White
Lichter Gem	National
Lightfoot	A. G. Mason Mfg. Co.
Lightning	National
Lillard	A. G. Mason Mfg. Co.
Lima House	White
Limestone	White
Limited	Free
Lincoln	National
Lindake	National
Lindel	National
Lindenheim	Standard
Lindheim	Standard
Lindholmes	National
Linator	Goodrich
Lion	National
Lipscomb	White
Lit's Rotary	White
Little Gem	National
Little Wonder	New Home
Little Worker	New Home
Litts	White
Liquid Cool	Free
Livestock	Goodrich
Livingstone	National
Llewllous	White
Lloyd	White
Lockman	Unknown
Locke	Standard
loeb	A. G. Mason Mfg. Co.
Loeser	Davis
Lowenstein	A. G. Mason Mfg. Co.
Loffers	A. G. Mason Mfg. Co.
Loflin	White
Loflin Bros	White
Logans Rotary	National
Logna Rotary	National
Lomax	A. G. Mason Mfg. Co.
Lonard	National
Lonestar	Davis
Lone Star A, B, C, D	Free
Long	National
Longin	A. G. Mason Mfg. Co.
Longmire	White
Longs	Standard
Longs Favorite	Free
Longtino	White
Lonkes Special	National
Lopez Pewa Cia	Standard
Lorain	A. G. Mason Mfg. Co.
Lorch	National
Lorena	National
Loretta	Davis
Lotions	Standard
Lottie	Standard
Lott-W-Co	White
Lott-Walker Co	A. G. Mason Mfg. Co.
Louise	National
Louisiana	Free
Lowe	A. G. Mason Mfg. Co.
Lowenberg	White
Lowenstein	A. G. Mason Mfg. Co.
Lowett	A. G. Mason Mfg. Co.
Lowery	Goodrich
Lowman	White
Lozier	National
Lubra	Goodrich
Lucas	National
Lucas	White
Luce	A. G. Mason Mfg. Co.
Lucerne	White
Lucille	National
Luckey Platt Co.	National
Lugers	White
Lugon	White
Lula	A. G. Mason Mfg. Co.
Lumpkin	A. G. Mason Mfg. Co.
Lunsford	White
Luth J. Y. Cia Sue	National
lybrando	White
Lyle	A. G. Mason Mfg. Co.
Luzon	A. G. Mason Mfg. Co.
Mab	Goodrich
Mable	A. G. Mason Mfg. Co.
Macey's Electric	National
Macey's Leader	New Home
Maceys New Empire	New Home
Maceys R. R. Red Star	Davis
Maceys Special	New Home
Mackiss	White
Macks	White
Macon	A. G. Mason Mfg. Co.
Macy	Davis
Macy's Rotary	White
Madagascar	White
Maddington	A. G. Mason Mfg. Co.
Maddox	A. G. Mason Mfg. Co.
Madison	Standard
Madison	National
Magill	White
Magnet	A. G. Mason Mfg. Co.
Magnolia	National
Magnolia	Standard
Mail & Breeze	National
Maine	Standard
Majestic	New Home
Major	Goodrich
Malba	A. G. Mason Mfg. Co.
Malcohns	Standard
Malcolm	Standard
Malones	Standard
Maloness	White
Malta	White
Maltnomer	National
Manavata	Standard
Manawater	Standard
Manchester	Goodrich
Mandels	National
Manfield	National
Manhattan	Davis
Manhattan	National
Manhattan	Standard
Manilla	National
Manistee	White
Manix	Standard
Manifair	White
Manlove	A. G. Mason Mfg. Co.
Manisfield	Free
Mansfield	White
Mansion	Davis
Mansion	National

Appendix G

Sewing-Machine Name	Sewing-Machine Company
McGlynns	White
McGraths	A. G. Mason Mfg. Co.
McGreery	New Home
McGuiston	A. G. Mason Mfg. Co.
McKay	A. G. Mason Mfg. Co.
McKeey, The	Unknown
McKelvey	Free
McKinley	A. G. Mason Mfg. Co.
McKinney	Unknown
McKissack	National
McLain's Best	A. G. Mason Mfg. Co.
McLarty	White
McLeods Store	A. G. Mason Mfg. Co.
McMeans Bride	A. G. Mason Mfg. Co.
McMeans Pride	A. G. Mason Mfg. Co.
Mcmitch	National
McMillen	A. G. Mason Mfg. Co.
McNeil	A. G. Mason Mfg. Co.
McNicols	National
McPetters	White
McRae	A. G. Mason Mfg. Co.
McReas	Davis
McSwean	A. G. Mason Mfg. Co.
McVay Special	A. G. Mason Mfg. Co.
McWherr	White
McWilliams	A. G. Mason Mfg. Co.
Meckes	Free
Medon	Unknown
Meldrum	National
Meller	National
Meller	Unknown
Melone	Davis
Melone	Unknown
Melrose	National
Melville	National
Melvin	White
Menda	Standard
Menelee	A. G. Mason Mfg. Co.
Menough	Standard
Merchant & E	A. G. Mason Mfg. Co.
Mercantile	Standard
Mercury	Goodrich
Meridan	Standard
Merrell	Free
Merrick	Standard
Mervin, K., Co.	White
Mesco	New Home
Messayen	A. G. Mason Mfg. Co.
Metcalf	A. G. Mason Mfg. Co.
Meteor	New Home
Metropolis	Standard
Metropolitan	National
Mexbo	Free
Meyer	A. G. Mason Mfg. Co.
Mhoon	White
Miami Mer. Co.	A. G. Mason Mfg. Co.
Michel	Free
Michigan	New Home
Michigan	White
Michigan Farmer	Davis
Midkiff	White
Midland	Davis
Midland	National
Midway	White
Millard	Standard
Mikady	Standard
Miiam	White
Millane	Standard
Millard	Standard
Miller	Standard
Miller	White
Miller & W	National
Milligan Cash	A. G. Mason Mfg. Co.
Milton	Free
Milwauka	Free
Milwauka	Goodrich
Minakif Leader	A. G. Mason Mfg. Co.
Mingers	Standard
Mine Door	A. G. Mason Mfg. Co.
Mone Dor	White
Manter	Goodrich
Manwestlake	New Home
Maple	White
Maple Leaf	Standard
Marathon	Davis
Maravana	Standard
March	White
March, J. B.	A. G. Mason Mfg. Co.
Marchona	A. G. Mason Mfg. Co.
Marcus	Free
Marcy	Unknown
Margareta	Standard
Margets	Standard
Marguerite	Household
Mariana Furniture Co.	A. G. Mason Mfg. Co.
Marilton	Goodrich
Marka Terbie	A. G. Mason Mfg. Co.
Markham	White
Mars	New Home
Marse	White
Marshall	A. G. Mason Mfg. Co.
Marshall Field	Standard
Marshall Wells	National
Martha	A. G. Mason Mfg. Co.
Martha Washington	White
Mart Heidrich	Goodrich
Martin	Free
Martin	National
Marvel	National
Marvel	Sandard
Mary, A. M. and Son	A. G. Mason Mfg. Co.
Maryland	National
Mascot	New Home
Mascota	Davis
Mason	A. G. Mason Mfg. Co.
Mason Rotary	A. G. Mason Mfg. Co.
Mason Rotary	White
Mason Special	A. G. Mason Mfg. Co.
Masonia	A. G. Mason Mfg. Co.
Master	National
Master, The	Standard
Matchless	Davis
Matchless	A. G. Mason Mfg. Co.
Matchless	Standard
Mathews	Davis
Matron, The	National
Maud	Davis
Maxfield	White
Maxwell	White
May and Graix	White
May Company, The	Standard
Mayfair	White
Mayfield	A. G. Mason Mfg. Co.
May Flower	Goodrich
Mayhen Lbr. Co.	White
May Queen	Goodrich
Mays Special	White
Maywood	Goodrich
McAlpin	Davis
Mc Alpin	White
McAnish	National
McCall	A. G. Mason Mfg. Co.
McCallum's Rotary	White
McCalm	A. G. Mason Mfg. Co.
McCalvin	A. G. Mason Mfg. Co.
McCarthy	A. G. Mason Mfg. Co.
McCaslin	A. G. Mason Mfg. Co.
McChesney	A. G. Mason Mfg. Co.
McClung A, C, D	Goodrich
McCormick	Standard
McCracken	A. G. Mason Mfg. Co.
McCuiston	White
McCurdy	White
McDaniel	Free
McDermot	Standard
McDonald	Standard
McDowell	A. G. Mason Mfg. Co.
McDowell	National
McEvans	White
McGill	A. G. Mason Mfg. Co.
Miner	A. G. Mason Mfg. Co.
Minerva	Standard
Minneapolis	National
Minneapolis	Standard
Minnehaha	National
Minnehaha	Standard
Minnesota	Davis
Minnesota H	Davis
Minnesota 1	New Home
Minnesota A9-3500000	Davis
Minnesota 2 & 3	Davis
Minnie, New	A. G. Mason Mfg. Co.
Miracle	Davis
Mirror and Farmer	Standard
Mission	Davis
Missouri	National
Mississippi	White
Mistree	Standard
Mistress	Standard
Mitchell	Standard
Mitchell	A. G. Mason Mfg. Co.
Mi-well Co.	White
Moberly	Standard
Mobery	Standard
Mobile	Davis
Model	Davis
Model	Goodrich
Model D	Davis
Model Queen	A. G. Mason Mfg. Co.
Model Sewer	Standard
Modern	Davis
Modern	A. G. Mason Mfg. Co.
Modern Wilson	A. G. Mason Mfg. Co.
Modern Woodsman	Goodrich
Modes	National
Modiste	Free
Moerbe	White
Moerle	A. G. Mason Mfg. Co.
Mohand	Davis
Mohawk	National
Moiser	White
Moister	A. G. Mason Mfg. Co.
Mollen Kamp	A. G. Mason Mfg. Co.
Moll Special	White
Moms	National
Momas	National
Monarch	Davis
Monarch	New Home
Modys Favorite	Standard
Money King	Standard
Monitor	Davis
Monitor	National
Monogram	Davis
Monroe	Davis
Monte-go	White
Montejo Rotary	White
Montemayor	New Home
Montgomery	Standard
Montgomery Ward	National
Moores	A. G. Mason Mfg. Co.
Morehouse	Davis
Morey	Standard
Morgan	Goodrich
Morley	A. G. Mason Mfg. Co.
Morris	A. G. Mason Mfg. Co.
Morrison	Davis
Morrison	A. G. Mason Mfg. Co.
Morrison Bros.	New Home
Morse	Free
Morton	White
Morum Bros.	New Home
Mosby	A. G. Mason Mfg. Co.
Moser	White
Moss	A. G. Mason Mfg. Co.
Mountaineer	Standard
Moyer Special	A. G. Mason Mfg. Co.
Moyers Pride	Standard
Moyles Special	A. G. Mason Mfg. Co.
Mt. Calm	A. G. Mason Mfg. Co.
Muelder	White

Appendix G

Sewing-Machine Name	Sewing-Machine Company
Mulcock, J. K.	A. G. Mason Mfg. Co.
Mulder Jewell	A. G. Mason Mfg. Co.
Mulleins	A. G. Mason Mfg. Co.
Mullins	Davis
Mund	Domestic
Mundo de Colon	National
Munn	A. G. Mason Mfg. Co.
Munroe	A. G. Mason Mfg. Co.
Murphys	Standard
Murphys and Allen	A. G. Mason Mfg. Co.
Murray	A. G. Mason Mfg. Co.
Murray, The	Standard
Muskegdon	Standard
Muskoka	Goodrich
Mussina	National
Myers	A. G. Mason Mfg. Co.
Myers	Standard
My Own	A. G. Mason Mfg. Co.
My Own	Standard
Myrtle	Goodrich
Nabob	Davis
Nacional	National
Nacional Standard	Standard
Nadbers	White
Nagorski	White
Namson	Davis
Namson	A. G. Mason Mfg. Co.
Nance	A. G. Mason Mfg. Co.
Napier	Standard
Nash	White
Nashville	Goodrich
Nath M.F. and Hub. Co.	White
National A, B, C, D, E, F, G, H, O	National
National Baptistiec	National
National Home	Free
National Rotary	National
National Supply Co.	National
Nation's Pride	Standard
Naura India	National
Navarre	Davis
Naylors Special	A. G. Mason Mfg. Co.
Nebraska	Free
Neely and C	A. G. Mason Mfg. Co.
Nellie	National
Nelson	New Home
Nesbit	National
Netzon	Davis
Neurva National	New Home
Neva	Standard
Neversuch	Standard
Neville	A. G. Mason Mfg. Co.
New Acme	Davis
New Acme	Standard
New Ane	National
New Albany	National
New Ally	National
New American	Davis
New American Lichlador	National
New Atlas	Standard
New Automatic	Free
New Avonia	New Home
New Bach	White
New Belle	National
New Belle	Standard
New Ben Hur	National
New Bevon	Free
New Bouquett	National
New Cambridge	New Home
New Carson	New Home
New Centenial	Davis
New Century	Standard
New Century	A. G. Mason Mfg. Co.
New Century Leader	New Leader
New Century Rotary	White
New Champion	New Home
New Chroicle	National
New Colonial House	Davis
New Columbia	New Home
New Columbus	Standard
New Comer	White
New Companion	New Home
New Concord	Standard
New Conover	Davis
New Cottage	Davis
New Cottage	National
New Damascus	A. G. Mason Mfg. Co.
New Daisey	A. G. Mason Mfg. Co.
New Davis	Davis
New Decatur	National
New Defender	White
New Departure	National
New Dixie	Davis
New Domestic	Domestic
New Devon	National
New Duplex	Free
New Easy Running	National
New Elgin	A. G. Mason Mfg. Co.
New Elmore	National
New Empire	National
New Empress	National
New England	Davis
New England	A. G. Mason Mfg. Co.
New England Queen	National
New England Rotary	National
New Equity	National
New Era	National
New Ermine	A. G. Mason Mfg. Co.
New Family	New Home
New Favorite	Davis
New Fillespie	National
New Fireside	Davis
New Fireside	National
New Firm	Standard
New Florence	A. G. Mason Mfg. Co.
New Florence Rotary	A. G. Mason Mfg. Co.
New Gold Dust	Davis
New Goodrich	Goodrich
New Gourley	Davis
New Havana	Standard
New Havan	New Home
New Haven	New Home
New Haven Imp.	Standard
New Hibbare	Davis
New Hickory	Davis
New Holmes	Standard
New Holmes	White
New Home	New Home
New Home Central	New Home
New Home 400	New Home
New Home Queen	New Home
New Home Rotary	New Home
New Home Star	New Home
New Homestead	Free
New Homestead	Standard
New Home Superior	New Home
New Home Victoria	New Home
New Hope	Davis
New Household	National
New Howard	Free
New Howe	Standard
New Idea	A. G. Mason Mfg. Co.
New Ideal	New Home
New Idemascus	White
New Jewell	National
New King	National
New Leader	New Leader
New Lennox	Standard
New Life	National
New Love	New Leader
New Mason	White
New Mason's	White
New Matchless	Standard
New Matthews	A. G. Mason Mfg. Co.
New May	A. G. Mason Mfg. Co.
New Merrick	A. G. Mason Mfg. Co.
New Method	Standard
New Method	A. G. Mason Mfg. Co.
New Mexicano	Standard
New Mode	National
New Model	Goodrich
New Monitor	Free
New Monroe	A. G. Mason Mfg. Co.
New Molution	Free
New More	Standard
New National	New Home
New National	White
New Netzow	Davis
New Oriole	National
New Oswald	A. G. Mason Mfg. Co.
New Pacific	National
New Paguet	National
New Palace	A. G. Mason Mfg. Co.
New Parish	Standard
New Peerless	Standard
New Peoria	National
New Perfection	A. G. Mason Mfg. Co.
New Pillsbury	National
New Pittsburgh B	Goodrich
New Post	National
New Premium	National
New Presto	National
New Principle	Free
New Progress	Davis
New Queen	A. G. Mason Mfg. Co.
New Rapid	Standard
New Reliable	Davis
New Rex	Davis
New Rival	Goodrich
New Rome	National
New Rotary	White
New Royal	Free
New Royal A	Free
New Royal Queen	Free
New Single	A. G. Mason Mfg. Co.
New Sinning	A. G. Mason Mfg. Co.
New Sincer	New Home
New South 1	Davis
New South 2	Goodrich
New South 3	National
New Star	Davis
New Star	Standard
New Star	A. G. Mason Mfg. Co.
New States	Free
New Sterling	Free
New Steward	Standard
New Stockman	Davis
New Success	Standard
New Superb	Davis
New Treasure	A. G. Mason Mfg. Co.
New Tremont	National
New Trip	National
New Triumph	Davis
New Tuxedo	Standard
New Tyler	A. G. Mason Mfg. Co.
New Vance	Davis
New Vassar	Davis
New Victor	National
New Victoria	New Home
New Victory	Davis
New Victory 9	Goodrich
New Waltham	Goodrich
New Warwick	A. G. Mason Mfg. Co.
New Way	Free
New Way Rotary, The	White
New Weed	Standard
New White Peerless	A. G. Mason Mfg. Co.
New White Rotary	White
New Whiteley	National
New Whitesley	A. G. Mason Mfg. Co.
New Willard	White
New Williams	Unknown
New Wilmont	Unknown
New Wilson	Davis
New Wilson	A. G. Mason Mfg. Co.
New Wilsons	A. G. Mason Mfg. Co.
New Winchester	New Home
New Winner	Davis
New Yale	Foley & Williams Mfg. Co.
New York	Goodrich
New York	White

Appendix G

Sewing-Machine Name	Sewing-Machine Company
New York Gem	A. G. Mason Mfg. Co.
New Z Pasquet	National
Newark	Goodrich
Newman	White
Newport	Standard
Newton	Davis
Newton	Free
Newton	Standard
Niagra	National
Nichols	A.G. Mason Mfg. Co.
Nicholson	White
Nimmons	White
Nofzinger	A.G. Mason Mfg. Co.
No Name	National
Nonequat	White
Nonpariel	National
Noonan	A.G. Mason Mfg. Co.
Nordica	Davis
Norcon	National
Norella	White
Norfolk	Standard
Norfolk	White
Norleigh Diamond	Davis
Norman	A.G. Mason Mfg. Co.
Norris	White
North American	National
Northcut	A.G. Mason Mfg. Co.
Northern	New Home
North Queen	National
North Western	National
Norwood	Standard
Not Nac	Davis
No-Try-On	National
Nova	National
Nova Machine Roses	Standard
Noxabee Queen	National
Noxall	National
Nox, X.L.	National
Nuerva	New Home
Nunnely	White
Nutflake	White
Oakdale	Standard
Oakland	Goodrich
Oakwood, A.B.	Davis
Oberlin	Davis
Observer	Goodrich
Occental	National
Odelbury	White
Oden	A.G. Mason Mfg. Co.
Oettinger	White
Ogle	National
Oglethorpe	Free
Ohio	Davis
Ohio Farmer	Foley & Williams
Ohio Farmer	Goodrich
Ohio Farmer Model D	Davis
Ohio Walley	Davis
Okeh	New Home
Okeh	New Home
Oklahoma	Davis
Oklahoma, The	Free
Old Homestead	National
Old Homestead Rotary	National
Old Reliable	A.G. Mason Mfg. Co.
Oldenberg	A.G. Mason Mfg. Co.
Olds Wothman Co.	Standard
Oldson Leader	A.G. Mason Mfg. Co.
Olive, The	A.G. Mason Mfg. Co.
Olney	Goodrich
Olney	Standard
Olympia	National
Olympia	Standard
Omaha	Free
Omega Rotary	White
Onachita Bell	Davis
Oneida	National
O'Neil Pride	P.E. Victor
O'Neil, The	Standard
O'Neil Rotary	White
Ongnard	A.G. Mason Mfg. Co.
Onondazo	Free
Ontarri	National
Oppenheimer	National
Oracle	New Home
Orade	New Home
Orange	Davis
Oransky	A.G. Mason Mfg. Co.
Orchid	Davis
Ordway	New Home
Oregon	Goodrich
Orient	National
Orient	Standard
Orient	White
Oreloe	Standard
Oretan	National
Oritana	National
Orleans	Standard
Orme Co.	A.G. Mason Mfg. Co.
Osborn	Unknown
Osborn	A.G. Mason Mfg. Co.
Oscar Hewett Rotary	White
Ostertag	A.G. Mason Mfg. Co.
Osvetta	A.G. Mason Mfg. Co.
Oswale	A.G. Mason Mfg. Co.
Ottowa	Household
Otto	Standard
Otto Klein	A.G. Mason Mfg. Co.
Ouatonna	White
Our Bonanza	A.G. Mason Mfg. Co.
Our Gem	White
Our Grand	Davis
Our Leader	Free
Our Model	Standard
Our Own	Free
Our Pet	National
Our Pride	National
Our Salesman	Free
Our Special	Free
Our Special	Goodrich
Our Troveler	National
Our Very Best	Standard
Our Wonder	Goodrich
Outlet Special	National
Overstreet	White
Owattona	A.G. Mason Mfg. Co.
Oxford	White
Oxford 1	Goodrich
Oxford 2	National
Oxford Singer	Unknown
Ozark	Free
Pace	A.G. Mason Mfg. Co.
Pacific	National
Pacific	Standard
Pacific Queen	Goodrich
Paddock	Davis
Page	A.G. Mason Mfg. Co.
Pagoma	Davis
Palace	National
Palcios and Zambreno	A.G. Mason Mfg. Co.
Palma	A.G. Mason Mfg. Co.
Palmer	National
Palmetto	National
Pan American	New Home
Pansor	National
Panton and Whit	Goodrich
Paragold	A.G. Mason Mfg. Co.
Paragon	Davis
Paragon	Standard
Paragon, The New	Standard
Paramount	Davis
Partridge	A.G. Mason Mfg. Co.
Parent	A.G. Mason Mfg. Co.
Parinas	Davis
Paris	A.G. Mason Mfg. Co.
Paris King	A.G. Mason Mfg. Co.
Parish Grand	Standard
Parisian	Davis
Park City	National
Parker	National
Parker	White
Parks	Standard
Parlor City	Davis
Parlor City	White
Parmao	White
Passaic	White
Passmore	A.G. Mason Mfg. Co.
Passmore Rotary	White
Pastime	Standard
Pate	White
Pates	New Home
Pates Special	Standard
Pathfinder	Davis
Pathway	Free
Pat-Mac	Davis
Patrick's Gem	A.G. Mason Mfg. Co.
Pattelos Special	A.G. Mason Mfg. Co.
Pattilo	White
Patten	Goodrich
Paul	National
Paul	A.G. Mason Mfg. Co.
Paveway	National
Pea-Body	Davis
Peabody	A.G. Mason Mfg. Co.
Peach Belt	A.G. Mason Mfg. Co.
Pearl	Davis
Pearl	New Home
Pearl	Standard
Pearlhaven	Standard
Pearline	National
Pecko Special	A.G. Mason Mfg. Co.
Peco Electric	New Home
Pee Dee	Davis
Pee-Gee	Davis
Peepless	White
Peepp	White
Peeress	Standard
Peerless	Free
Peerless	National
Peerless Rotary	National
Peerless Rotary	A.G. Mason Mfg. Co.
Pelantense	White
Pelham	National
Pelican	Free
Pelican	Standard
Pelleter	Free
Pellerin	National
Pelotence	A.G. Mason Mfg. Co.
Pelton	A.G. Mason Mfg. Co.
Pemberton	Davis
Peninsular	National
Penman, H.D.	A.G. Mason Mfg. Co.
Penn	A.G. Mason Mfg. Co.
Penn, The	A.G. Mason Mfg. Co.
Pennsylvania	Goodrich
Penny	Davis
Pensylvania	Goodrich
People, The	Standard
Peoples Furniture Company	A.G. Mason Mfg. Co.
Peoria	Davis
Peoria	New Home
Perer	White
Perfect	A.G. Mason Mfg. Co.
Perfecta, The	Standard
Perfection	Davis
Perfection	Standard
Perfection	White
Perfecto	Goodrich
Perkins	White
Perla-de-la-Casa	Standard
Perpetual	National
Perrless Rotary	White
Perry and Henry	A.G. Mason Mfg. Co.
Pet	Davis
Pettis	Davis
Pettis	Free
Petty Brothers	White
P.E. Victor	Free
Pfeuffer, H., Co.	White
Pfleger	A.G. Mason Mfg. Co.
Phar Bros.	A.G. Mason Mfg. Co.

Appendix G

Sewing-Machine Name	Sewing-Machine Company
Phelans	White
Philadelphia	A.G. Mason Mfg. Co.
Phila-Singer	Unknown
Phillip	A.G. Mason Mfg. Co.
Phillips	Standard
Phillippine	Davis
Phillopene	Davis
Phoenix	National
Phoenix	White
Pickering	Standard
Piedmont	Davis
Piedmont	Goodrich
Piedmont Electric	New Home
Pierce	White
Pierce Gold	Standard
Piffer Special	A.G. Mason Mfg. Co.
Pilgrims	National
Pillsbury	National
Pilot	Standard
Pilsbury	National
Pinnens Pride	Free
Pinnic Kinick	Davis
Pinnock	Goodrich
Pioneer	National
Pioneer	Standard
Pioneer Press	National
Piper	Standard
Piquett	Goodrich
Pittman	A.G. Mason Mfg. Co.
Pitts	White
Pittsburgh Electric	A.G. Mason Mfg. Co.
Plain	National
Plainview	White
Planet	Goodrich
Planters	Standard
Planters	A.G. Mason Mfg. Co.
Platt	Davis
Plymouth	Davis
Plymouth	National
PlyQueen	White
Polk and Co.	A.G. Mason Mfg. Co.
Polly	Standard
Polytype	National
Pointer Gem	A.G. Mason Mfg. Co.
Pommer	National
Popes Queen	A.G. Mason Mfg. Co.
Poplar	National
Popular	Davis
Porch Privetts	White
Portage	A.G. Mason Mfg. Co.
Porter	Davis
Post Electric	National
Potts, W. A.	A.G. Mason Mfg. Co
Potzer	Davis
Powell	A.G. Mason Mfg. Co.
Practical Farmer	Standard
Praire Queen	Free
Prairie Queen	Free
Pratts	A.G. Mason Mfg. Co.
Premier	Davis
Premier	New Home
Premier	National
Premier	Standard
Premium Chronicle	Goodrich
Premium Chronicle, New	National
Premium Dallas	Unknown
Premium Galveston	National
Premium Houston	Goodrich
Prescot Hardware Co.	A.G. Mason Mfg. Co.
President	Davis
Press Pub. Assn.	Standard
Presto	A.G. Mason Mfg. Co.
Prewitt	A.G. Mason Mfg. Co.
Price and Allen	A.G. Mason Mfg. Co.
Priscilla	New Home
Pride of Home	A.G. Mason Mfg. Co.
Pride of Kentucky	Standard
Pride of Milwaukee	Free
Pride of Poteau	A.G. Mason Mfg. Co.
Pride of Virginia	A.G. Mason Mfg. Co.
Price of World	A.G. Mason Mfg. Co.
Primmer	A.G. Mason Mfg. Co.
Primor	New Home
Princess	National
Princeton	National
Principle	Goodrich
Pringle	Davis
Printzlaff	Free
Priscella	Davis
Priscilla	A.G. Mason Mfg. Co.
Priscilla	Unknown
Priscilla	New Home
Pritzlaff	Davis
Prize Model	Goodrich
Prize, The	National
Process	National
Progress	Standard
Progress	A.G. Mason Mfg. Co.
Prospect	A.G. Mason Mfg. Co.
Prosperity	White
Protens	National
Providence	National
Provodero del Hagar	A.G. Mason Mfg. Co.
Public Service	White
Pullman	A.G. Mason Mfg. Co.
Punxsutawney	White
Purdin	Goodrich
Puregold	Free
Puritan	National
Puritan	White
Purity	National
Pursero	White
Putnam	A.G. Mason Mfg. Co.
Pyramid	Goodrich
Quackenbush	Davis
Quaker	National
Quaker City	Free
Quality	Davis
Quality	National
Quality	Standard
Quapa Special	National
Queen	Davis
Queen	A.G. Mason Mfg. Co.
Queen American	National
Queen Anne	Standard
Queen Bee	National
Queen Bess	Davis
Queen Bess	Free
Queen City	Davis
Queen City	National
Queen City	Unknown
Queen Cottage	National
Queen Family	A.G. Mason Mfg. Co.
Queen Fairest	National
Queen Home	Davis
Queen Kentucky	National
Queen May	National
Queen Modern	A.G. Mason Mfg. Co.
Queen, New	A.G. Mason Mfg. Co.
Queen New England	A.G. Mason Mfg. Co.
Queen North	National
Queen Tuxubee	National
Queen Pacific	Standard
Queen Plymouth	A.G. Mason Mfg. Co.
Queen Royal	A.G. Mason Mfg. Co.
Queen Southern	A.G. Mason Mfg. Co.
Queen Smoth	A.G. Mason Mfg. Co.
Queen Texas	A.G. Mason Mfg. Co.
Queen Toronto	National
Queen Western	National
Queen	White
Sewing Machine Co.	A.G. Mason Mfg. Co.
Queen of the West	National
Queen Winner	A.G. Mason Mfg. Co.
Queen 12	Free
Quickel's Best	Standard
Quickstitch	Standard
Quiller, P.R.	A.G. Mason Mfg. Co.
Quinan Och Hemmett	New Home
Quincy	Davis
Quincy	Goodrich
Quinn	A.G. Mason Mfg. Co.
Quison	Standard
Raders	A.G. Mason Mfg. Co.
Radiant	Standard
Radio	Davis
Radior	A.G. Mason Mfg. Co.
Radior Rotary	White
Radner Special	A.G. Mason Mfg. Co.
Raesford Hardware Co.	A.G. Mason Mfg. Co.
Railway	National
Rainbow	Free
Rainer	White
Rainha	White
Rainwater	Goodrich
Raleigh	National
Ralston B	A.G. Mason Mfg. Co.
Ramand	National
Ramco Rotary	White
Ramons	National
Ramsdells Best	A.G. Mason Mfg. Co.
	National
Ranberry	Goodrich
Randchier	A.G. Mason Mfg. Co.
Randville	A.G. Mason Mfg. Co.
Raney	A.G. Mason Mfg. Co.
Ranger	Davis
Rankin	A.G. Mason Mfg. Co.
Ranks	A.G. Mason Mfg. Co.
R.D. Masayeh R.	White
Read, The	Free
Read, The	Standard
Read Rotary	White
Read & Snyder	National
Reading Special	A.G. Mason Mfg. Co.
Reagan	White
Reams	White
Record	National
Rectors	White
Red Buza	Free
Red Cross	Davis
Red Cross	Standard
Redgeton	National
Red Star	National
Read & Son	A.G. Mason Mfg. Co.
Reed Special	Standard
Regal	Davis
Regal	A.G. Mason Mfg. Co.
Regal B, C, D Rotary	National
Regent	Free
Regina	Goodrich
Rehan	Davis
Reich	A.G. Mason Mfg. Co.
Reimer	White
Reimer Special	A.G. Mason White. Co.
Reina	Standard
Reliable	National
Reliable	Standard
Reliable A	Free
Reliance	Davis
Reliance	Free
Reliance	Standard
Reliance	A.G. Mason Mfg. Co.
Reliance Hardware Co.	New Home
Remaly	Standard
Remington	National
Renan	A.G. Mason Mfg. Co.
Renfreu	Davis
Reno	Goodrich
Renown	National
Republic	Davis
Republic	National
Reputation	National
Revalation	National
Rev-O-Nue	National
Revork	Davis
Rex	National
Rexford	National
Reynolds	Free
Reynolds	Free
Reznoir Rotary	A.G. Mason Mfg. Co.

Appendix G

Sewing-Machine Name	Sewing-Machine Company
Reznor Rotary	White
Rhenania	Goodrich
Rhoda and Happe	Standard
Rhodesia	Standard
Rhone Hardware Co.	A.G. Mason Mfg. Co.
Rhyne Brothers	A.G. Mason Mfg. Co.
Rialto	National
Rice, The	Free
Rice's	White
Richard, J.D.	A.G. Mason Mfg. Co.
Richard's	White
Richardson	Standard
Richland	Standard
Richland	A.G. Mason Mfg. Co.
Richmond	Davis
Richmond A, B, C, D, E	Free
Richter	Free
Richters	Standard
Rickoff	White
Ridder	National
Ridgeway	National
Riegle, The	A.G. Mason Mfg. Co.
Rierson	A.G. Mason Mfg. Co.
Rierson, W. and S.	White
Rightway	Standard
Rikes	Davis
Riley	A.G. Mason Mfg. Co.
Ripley Belle	A.G. Mason Mfg. Co.
Ritchable	National
Ritchdale	A.G. Mason Mfg. Co.
Ritchie Hardware Co.	Standard
Ritman	White
Rittenhouse	Free
Ritter	Standard
Ritters	Goodrich
Rival	Free
Rival	Standard
Rival Sin	A.G. Mason Mfg. Co.
Riverside	National
Riverside Extra	Standard
Riverton	Household
Rivore	A.G. Mason Mfg. Co.
Roanoke	Davis
Rober	Standard
Roberta	National
Roberta	A.G. Mason Mfg. Co.
Robert Lee	White
Roberts	Goodrich
Roberts	Standard
Robertson	Goodrich
Robins	National
Robinson	A.G. Mason Mfg. Co.
Rockford	Free
Rockford	Standard
Rock City	National
Rockford	Free
Rockland	A.G. Mason Mfg. Co.
Roding	National
Roeser	Standard
Rogers	A.G. Mason Mfg. Co.
Rogers, E.M.	Standard
Roiz	Standard
Roland, J.A.	A.G. Mason Mfg. Co.
Roman	White
Rome	A.G. Mason Mfg. Co.
Rominger	A.G. Mason Mfg. Co.
Romish Special	A.G. Mason Mfg. Co.
Ronaldson	Standard
Ronans	White
Rood	Standard
Roops	A.G. Mason Mfg. Co.
Roos	White
Roots	National
Rose	National
Roselyn	A.G. Mason Mfg. Co.
Rosemary	National
Rosenbaum	Davis
Rosenberg	A.G. Mason Mfg. Co.
Resenburg and H	Standard
Rosenblum	Free
Rosendale	Standard
Rosenbush	A.G. Mason Mfg. Co.
Rosenthal Gem	A.G. Mason Mfg. Co.
Rosenwald	A.G. Mason Mfg. Co.
Rosenwater	Standard
Ross	A.G. Mason Mfg. Co.
Rossman	White
Ross Perfection	Standard
Rossenback	Standard
Rotary Special	A.G. Mason Mfg. Co.
Rotative A	National
Roth Special	Standard
Rothchild	Standard
Rotiscillo	Free
Rotoro	National
Rottenberg	Goodrich
Rover	Standard
Rowe Brothers	A.G. Mason Mfg. Co.
Rowel	A.G. Mason Mfg. Co.
Rowell	White
Rowland	A.G. Mason Mfg. Co.
Rowland King Co.	Standard
Rowley	White
Royal	Free
Royal Electric	Free
Royal Leader	A.G. Mason Mfg. Co.
Royal New	Free
Royal Oak	Free
Royal Palm	A.G. Mason Mfg. Co.
Royal Ruby, The	New Home
Royal St. John, New	Free
Royal Sant John O.S.	Free
Royal St. John O. S. H.	Free
Ruby	New Home
Rudolph A, B, C	Goodrich
Rudy	Free
Rugby	Davis
Rugby	Free
Rule	A.G. Mason Mfg. Co.
Run Easy	National
Rural	A.G. Mason Mfg. Co.
Rush	A.G. Mason Mfg. Co.
Rusmark	Free
Russell	A.G. Mason Mfg. Co.
Russer	A.G. Mason Mfg. Co.
Ruther	White
Rutherford	White
Rygresco Rotary	A.G. Mason Mfg. Co.
Rygroco Rotary	White
Rylando	A.G. Mason Mfg. Co.
Ryno, C. V.	A.G. Mason Mfg. Co.
Sabin	Davis
Sacket Studio	A.G. Mason Mfg. Co.
Sackett	White
Sacremento Star	Goodrich
Sadie	Standard
Sadler Special	A.G. Mason Mfg. Co.
Saidon	Free
St. Clair	Goodrich
St. Hyacinthe	Goodrich
St. Jcobs	Standard
St. James	Standard
St. John Royal	Free
St. Lawrence	Standard
St. Louis	National
Saint Marys	National
St. Paul	Goodrich
Salt City	A.G. Mason Mfg. Co.
Salt Lake	Davis
Sltman	National
Salva Hos	National
Samaornials	National
Sambrooks	A.G. Mason Mfg. Co.
Sampson	Standard
Sampson	White
Samuel	New Home
Samuels	A.G. Mason Mfg. Co.
Sanchez M. Y. Hno	National
Sanders Co.	A.G. Mason Mfg. Co.
Sanderson Co.	A.G. Mason Mfg. Co.
Sangaman	Davis
Sanger	National
Sanger Grand B	National
Sans Favorite	Standard
Sarver and Spencer	A.G. Mason Mfg. Co.
Saskatchewan	A.G. Mason Mfg. Co.
Sancer Special	Free
Savage	National
Savory	A.G. Mason Mfg. Co.
Saxon Special	A.G. Mason Mfg. Co.
Scandanavian	Goodrich
Scar	A.G. Mason Mfg. Co.
Scarborough	National
Schackeford	Standard
Schafer	A.G. Mason Mfg. Co.
Scheats	A.G. Mason Mfg. Co.
Scheets	A.G. Mason Mfg. Co.
Schelemer	A.G. Mason Mfg. Co.
Schelnk	Standard
Schelton's Pride	A.G. Mason Mfg. Co.
Schertz	A.G. Mason Mfg. Co.
Scheusseers Queen	A.G. Mason Mfg. Co.
Schlemier	A.G. Mason Mfg. Co.
Schmidt	A.G. Mason Mfg. Co.
Schilz	National
Schmit & S.	A.G. Mason Mfg. Co.
School-Rotschild	Davis
Schoonmaker	National
Schremie Co.	A.G. Mason Mfg. Co.
Schultz	White
Schultz & Howe	A.G. Mason Mfg. Co.
Schultze's Gem	A.G. Mason Mfg. Co.
Schuman	A.G. Mason Mfg. Co.
Schwartz Kopp	National
Scientific	Standard
Scio	A.G. Mason Mfg. Co.
Scanavely, C. C.	National
Scofield	A.G. Mason Mfg. Co.
Scott	Standard
Scott L.G.	A.G. Mason Mfg. Co.
Scoville New Era	National
Scruggs	Free
Scully	National
Seagal Special	A.G. Mason Mfg. Co.
Seal's Pride	Standard
Seamstress	Davis
Seamstress, New	New Home
Seamstress, Old	Goodrich
Sea Side	A.G. Mason Mfg. Co.
Seasons 4	A.G. Mason Mfg. Co.
Sears, H.D.	A.G. Mason Mfg. Co.
Sears, Roebuck	National
Seaver's Special	A.G. Mason Mfg. Co.
Seavoy	Standard
Secora	National
Security	Davis
Security	A.G. Mason Mfg. Co.
Sedwig, J.	A.G. Mason Mfg. Co.
Sefton	A.G. Mason Mfg. Co.
Segal Special	National
Segnor	Standard
Selecta	Standard
Selecto	White
Selma C., D., E.	Free
Selsers Pride	Standard
Semense	Standard
Seminole	Free
Seneca	Free
Seneca Chief	A.G. Mason Mfg. Co.
Senorita	Standard
Sentinel	National
Sequoia	Davis
Serata	New Home
Seimshans	White
Seroco	National
Service	Davis
Service	Free
Sewards	A.G. Mason Mfg. Co.
Sew Easy	A.G. Mason Mfg. Co.
Sew Easy	White

Appendix G

Sewing-Machine Name	Sewing-Machine Company
Sew Right	A.G. Mason Mfg. Co.
Sewell	A.G. Mason Mfg. Co.
Seybold	Davis
Seybold Bros.	Standard
Shamrock	Standard
Shapleigh	Davis
Sharon	Sharon, Sharon, Ohio (1907)
Sharwick	Standard
Shawnee Chief	Davis
Sheffield	White
Shelby	Goodrich
Sheldon	National
Sheller	White
Shenley, The	National
Sheppard	Standard
Sheppard Special	A.G. Mason Mfg. Co.
Sheppars Favorite	Standard
Sherman	Standard
Shettucket	Davis
Shifley	A.G. Mason Mfg. Co.
Shinks	White
Shipkonsky	Standard
Shipley and Boht	A.G. Mason Mfg. Co.
Shoneman	Standard
Shook and Shook	Davis
Shook and Shook	White
Shordemanden	Goodrich
Shyrock	New Home
Shyrock	White
Syrock, The	A.G. Mason Mfg. Co.
Shuff's Own	Standard
Shurley	A.G. Mason Mfg. Co.
Sidders	Free
Siebold Special	A.G. Mason Mfg. Co.
Siegel	Free
Siegfried	White
Sierers	White
Sigman	A.G. Mason Mfg. Co.
Signal	Davis
Signal	Standard
Signor	Goodrich
Silco	Free
Silent	Davis
Silent Princess	National
Silent Stitcher	Davis
Silvens	A.G. Mason Mfg. Co.
Silver	Free
Silver King	Davis
Silver Medal	National
Silver Spray	Davis
Silver Star A, B, C, D, II	Davis
Silveus	White
Simmons Co.	National
Simon	A.G. Mason Mfg. Co.
Simplex	Davis
Simplex	Free
Simpson and Will	A.G. Mason Mfg. Co.
Sine, H.L.	A.G. Mason Mfg. Co.
Singleton	White
Sin Par	White
Sinsel	White
Sit-Easy	White
Sitright Franklin, The	Domestic
Sit-Straight	White
Skandanavian	Davis
Skeens	White
Skeleton	National
Skinner's	White
Skitler	A.G. Mason Mfg. Co.
Slane, The	National
Slater	Standard
Slaughter	White
Slavic	National
Sleepine	White
Slidell	Standard
Sluder	White
Smalley	National
Small, M.	White
Smathers	White
Smith	Davis
Smith	White
Smith Special	New Home
Smith and Caugheys	Standard
Smith and Wesson	Free
Smytha	White
Smythe and Co.	National
Snodgrass	A.G. Mason Mfg. Co.
Snow	A.G. Mason Mfg. Co.
Snavely	National
Snellenburg	New Home
Snyder	A.G. Mason Mfg. Co.
Soden	Davis
So Easy	Free
Soeasy	National
So-Ezy	Davis
So-Ezy	New Home
Solomons	Standard
Solon	A.G. Mason Mfg. Co.
Sonora	Standard
Sonoria	National
Soo Special	National
Sorosis	National
Souder	White
South Bend	White
Southern	Davis
Southern	White
Southern Belle	Davis
Southern Novelty	Free
Southwell	National
Sowerset	White
Spalding	Standard
Spartan	Free
Spear Edge	National
Special	A.G. Mason Mfg. Co.
Special	Standard
Spee Dee	Standard
Speedway	National
Speedwell	National
Spell, F. C.	A.G. Mason Mfg. Co.
Spencer	Davis
Spencer	A.G. Mason Mfg. Co.
Spetnagel	Davis
Spicer	A.G. Mason Mfg. Co.
Spike Nash Co.	A.G. Mason Mfg. Co.
Spill Brothers	White
Spindall	A.G. Mason Mfg. Co.
Spitler	White
Splendid	Free
Spokane	New Home
Spotless	National
Sprague	A.G. Mason Mfg. Co.
Spring City	Standard
Spring City	White
Spurlin	White
Square Deal	A.G. Mason Mfg. Co.
Srojan	National
Srormost	Goodrich
Stag	Davis
Stahns Favorite	Standard
Stahn's, E.A.	A.G. Mason Mfg. Co.
Standart	Davis
Stand, New	A.G. Mason Mfg. Co.
Standard (after 27500)	Standard
Standard Electric	Standard
Standard Favorite	Standard
Standard, J.W.	A.G. Mason Mfg. Co.
Standard Norwood	Standard
Standard Paragon	Standard
Standard Rotary	Standard
Standard Vibrator	Standard
Standfield, J.W.	A.G. Mason Mfg. Co.
Stanffer	White
Stanley	National
Stanly	Standard
Stapp	A.G. Mason Mfg. Co.
Star	Davis
Star	A.G. Mason Mfg. Co.
Star Capoc	A.G. Mason Mfg. Co.
Star Golden	A.G. Mason Mfg. Co.
Star Installment	A.G. Mason Mfg. Co.
Star New Home	New Home
Staufer	Davis
Stee Merc. Co.	A.G. Mason Mfg. Co.
Steel's Favorite	A.G. Mason Mfg. Co.
Steengagen	Standard
Stager	National
Stegman Electric Rotary	White
Stein	Davis
Stein	A.G. Mason Mfg. Co.
Stein Furniture Company	Standard
Steinkamp	White
Stella	National
Stemkamp	Standard
Stemway	National
Stephenson	A.G. Mason Mfg. Co.
Stepp, J.M.	A.G. Mason Mfg. Co.
Sterch	A.G. Mason Mfg. Co.
Sterling	Davis
Sterling	Standard
Sterling A, B, C, D, E, F	Goodrich
Stern	Davis
Sternberg	A.G. Mason Mfg. Co.
Sternikamp	A.G. Mason Mfg. Co.
Stevens	National
Stewart	A.G. Mason Mfg. Co.
Stewart Special	Free
Stier Speical	A.G. Mason Mfg. Co.
Stigall and Potts	A.G. Mason Mfg. Co.
Stilles	White
Stilleto	Free
Stimulator	New Home
Stitchwell	National
Stitchwell	Standard
Stockdale	A.G. Mason Mfg. Co.
Stockdale Rotary	White
Stockman	A.G. Mason Mfg. Co.
Stockman & Farmer	A.G. Mason Mfg. Co.
Stone	A.G. Mason Mfg. Co.
Stoops	Standard
Store Big Special	Goodrich
Stores Grenada	National
Stork	New Home
Stouffer	White
Stoval	A.G. Mason Mfg. Co.
Strahn's Favorite	Standard
Straightway	Standard
Strange	National
Strangburg	A.G. Mason Mfg. Co.
Strand's Electric	A.G. Mason Mfg. Co.
Straco	Free
Stratton	White
Strawbridge Clothier	National
Street	A.G. Mason Mfg. Co.
Streets	White
Strelezpk	White
Srong Rotary Electric	White
Strongs Favorite	A.G. Mason Mfg. Co.
Stronds Electric	A.G. Mason Mfg. Co.
Stroud Rotary Electric	White
Struthers Best	Standard
Stubbo	White
Stulco	White
Style Mode	Davis
Success	Free
Successful	National
Sullivan	Davis
Sullivan Slade Co.	A.G. Mason Mfg. Co.
Sultan	Davis
Sultana	National
Summers	A.G. Mason Mfg. Co.
Summit	A.G. Mason Mfg. Co.
Sun and Voice	Davis
Sunbeam	White
Sunflower	National
Suniers	White
Sunoria	Free
Sunray	Davis
Sunset	A.G. Mason Mfg. Co.
Sunset	Davis
Sunshine	Davis

Appendix G

Sewing-Machine Name	Sewing-Machine Company
Sunshine	Goodrich
Superb	Davis
Superb	White
Superba	Davis
Superior	Davis
Superior	New Home
Superior	Standard
Super Quality	Standard
Supplies 2	Davis
Supreme	Davis
Supreme	Goodrich
Surasky Special	Free
Surelock Rotary	National
Surety	Davis
Surprise	Standard
Surprise	A.G. Mason Mfg. Co.
Surviver, J.S.	A.G. Mason Mfg. Co.
Sutton Bros.	A.G. Mason Mfg. Co.
Swan	A.G. Mason Mfg. Co.
Swan	Goodrich
Swank	Davis
Swastika	Standard
Sweeton and B.	White
Swift	Standard
Swinton	Standard
Suwanee, A.C.	Free
Sweden	A.G. Mason Mfg. Co.
Symonds	Standard
Syndicate	National
Syracuse	National
Tabin	White
Taff	Goodrich
Tallulah, The	A.G. Mason Mfg. Co.
Tanek, M.	A.G. Mason Mfg. Co.
Target	Standard
Tarnocks	A.G. Mason Mfg. Co.
Tarver	A.G. Mason Mfg. Co.
Tates	A.G. Mason Mfg. Co.
Taylor	Davis
Taylor	A.G. Mason Mfg. Co.
Taylor	Standard
Teague	Davis
Tecco	Standard
Tedstorm	White
Tedstrom	A.G. Mason Mfg. Co.
Tellico	National
Temple	National
Tenks	Davis
Tennessee	A.G. Mason Mfg. Co.
Tenn Furniture Co.	A.G. Mason Mfg. Co.
Terrebone	A.G. Mason Mfg. Co.
Teutonia	New Home
Texas	A.G. Mason Mfg. Co.
Texas	White
Therlaigs	A.G. Mason Mfg. Co.
Thelma	Standard
Thelma's Favorite	A.G. Mason Mfg. Co.
Thistle	National
Thomas	Davis
Thompson	A.G. Mason Mfg. Co.
Thompson	Standard
Tidente	New Home
The 400	Standard
The Tiger	Davis
Ti-Ki	Goodrich
Tillsworth	A.G. Mason Mfg. Co.
Tisbest	A.G. Mason Mfg. Co.
Tissier Special	A.G. Mason Mfg. Co.
Tobin Bros.	A.G. Mason Mfg. Co.
Todd, H.E.	A.G. Mason Mfg. Co.
Toledo	Goodrich
Tomanis	National
Tom Cummins	National
Tomec, The	A.G. Mason Mfg. Co.
Tondy	Standard
Townley	Davis
Trabue	A.G. Mason Mfg. Co.
Treasure	Goodrich
Treasurer	A.G. Mason Mfg. Co.
Tremont	Davis
Trennan	A.G. Mason Mfg. Co.
Trenton	New Home
Trice	A.G. Mason Mfg. Co.
Trice Bros.	National
Tri-City	National
Tinacria	Standard
Trip Imp.	National
Tristate	Davis
Triumph	Davis
Triumph	New Home
Trotter	National
Tuapecka	Standard
Tucker	National
Tuckwell	Standard
Tude 7A	Standard
Tuggers	A.G. Mason Mfg. Co.
Tuggle, H.D.	A.G. Mason Mfg. Co.
Tupelo Mer. Co.	National
Turn City	National
Turners	A.G. Mason Mfg. Co.
Turnocks	A.G. Mason Mfg. Co.
Turpin's Pride	A.G. Mason Mfg. Co.
Tuscarawwas	A.G. Mason Mfg. Co.
Tuxedo	New Home
Tuxhorns	A.G. Mason Mfg. Co.
Twentieth Century	A.G. Mason Mfg. Co.
Twews	White
Tyanko	National
Tyler	A.G. Mason Mfg. Co.
Tyrholm	A.G. Mason Mfg. Co.
Ulasta	Goodrich
Ulmer	A.G. Mason Mfg. Co.
Unaka	Free
Unanzst	Standard
U-Need-Me	A.G. Mason Mfg. Co.
Uni	A.G. Mason Mfg. Co.
Unica	A.G. Mason Mfg. Co.
Unicorn	A.G. Mason Mfg. Co.
Union	Davis
Union	New Home
Union 24	Standard
Union Advance	Davis
Union Grand	Free
Union Leader	National
Union Merc. Co.	A.G. Mason Mfg. Co.
Unique	Davis
Unique	A.G. Mason Mfg. Co.
United	National
United States	A.G. Mason Mfg. Co.
Unito	National
Unity	A.G. Mason Mfg. Co.
Universal	Davis
Universal	New Home
Universal	Standard
Up-To-Date	Davis
Up-To-Date	New Home
Upright	Standard
U.S. Dailey	Standard
Utah	Free
Utica	Davis
Utility	Davis
Utility	Standard
Utopia	Goodrich
Vallarena	National
Valley City	Free
Van Allen	A.G. Mason Mfg. Co.
Van Loon Special	Free
Vance A	National
Vance, The	Davis
Vancello	National
Vanderbilt	Davis
Vanters	Goodrich
Varnado	Standard
Vassar	National
Vassar	Standard
Vasumpaur	Free
Vaughan	Davis
Vaughan	Standard
Velox	National
Velox 2	Davis
Velox A & B	New Home
Venango	Goodrich
Vendome	National
Venture	Davis
Venus	National
Verhart, F.M.	Standard
Veribest	Standard
Vertical Feed	Davis
Via and Steman	A.G. Mason Mfg. Co.
Vibra	Davis
Vibrant	Standard
Vibrator	Standard
Vibratorio	A.G. Mason Mfg. Co.
Viceroy	National
Vicellio	A.G. Mason Mfg. Co.
Victor	Davis
Victor, New	A.G. Mason Mfg. Co.
Victor 03	Free
Victoria	Standard
Victoria	A.G. Mason Mfg. Co.
Victoria Caniff	National
Victorio	Davis
Victory	Davis
Victory	Free
Victory, New, 9	Goodrich
Vigo	Davis
Viking	Davis
Viking	A.G. Mason Mfg. Co.
Vini Model	National
Vindex	National
Vinegard	A.G. Mason Mfg. Co.
Virginia	National
Virginian	National
Vittorio, E.M.	A.G. Mason Mfg. Co.
Voekel	A.G. Mason Mfg. Co.
Vogel	A.G. Mason Mfg. Co.
Vogelsburg	A.G. Mason Mfg. Co.
Vogue	Free
Vogue	A.G. Mason Mfg. Co.
Vola	National
Volksfriend	National
Volkspost	National
Volo	Davis
Volo	National
Volunteer	Davis
Volunteer	A.G. Mason Mfg. Co.
Vords	National
Vose, V.S.	A.G. Mason Mfg. Co.
Voucher	Standard
Vulcan	National
Vulcan	Standard
Wabash	Davis
Wabash	New Home
Wabash	Standard
Wa-Car-Co	A.G. Mason Mfg. Co.
Wacerly	National
Wade	A.G. Mason Mfg. Co.
Wagener	Goodrich
Wagley	A.G. Mason Mfg. Co.
Wagner H	Free
Wah Wah	National
Wako	National
Wainright	Standard
Walbert	Goodrich
Walbridge	Davis
Walcot	A.G. Mason Mfg. Co.
Waldo	Goodrich
Waldorf	Davis
Waldorf	A.G. Mason Mfg. Co.
Walker	Davis
Walker	National
Wallace	Free
Wallavok	Goodrich
Walters	A.G. Mason Mfg. Co.
Waltham	Davis
Waltham	Free
Waltham Rotary	National
Walton	A.G. Mason Mfg. Co.
Wanamaker Rotary	White
Wanamaker, S.R.	White

Appendix G

Sewing-Machine Name	Sewing-Machine Company
Wanda	Goodrich
Wanemaker	New Home
Wankon	White
Wanless	Goodrich
Wannamaker	Davis
Wannamaker	New Home
Wanzer C	Standard
Wapello Chief	A.G. Mason Mfg. Co.
Warbler	Free
Ward	Unknown
Ward, New	National
Wardell	A.G. Mason Mfg. Co.
Wardlan	A.G. Mason Mfg. Co.
Ware	A.G. Mason Mfg. Co.
Warewell A, C, E, G, H	National
Warkatz	Standard
Warnell	A.G. Mason Mfg. Co.
Warner, The	A.G. Mason Mfg. Co.
Warnocks	A.G. Mason Mfg. Co.
Warren	A.G. Mason Mfg. Co.
Warren	Standard
Wartanberg	A.G. Mason Mfg. Co.
Warwick, New	A.G. Mason Mfg. Co.
Wasans	A.G. Mason Mfg. Co.
Washington	New Home
Washington	Standard
Washtenaw	National
Watango	Goodrich
Watchman	National
Watkins	A.G. Mason Mfg. Co.
Watson	National
Wauson	National
Waverly	A.G. Mason Mfg. Co.
Waxahacie Hardware Co.	A.G. Mason Mfg. Co.
Wayne	National
Waywick New	Free
Weal	National
Wearwell	National
Weatherford	A.G. Mason Mfg. Co.
Weathers	White
Weatherspoon	A.G. Mason Mfg. Co.
Weaver	Goodrich
Weaver	White
Webb	A.G. Mason Mfg. Co.
Weber	Standard
Weber	White
Weber Special	Free
Weels	White
Weerooms	White
Weesmer	White
Wessner Ream Co.	Standard
Weeter	Davis
Weichers	A.G. Mason Mfg. Co.
Weigand	A.G. Mason Mfg. Co.
Weig and Schultz	Standard
We'ils	White
Weiners	White
Weirs	A.G. Mason Mfg. Co.
Weisberger	Davis
Weise	Davis
Wellborn Bros.	Standard
Welch	White
Welcome	A.G. Mason Mfg. Co.
Welcome	Standard
Weldin	Standard
Wellington	Davis
Wellington	Free
Wells	A.G. Mason Mfg. Co.
Wellworth	Free
Wellworth E.	National
Welsh John	A.G. Mason Mfg. Co.
Wentworth	National
Werner	Davis
Werner	A.G. Mason Mfg. Co.
Werner, The	Standard
Wertenberger	A.G. Mason Mfg. Co.
Wertz, W.D.	A.G. Mason Mfg. Co.
Wet	White
West Brothers	A.G. Mason Mfg. Co.
Western	A.G. Mason Mfg. Co.
Western Electric	National
Western Queen	A.G. Mason Mfg. Co.
Western Union	A.G. Mason Mfg. Co.
Westlake	National
Westinghouse	National
Westmoreland	National
Westraiila	A.G. Mason Mfg. Co.
Wetherbee	White
Wetherbee, H., and Co.	A.G. Mason Mfg. Co.
Weyand Bros.	A.G. Mason Mfg. Co.
Weyth	National
Wheeler	Free
Wheeler	White
Wheeler A, B, C, E, P, W	New Home
Wheeling	Davis
White, A.J. Ltd.	Standard
White-Cross	Davis
White Diamond	Standard
White Family Rotary	White
White Family Shutle	White
White Furniture Co.	A.G. Mason Mfg. Co.
White House	Davis
White King	Standard
White New Family Sewing Machine	White
White Peerless	A.G. Mason Mfg. Co.
White Pet	A.G. Mason Mfg. Co.
White Pet	White
White Star	Free
White Vibrator	White
Whitehall, New	Free
Whitehall, Old	Unknown
Whitehead	National
Whitehead	White
Whitehouse	A.G. Mason Mfg. Co.
Whitelau	A.G. Mason Mfg. Co.
Whitely	A.G. Mason Mfg. Co.
Whitemarsh	White
Whiteside	A.G. Mason Mfg. Co.
Whiting	Standard
Whitner & R	A.G. Mason Mfg. Co.
Whitsett	A.G. Mason Mfg. Co.
Wigginton	A.G. Mason Mfg. Co.
Wild Rose	National
Wilks	A.G. Mason Mfg. Co.
Wilkins and Field	Standard
Will C. Free	Free
Willamette	National
Willard	Davis
Willford	National
William Penn	Free
Williams	National
Williams	White
Williams, New	Unknown
Williams Singer Model	Unknown
Williamson	A.G. Mason Mfg. Co.
Willington	A.G. Mason Mfg. Co.
Willis	Standard
Willis and Co.	A.G. Mason Mfg. Co.
Willis, J.M.T.A.	Standard
Wilmot	National
Wilson	A.G. Mason Mfg. Co.
Wilson Rotary	A.G. Mason Mfg. Co.
Will Ranciers	A.G. Mason Mfg. Co.
Winchester	Davis
Winchester	Goodrich
Winchester	Free
Winchester	White
Wingold	Goodrich
Winn	A.G. Mason Mfg. Co.
Winnepag	Free
Winnepeg	Free
Winner	Davis
Winner	Free
Winner, New	A.G. Mason Mfg. Co.
Winslow Special	A.G. Mason Mfg. Co.
Wise, The	A.G. Mason Mfg. Co.
Wise-Rotary, The	White
Witherbee	A.G. Mason Mfg. Co.
Witherow	Goodrich
Witners	National
Wittes Rotary	National
Wizard	Davis
Wolfe	A.G. Mason Mfg. Co.
Wolters	A.G. Mason Mfg. Co.
Wolverine	Free
Wolverine	A.G. Mason Mfg. Co.
Woman and Home	New Home
Woman & House	New Home
Women's Institute Rotary	White
Wonder	Davis
Wonder	Free
Wonder, The	A.G. Mason Mfg. Co.
Wonder Worker	Standard
Wood	A.G. Mason Mfg. Co.
Woodbert	A.G. Mason Mfg. Co.
Woodhill	Standard
Woodidle	White
Woodman	New Home
Wood's Special	A.G. Mason Mfg. Co.
Woodrill	A.G. Mason Mfg. Co.
Woodruff	Davis
Woodward	Davis
Woodworth	Standard
Woolbert	A.G. Mason Mfg. Co.
Woolsey	A.G. Mason Mfg. Co.
Wootherspoon	Standard
Workwell	Standard
World Rotary	A.G. Mason Mfg. Co.
Worlds Best	Davis
Worlds Fair	National
Worlds Fair Premium	A.G. Mason Mfg. Co.
Worlds Rotary	White
Wormack, R.V.A.	A.G. Mason Mfg. Co.
Wornell	White
Worthmore, E	Free
Worthmore, E	National
Wright	A.G. Mason Mfg. Co.
Wrights	Davis
Wrigley	Free
Wrinkle, M. Co.	A.G. Mason Mfg. Co.
Wu Yeo Co.	Standard
Wyandott Furniture Co.	A.G. Mason Mfg. Co.
Wyatt	White
Wyeth	National
Wymes	White
Wyness	White
Wyoming	Standard
Xmas	Goodrich
Xmas	Standard
Yahrborough	White
Yale	Davis
Yale	Free
Yankee	Standard
Yarborough	A.G. Mason Mfg. Co.
Yates	White
Yews	National
Yoder and McLean	A.G. Mason Mfg. Co.
York	A.G. Mason Mfg. Co.
York Music Co.	A.G. Mason Mfg. Co.
York and Wadsworth	A.G. Mason Mfg. Co.
Young Blood	A.G. Mason Mfg. Co.
Young Brothers	Standard
Young's Favorite	A.G. Mason Mfg. Co.
Young's Reliable	A.G. Mason Mfg. Co.
Young and Chaffee	National
Young and Maritin	A.G. Mason Mfg. Co.
Young and McComb	National
Youman and Leete	A.G. Mason Mfg. Co.
Youth's Companion	New Home
Yvins Leader	Goodrich
Zachman	A.G. Mason Mfg. Co.
Zawadski	White
Zenith	National
Zenith A	Free
Zenobla	A.G. Mason Mfg. Co.
Zephyr Mer. Co.	National
Ziberna	White
Zinco	National
Zinco City	National
Zuberma	National
Zulema	National

Appendix G

The item names in the lists that follow are taken directly from a 1932 Torrington catalog of sewing machine parts. Although there are only three actual manufacturers given, this list is probably rather accurate. Furthermore, based upon other information in the catalog, one can conclude that the machine names given in the list are machines that were manufactured as far back as 1900.

Note that between the Torrington list and Cooper's data, there is not total correspondence among the names and their makers. This is possibly due to the evolution of sewing machine names as the century advanced, but there are some other discrepancies. The source for Cooper's list is partially unknown, but it is believed to have been created from several catalogs dating from the early 1900s (see page 384).

The bottom line: use these lists with caution; they are useful, but may not be ironclad in their accuracy.

Made by the Davis Sewing Machine Company

Aeronaut	Crawford	Honeymoon	New Century	Silent
Ajax	Crescent	Howland	New Conover	Southern
Albion	Cumberland	Lake View	New Cottage	Southern Bell
Alexander	Daytonia	Laurel	New Hibbard	Standart
Alexandra	Delaware	Lauretta	New Idea	Star
Bartlett	Dunham	Lexington	New Leader	Sterling N. S.
Bee Hive	Eclipse	Liberty	New Rex	Sterling O. S.
Belmont	Electro No. 2	Manhattan	New Vance	Sultan
Ben-Hur	Elite	Marathon	New Victory	Sunray
Blue Ribbon	Essex	Mascota	Parisian	Sunshine
Boston	Excelsior	Matthews	Pearl	Superb
Burdick	Fall City	Minnesota A.	Pemberton	Tiger
Capitol	Fireside	Minnesota B.	Peoria	Tremont
Centuria	Flyer	Minnesota C.	Progress	Triumph
Century	Fulton	Minnesota D.	Quality	Unique
Challenge	Garden City	Minnesota G.	Ranger	Victoria
Champion	Gem City	Modern	Red Cross	Victory
C. and C.	Gold Hibbard	Monarch D	Regal	Western
Chattanooga	Gulf Queen	Monitor	Renfrew	White House
Conover	Halcyon	Naravie	Royal	Winner N. S.
Coronell	Henrietta	Netzow	Sequoia	Winner O. S.
Coronet	Homan	New Baldwin	Shetucket	Yale

Made by the New Home Sewing Machine Company

American-Majestic	Electric Ideal	Majestic	Pan-American (Hand)	Sterling-Majestic
American Union	Eureka	Mars-Ideal	Pearl	Teutonia
Appleton	Falcon	Monarch-Majestic	Peninsula	Tuxedo
Cambridge	Favorite	New Carson	Peoria	Up-To-Date Majestic
Champion Ideal	Fireside	New Century	Perfection	Wabash
Climax	Free Trade-Niobe	New Ideal	Pioneer	Washington
Columbia	Garland	New National	Reliance	Western-Ideal
Columbus	Governor	New Peoria	Ruby	Whitsett
Companion	Hudson-Ideal	Niobe	Spokan-Majestic	Woman's Home-Ideal
Dandy	Ideal	Ordway	Star-Ruby	Woodman

Made by the National Sewing Machine Company

Abbott
Acme C.
Adams
Alamanche
Albemarle
Alpha
American Imp. H.A.
Anglo-American
Apex
Appleton
Arcade Special
Arlington Queen
Atlantic Queen
Aurora
Banner
Bay State
Beauty
Beaver
Ben-Hur
Blue Ribbon
Boston Special
B. Special
Buckeye
Busy Bee
Cadillac
Centennial No. 1
Centennial D.
Century Mfg. Co.
Christy
Colanzo
Colonial
Colorado
Comus
Continental C.
Crescent
Cumberland
Cuyahoga
Daisy
Daniels
Dauntless
Defender
Defiance
Delmar
Denver
Diamond
Diana
Dixie
Dixie Special
Dixon
Duncan
Durham
Eagle
Eatonia
Eclipse A.
E.E. Forbes' Special
Elberta
El Capitan
El Dorado D.
El Dorado E.
Electric City
Elgin
Elmhurst
Elmira
Emmons
Emperor
Empire
Englewood
Enterprise
Eudora
Excelsior
Excelsior B.B.
Family Favorite
Family Jewelry
Famous No. 1
Famous No. 2
Faultless
Favorite
Fayette
Fidelity
Florida
Garland B.
Gasco
Gem
Geneva
Georgia
Glenwood
Globe
Golden Rod
Gold Medal
Goldsmith
Guilford
Harvard
Home Favorite
Imperial Special
Improved Reliable
Indiana Farmer
Innovation
Invincible
Iowa No. 1
Iowa Queen
Jefferson
Jerome
Kansas
Kaufman Special
Keystone
Laclede
Lakeshore
Lakeside
Laurel
Lesley
Liberty
Lindell
Magnolia
Majestic Special
Manhattan
Mars
Mascott
Mayflower
Mohawk
Monitor
Moore Special
National
Nebraska
New Acme
New Alley
New Columbia
New Departure
New Empire
New Era
New Fireside
New Kensington
Newman
New National
New Peerless
New Perfection D.
New Queen
New Rival
New Sterling
New Victoria
Norfolk Special
Olympia
Olympic
Orient
Oriole
Oxford
Pacific
Parson's Special
Pearline
Peerless
Perfecta
Plymouth Queen
Portland Special
Prairie Queen
Premier
Premium
Princess
Princeton
Priscilla
Progress
Quaker
Queen City
Raleigh
Ramous
Record
Regal
Regent
Reliable
Reliance
Rialto
Rival
Riverside
Run Easy
Sentinel
Simplex
Simplex C
Simplex D
Sorosis
Southern Gem
Splendid
Sterling
Sunflower
Superior
Temple
The Elliott
The Everett
The Helena
The Journal
The Richmond
The Toledo
Treasure
Triumph
Union Leader
Veda
Venture
Viceroy
Victoria
Victory
Vulcan
Wadley
Wanamacker Special
Warner
Washtenaw
Waverly
Wayne
Webster
Whitehouse
Windsor
Wizard
York Special

Appendix H

Some Photographs of Vintage Sewing Machines

On the next few pages are some photographs of vintage sewing machine heads. They are arranged alphabetically and were manufactured between 1890 and 1930. It would be impossible to illustrate every sewing machine name made during that period, for there were thousands. But the selection that follows typifies machines produced for home use at that time. Note the gradual appearance of the electric motor. Initially, motors were attached to machines with a special mounting device; later, they became an integral part of the machine (see the Free sewing machine).

The table given here shows, according to the lists of the previous appendix, just who actually manufactured which machine. Note that there are some innacuracies and omissions; hence, one is urged to use the two lists of appendix G with caution. Also, note that the Torrington list only contains data for three manufacturers.

Machine Name	Manufacturer, Cooper List	Manufacturer, Torrington List	Actual Manufacturer
Climax	New Home	New Home	New Home
Cumberland	Davis	Davis	Davis
Eatonia	National	National	National
Ever Ready	Foley & Williams Goodrich		New Home
Free	Free		Free
Gilchrist			New Home
Goodrich			Foley & Williams
Lady Washington			New Home
Mansion	National		Probably National
New Ideal	New Home	New Home	New Home
New Treasure	A. G. Mason		Probably A. G. Mason
New Wilson	Davis A. G. Mason		
R. H. Macy	Davis		Domestic and others
Rockford	Free Standard		
Run Easy	National	National	National
Standard	Standard		Standard
Surprise	Standard A. G. Mason		
Windsor B		National	National
Winner	Davis Free A. G. Mason		Probably New Home

Appendix H

Appendix H

410

Appendix H

412

Appendix H

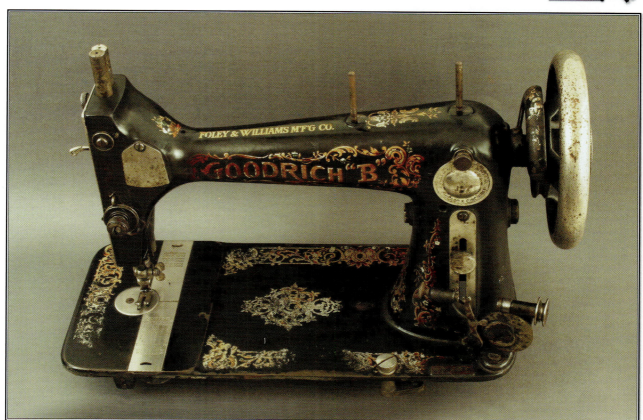

Appendix H

Appendix H

The fan supposedly kept the seamstress cool.

Appendix H

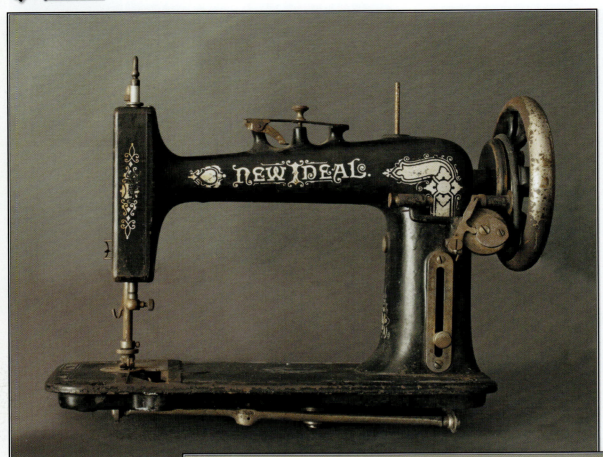

Appendix H

Appendix H

Appendix H

Appendix I

Early Photographs

Early photographs of people and their sewing machines are rather difficult to find, with the difficulty increasing as we go further back in time. The following figures represent a selection of such photos — some depict people at their work, others are posed photos using sewing machines as props, and still others have a whimsical nature.

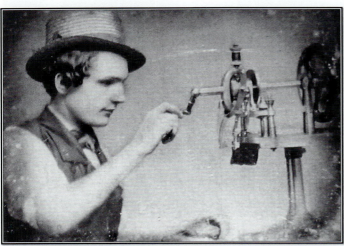

Figure I-1. A gentleman and a Blodgett and Lerow prototype, 1849. This is the earliest known photograph of an American sewing machine. Quite likely it is the very machine illustrated in figure 2-35 of this book.

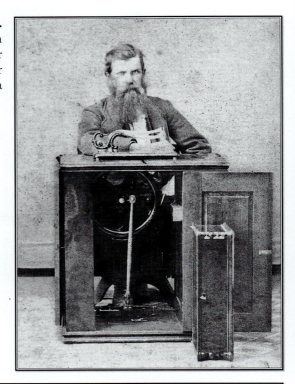

Figure I-2. A gentleman and a Grover and Baker machine, circa 1865.

Figure I-3. Man, son, and Singer #2, circa 1865.

Figure I-4. Lady and Singer, circa 1870. She does not appear to be very interested in sewing.

Figure I-5. A gentleman and a Wheeler & Wilson, circa 1870. This may have been a prop used by a photo studio.

Figure I-7. Display room, Howe Sewing Machine Co., circa 1870. This is half of a stereoscopic view, apparently from the same series as figure I-6.

Figure I-6. Display room, "Howe Sewing Machine Co.," circa 1870. This is a stereoscopic view, designed to be visualized in three dimensions with a proper viewing device. The company was actually called the Howe Machine Company, but the photograph is labeled as indicated.

Figure I-8. A lady who appears to be sewing, circa 1872. The room is rather uncluttered for a sewing room and may have been a photographer's studio.

Figure I-9. A gentleman and a Weed Family Favorite, circa 1872.

Figure I-11. A gentleman in uniform and a Singer New Family look-alike, circa 1875.

Figure I-10. A lady and a Grover & Baker, circa 1872. Note the pink ribbon, which was obviously colored by hand.

Appendix I

Figure I-12. A gentleman and a heavy duty Wheeler & Wilson, circa 1877. He had better pay more attention or he'll run the needle through his hand.

Figure I-13. Two ladies and a Victor, circa 1877. The pillar at the right looks suspiciously like a prop.

Figure I-14. A dolly and her Howe, ambitiously sewing a ruffle onto her dress. Like the gentleman in figure I-12, she'd better pay more attention to her work.

Figure I-15. This lady knows what to do. She is dressed in full seamstress attire and is keeping her paw clear of the needle. Circa 1880.

Figure I-16. Circa 1880. One would like to know the story behind this photo. Could it be "Little Red Riding Hood"?

Figure I-17. Circa 1880. The little girl does not seem amused. Again, note the pillar at right.

Appendix I

Figure I-18. Circa 1880. This actually looks like a sewing room.

Figure I-19. A dolly taking a break, circa 1880. The machine could be a Little Tot, but there are some minor differences in the stand.

Figure I-20. The cloth has embroidered upon it "Wheeler and Wilson/John Malone/Agent/Springfield Mass./July 16 1883."

Appendix I

Figure I-21. A lady hard at work while her disinterested husband amuses himself, circa 1885.

Figure I-22. A young tailor displaying the fruits of his labor, circa 1890.

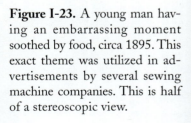

Figure I-23. A young man having an embarrassing moment soothed by food, circa 1895. This exact theme was utilized in advertisements by several sewing machine companies. This is half of a stereoscopic view.

Appendix I

Figure I-24. Same theme as figure I-23. Perhaps a few years later, different actors. Again, this is half of a stereoscopic view.

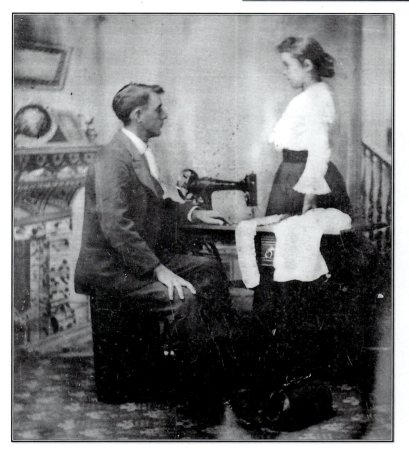

Figure I-25. Circa 1905. Could he be proposing?

Figure I-26. 1907. This speaks for itself.

Appendix I

Figure I-27. A German shoe factory, circa 1910. The stereoscopic view was published by the Underwood Works of New York, Ottawa, Kansas, and Arlington, NJ.

Figure I-28. A genuine home scene, 1916. "Neva at Her Sewing Machine. Taken in a bedroom of an apartment in Los Angeles."

Appendix I

Figure I-29. Circa 1900 – 1920. Half of a stereoscopic view. The caption says, "General View of Stitching and Fitting Department in a Large Shoe Factory, Syracuse, N. Y."

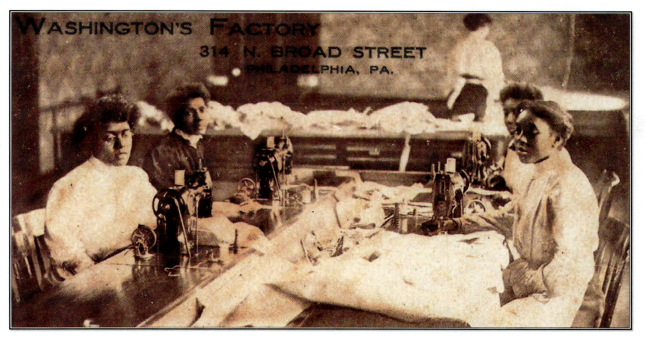

Figure I-30. A postcard advertisement, circa 1920.

Index

Aetna	21
Akins & Felthousen	21
American	21
American Eagle	26
American Gem	292
American Girl	299
American Hand	26
American Magnetic	26
Ashland	26
Atwater	26
Baby	291
Baby Grand	294
Banner	26
Bartholf	26
Bartlett	30
Bartram & Fanton	30
Battelle	36
Beckwith	36, 41 – 42
Belle	36
Betsy Ross	300
Bird	36
Bishop	39
Blees	39
Blodgett & Lerow	39
Bosworth	48
Boudoir	48
Boynton	48
Bradford & Barber	48
Buckeye	48
Buell	48
Busy Bee	48
Casige	299
Centennial	48
Cherub	56
Chicopee	56
Clark's Revolving Looper	56
Common Sense	56
Cupid	294, 306
Cute	56
Daisy	60
Davis	60
Demorest	60
Diamond	60
Domestic	60
Dorcas	63
Elastic Motion	63
Eldredge	63
Elliptic	66
Empire	68
Englewood Junior	296
Erie	78
F & W Automatic	78
F. A. O. Schwarz	286
Fairy	78
Family	78
Family Gem	78
Fetter & Jones	78
Figural	78
Finkle & Lyon	78
Florence	80
Foley & Williams	279
Foliage	80
Folsom	88
Franklin	88
Gem	281, 292, 301
Gibbs	91
Globe	91
Gold Medal	91
Goodbody	94
Goodes	280
Goodrich	94
Goodspeed & Wyman	30
Grant Brothers	160
Greenman & True	98
Griswold	98
Grover & Baker	99
Hancock	113
Hardie	113
Heberling	113
Hendricks	113
Hodgkin's	113
Holly	113
Home Shuttle	113
Hook	113
Horse	113
Household	113
Howe	120
Hunt & Webster	120
Ideal	300
Independent	120
Jameson's Automatic	120
Jennie June	120
Johnson	122
Keystone	122
Kruse	122
Ladd & Webster	122
Lake	127
Landfear	127
Lathrop	127
Leavitt	130
Lester	130
Letter A	209
Liberty	282
Linnea	297
Little Comfort	285
Little Daisy	303
Little Giant	130
Little Hustler	284
Little Lady	283
Little Monitor	130
Little Tot	305
Little Worker	130
Mack	136
Madame Demorest	136
Manhattan	139
Mary	296
McLean & Hooper	139
Medallion	139
Midget	281
Monitor	139
Mueller	289
Murphy	139
National	139
National Wax Thread	139
Ne Plus Ultra	139
Nettleton & Raymond	139
New England	154
New Family	210
New Home	154
Novelty	154
Ormond	154
Our New No. 10	293
Pansy	291
Parham	155
Parker	155
Paw Foot	155
Pearl	293
Peirce & Ruddick	155
Perfection	286
Pixie	298
Planer & Kayser	155
Pocket	186
Pond	186
Pony	282, 286
Pratt	186
Princess	301
Quaker City	186
Reese	189
Reliable	281
Remington	189
Rival	189
Robinson and Roper	189
Scovel & Godell	190
Seamstress Friend	190
Secor	190
Sewing Shears	190
Shaw & Clark	190
Shaw's Patent	209
Simplicity	209
Singer	209, 288
Smith, E. H.	226
Smith, W.	226
Smith & Egge	285
Snake	164
Soezy	293
Spenser	290
Springsteen	226
Squirrel	226
Stebbins	226
Stevens	227
Stitchwell	283, 302
Strange & Huntley	227
Tabitha	293
Taggart & Farr	227
Thompson	227
Thomson	227
Tourist	288
Triumph	287
Triune	227
Turtleback	209
Uhlinger	227
Union	227
Universal	231
Victor	231
Wannamaker	231
Wardwell	231
Washington	231
Watson	231
Wee	283
Weed	244
West & Willson	244
Western Electric	244
Wheeler & Wilson	244
White	263
Whitney	263
Willamette	283
Willcox & Gibbs	263
Williams & Orvis	263
Wilson, W. G.	274
Wood	284
Woodruff	274
Yale	297
Yankee	287
Xray	274

Rarity/Value Codes: A Price Guide

An attempt has been made to quantify the rarity and value of the sewing machines of chapters 2 and 3. This is difficult enough in the case of estimating rarity, and much more so when it comes to assigning prices. Hence, although the rarity codes come somewhat close, the value codes can only be considered educated guesses, and are therefore rather broad. As has been pointed out, much of the value can be derived from, in addition to rarity, the eye appeal of a machine and its condition. Hence, even a common Singer New Family machine, if in perfect condition, will command a premium price.

The rarity codes are explained in the table below:

Rarity Scale	Number of Surviving Examples
X (Extemely Rare)	0 – 5
R (Rare)	6 – 30
O (Occasionally found)	31 – 200
F (Frequently found)	201 – 600
A (Abundant)	more than 600
U (Cannot establish rarity due to insufficient data)	

A value code table follows. This table must be used with caution, as values will vary considerably over time and from machine to machine.

Value Code	Dollar Value Range
1	$10.00 – 200.00
2	$25.00 – 300.00
3	$75.00 – 500.00
4	$125.00 – 750.00
5	$200.00 – 1,200.00
6	$400.00 – 2,500.00
7	$800.00 – 4,000.00
8	$1,500.00 – 6,000.00
9	$3,000.00 – 10,000.00
10	$6,000.00 and up

The highest known price paid for an American – made sewing machine as of 2004 was $32,000.00.

From the above table, one can conclude, for example, that if a machine has a value code of 2, its value might be as little as $25.00 or perhaps as high as $300.00. A value code of 6 would lead one to conclude that the machine is worth between $500.00 and $2,500.00. Although this is a large range, it is the only plausible way to deal with actual dollar values.

The best way to regard value is to look at it as a relative measure. In other words, a machine with a value code of 6 will be worth more than one with a value code of 4. Naturally, a given machine could vary considerably from collector to collector.

GODEY'S FASHIONS.

FOR DESCRIPTION SEE FASHION DEPARTMENT.